I-80 W →

Merle Hay S towards town

Bennegan's - 3rd stop light

1st Main intersection -

Meredith Quick Trip

R - W → 2nd right is 62nd st.

R on Goodman Dr.

6100 Goodman on John Side

light Blue

LET GOD BE GOD!

As for the slanders and evil names with which my person is assailed, although numerous enough . . . they do not trouble me. It has never been my intention to avenge myself on those who rail at my person, my life, my work, my doings. That I am not worthy of praise, I myself know full well. . . . Whoever will, let him freely scold, slander, condemn my person and my life; it is already forgiven him. But let no one expect from me either grace or patience who would make my Lord Christ, whom I preach, and the Holy Ghost, to be liars. I am nothing at all, but for the Word of Christ I give answer with joyful heart and vigorous courage, and without respect of persons. To this end God has given me a glad and fearless spirit, which they shall not embitter, I trust, not in all eternity.

LUTHER.

AETHERNA IPSE SVAE MENTIS SIMVLACHRA LVTHERVS
EXPRIMIT·AT VVLTVS CERA LVCAE OCCIDVOS·

·M·D·X·X·

MARTIN LUTHER

LET GOD BE GOD!

*An Interpretation of
the Theology of Martin Luther*

By

PHILIP S. WATSON, M.A.

*Tutor in Systematic Theology and
Philosophy of Religion,
Handsworth College, Birmingham*

Reproduced by permission of
The Methodist Bookroom

Wipf and Stock Publishers
150 West Broadway • Eugene OR 97401
2000

Let God Be God
An Interpretation of the Theology of Martin Luther

By Watson, Philip S.

Copyright© 1947 by The Methodist Bookroom

Reprinted by *Wipf and Stock Publishers*
150 West Broadway • Eugene OR 97401

PREFACE

IT is now over a quarter of a century since the publication in Germany of Karl Holl's epoch-making studies of Luther. They have been followed both on the Continent and more notably in Scandinavia by a veritable Luther renascence. Modern research has led to a new understanding and appreciation of Luther and shown the need for a thorough revision, not only of non-Lutheran, but also of traditional Lutheran conceptions of his reforming work.

The change of outlook has scarcely been noticed in this country, in spite of a marked quickening of interest in the Reformation in recent times. English discussions of Luther still largely reflect the interpretations of Adolf Harnack and Ernst Troeltsch, while English acquaintance with Luther himself all too rarely extends beyond the Wace and Buchheim edition of his *Primary Works*. This does much to explain the ease with which some eminent Churchmen were lately beguiled by the efforts of a modern Cochlaeus to persuade us that Martin Luther was Hitler's spiritual ancestor. It is particularly unfortunate that Troeltsch's *Soziallehren*, which displays a singular lack of insight in its treatment of Luther, should have found a translator (twenty years after its original publication), whereas we still have no English version of Holl's *Gesammelte Aufsätze*, which contains some penetrating criticisms of Troeltsch and is based on a far greater knowledge of the sources.

Holl did not say the last word on the subject, of course, nor has it yet been said. If it is ever spoken, it will be due not least to the work of a number of Swedish theologians, to whom the leadership of Lutheran scholarship has passed in recent years. Something of their contribution to this Fernley-Hartley Lecture will be apparent from the Notes at the end of each chapter, but it is fitting here to record a wider indebtedness to them both for personal friendships and for books on subjects other than the Reformation.

It was in Sweden a dozen years ago that I found a Luther in many ways other and greater than I had heard of in either England or Germany; and in this lecture I have tried to show where his greatness essentially lies. An exhaustive account of his theology could not, of course, be given here, but all the main issues have at least been touched upon. I hope to discuss in a further volume several questions that call for fuller treatment—particularly those of 'reason', 'good works' and 'free will'.

In this lecture, Luther has been allowed as much as possible to speak for himself. If any error should prove to have crept into the references to his works, it will be remembered that these are not easily available in this country. I have had to rely a good deal on notes taken from them as opportunity has offered, and it has not been possible to make a final verification before going to press. For the translation of passages from the Weimar and Erlangen editions I must bear responsibility; and in quotations from translated sources I have occasionally taken the liberty of modifying spelling, capitalization, and punctuation to conform more nearly to modern English usage.

The quotation on page ii comes from *The Papacy at Rome* (*W.M.L.*, I, 393)—Luther's reply in 1520 to the scurrilities of the Franciscan monk Alveld. The frontispiece reproduces an engraving by Lukas Cranach in the same year.

The following pages owe much to the kindness of friends and colleagues. My special thanks are due to Principal Wilbert F. Howard, M.A., D.D., for his unfailing interest and many hours generously given to discussion of the work; to the Reverend Harold S. Darby, M.A., for valuable criticism of the first draft of the manuscript, and the Reverend E. Gordon Rupp, M.A., B.D., for his approval of the second draft; and to the Reverend George W. Anderson, M.A., and the Reverend Michael J. Skinner, M.A., for assistance with the reading of proofs and the compilation of indexes.

                                                        PHILIP S. WATSON

HANDSWORTH COLLEGE
Whitsuntide 1947

CONTENTS

ABBREVIATIONS

W.A., Luther, *Werke.* Kritische Gesamtausgabe. Vols. Iff. (Weimar, 1883ff.)

E.A., Luther, *Sämmtliche Werke.* 67 vols. (Erlangen, 1826-57.)

Römerbr., *Luthers Vorlesung über den Römerbrief*, 1515-16. Ed. J. Ficker. 4th edn. (Leipzig, 1930.)

Tischr., *Martin Luther, Tischreden.* Ed. H. Borcherdt and W. Rehm. (München, n.d.)

W.M.L., *Works of Martin Luther* with introductions and notes. 6 vols. (A. J. Holman Company, Philadelphia, 1915-32.)

S.W., *Select Works of Martin Luther.* Tr. by H. Cole. 4 vols. (London, 1826.)

W.B., *Luther's Primary Works.* Ed. Wace and Buchheim. (London, 1896.)

Gal. E.T., *A Commentary on St. Paul's Epistle to the Galatians*, by Martin Luther. Ed. Erasmus Middleton. (London, 1807.)
(Figures in brackets following references to this work indicate chapter and verse on which Luther is commenting.)

B.o.W., *The Bondage of the Will*, by Martin Luther. Tr. by H. Cole. (Ed. H. Atherton, London, 1931.)

Sermons, *Sermons on the most interesting doctrines of the Gospel*, by Martin Luther. (London, 1830.)

Letters, *The Letters of Martin Luther.* Selected and translated by M. A. Currie. (London, 1908.)

M.H.B., *The Methodist Hymn-book.* (London, 1933.)

S.T., *The Summa Theologica of St. Thomas Aquinas.* Tr. by the Fathers of the English Dominican Province. 2nd and revised edn. (London, 1922.)

(Particulars of other works cited are to be found by reference to the authors' names in the list on page 190.)

Part One

The General Character of Luther's Theology

CHAPTER ONE

LUTHER AS A THEOLOGIAN

I. THE TASK OF THE INTERPRETER

A DISTINGUISHED Lutheran Church historian has written of
Methodism that it can be described as 'the Anglican translation of the Evangelical-Lutheran doctrine of salvation'.[1]
If that is so, the People called Methodists may well be expected
to show sympathy and understanding for the genius of Martin
Luther, and it is not inappropriate that a Methodist lecture should
be devoted to an interpretation of his theology.

The Founders of Methodism were profoundly, if in the main
indirectly, influenced by Luther's doctrine. It was with his
accents that Spangenberg spoke in Georgia and Peter Böhler
in Oxford; and it was his *Commentary on the Epistle to the Galatians*
and his *Preface to the Epistle to the Romans* that proved decisive in
the historic month of May 1738. There is, moreover, a permanent
Lutheran contribution to Methodist piety in John Wesley's
translations of German hymns, and to Methodist theology in his
standard *Notes on the New Testament*, of which he derived the major
portion from the *Gnomon Novi Testamenti* of Bengel, 'that great
light of the Christian world', as he calls him. John and Charles
Wesley did not, of course, become Lutherans, nor yet Moravians;
and Methodism both had and has its own peculiar ethos. Yet
deeper than all differences is the essential spirit, in which the
Wesleys are more nearly akin to Luther than to any other great
exponent of the Christian faith and life. There is an extraordinary
similarity between the spiritual evolution of the sixteenth-century
monk into the Reformer and that of the eighteenth-century
Oxford Anglicans into leaders of the Evangelical Revival; and
the Revival itself is aptly named, for it was fundamentally a
renewal and extension of the work of Luther's Reformation.

It is true that John Wesley, who spoke of the Reformer as a much
greater man than himself,[2] was also sharply critical of him on
certain points. We shall have occasion to notice and to criticize his
criticisms in due course; but it is only fair to say here that he had
some excuse for making them. He possessed little or no first-hand

knowledge of Luther's teaching, and he was misled by the errors of men whom he imagined, as they imagined themselves, to be faithful exponents of Luther. More important than these matters, however, is the fact that Wesley stands together with Luther on the same solid ground of the doctrine of salvation by faith, about which the two men often speak in almost identical terms. Writing in 1740, Wesley describes this doctrine as 'the *old way*, of salvation by faith only', and opposes it to 'the *new path*, of salvation by *faith and works*'.³ Two hundred years earlier, Luther was urging the defence of 'the old faith against new articles of faith' and—which is the same thing—of 'the old good works against the new good works'.⁴ In the first of the *Standard Sermons*, where Wesley presses the need for preaching it, he asserts that it was

this doctrine, which our Church justly calls *the strong rock and foundation of the Christian religion*, that first drove Popery out of these kingdoms; and it is this alone can keep it out.

In the same way, Luther declares that

the doctrine of faith and justification, or how we become righteous before God . . . drives out all false gods and idolatry; and when that is driven out, the foundation of the Papacy falls, whereon it is built.⁵

There are scores of passages in John Wesley's writings that could thus be paralleled with quotations from Luther; and the same can be said of his brother's hymns. Indeed, anyone who is but familiar with Charles Wesley's hymns has already a fair acquaintance with Luther's theology, albeit in its Anglican translation. With the translation, however, we are not here proposing to deal, but with the original, to which we must now turn.

We have spoken of interpreting the theology of Luther; but the question may perhaps be raised, whether any such thing exists. There is a very common opinion that it does not; and in some quarters it is almost proverbial that Luther was 'no theologian'. Even a friendly critic thinks it scarcely too much to say, that to speak of the 'Theology of Luther' is to use a phrase without a meaning.⁶

Luther's contribution, we are told, was to religion, not to theology. He was a 'religious genius', a man of profound experience and vivid intuitions, who expressed what he felt and saw in paradoxical speech which defies systematization. His religion, it is alleged, is simple, not to say naïve, and can be easily understood by anyone who will read his Primary Treatises and Catechisms; but his 'theology' evades description. He introduced no new doctrines, and his revival of a number of old ones scarcely enhances his claim to theological distinction. His writings contain, not a theology, but statements of doctrine, which cannot be reduced to an ordered and coherent system. If his work has been of vital and lasting importance for religion, he has left for theology only problems to solve, not solutions of problems.

Such an estimate of Luther would no doubt be widely accepted; and the grounds for it are apparent. Yet it cannot be said to reveal more than a very slender acquaintance with Luther himself and an unnecessarily narrow conception of what we are to understand by theology.

If the essential art of a theologian is to elaborate a comprehensive and logically ordered system of doctrine, then Luther is certainly 'no theologian'—nor, we may add, is Saint Augustine or many another of the Fathers of the Church. His work is far from systematic in that sense of the term. He wrote largely as occasion demanded, in fulfilment of his duties as professor, preacher, and pastor, or in defence of his position against its assailants. He made no attempt to construct a Lutheran *Summa* or *Institutes*; and the *Loci communes*, although his work was their inspiration, are not his own, nor do they adequately represent his outlook.[7] But that is no sufficient reason for saying that Luther presents us only with a number of disconnected statements of doctrine. He is, in fact, never concerned merely with particular points of doctrine in isolation from each other or from the Christian Faith as a whole. In his own view, at any rate, every single doctrine is inseparably bound up with all the rest, so that 'no one article of faith is believed without all the other articles';[8] and he believes that, just as 'in philosophy a small fault in the beginning is a great and foul fault in the end, so in divinity one little error overthroweth the whole doctrine'.[9]

When Luther selects some particular doctrine for special emphasis, he does so primarily because it crystallizes the fundamental controversy between himself and his opponents. But just for that reason he cannot regard it as an isolated issue, but believes that upon a true understanding of it the whole of Christianity depends. It is in this sense he claims that the distinction between

B

the Law and the Gospel 'contains the sum of all Christian doctrine',[10] or describes the doctrine of justification as 'master and prince, lord, ruler, and judge over all kinds of doctrine, which preserves and governs all ecclesiastical doctrines'.[11] These were points at which the vital difference between Luther's understanding of Christianity and that of the medieval theologians inevitably emerged in open conflict. Elsewhere it often remained latent, though it was no less real. There was, for instance, as it is expressly stated in the Articles of Schmalkald, no controversy about 'the supreme articles concerning the Divine Majesty'; but it cannot be said that these were viewed in the same light by both parties. Luther and his followers had no quarrel with the great Christological and Trinitarian formulations of the traditional Creeds; indeed, they regarded them as beyond dispute and valued them highly as evidence of their own continuity with the ancient Church. Yet it would be idle to assert that the significance of Christ was precisely the same for Luther as for his contemporary opponents, or that they held the same conception of the nature and the ways of God as he. In his reforming work, Luther was not seeking simply to correct an error here and there, but his task was such, in his own view, as to 'alter the whole religion of the Papacy'.[12] The Christian Faith is a unity, and if 'one little error' corrupts the whole, then the correction of error in any part cannot leave the rest unaffected.

Now since the unity and wholeness of the Christian Faith are something of which Luther himself is convinced, we have good reason to expect some coherence and consistency in his own presentation of it, despite the absence of an orderly account of it from his pen. Yet it must be admitted that, at first sight, his thought appears to be as unsystematic as his writings, and it is not easy to see how it can be presented as a homogeneous whole. Even at the most central points of Christian doctrine, he expresses his convictions with what seems to be a complete indifference to formal consistency. On the Work of Christ, for instance, some of his statements appear to imply an Anselmian theory; others reproduce the dramatic imagery, often in its most fantastic forms, of the Patristic view; while others are reminiscent of mystical ideas. Again, his doctrine of God itself contains seemingly contradictory elements. For how is it possible to reconcile the monistic conception of a Divine omnipotence that moves even the devil and wicked men, with the dualistic idea of a conflict between God and the devil, in which the latter is vanquished through Christ? Or how can the thought of a 'hidden God', who predestines both the elect and the damned, be harmonized with that of the Divine love and grace revealed in Christ?[13] In view of such problems, which quite overshadow the deliberately paradoxical theses for which Luther is notorious, it is hardly surprising that we should be advised to abandon discussion of his 'indescribable' theology in favour of the alleged simplicity of his religion.

But it is highly questionable whether Luther's theology—his thought and speech about God—can be quite as readily divorced from his religion—his faith in God and experience of communion with Him—as has been suggested. Theological precision and religious insight do not always go hand in hand, it is true, but if Luther's religion is easily comprehensible, it would be strange if his own understanding of it were so slight as to render his theological expression of it entirely inharmonious. Presumably he did not mean to contradict himself, and we may assume that he was not aware of any fundamental incongruity in his various statements, especially with regard to the most central doctrines of the Faith. From his own point of view, at any rate, there was no inconsistency; and the question arises, whether it is not simply the failure to grasp his point of view that has led to the criticisms we have described. It is possible that if they were rightly understood, both his religion would prove less naïve and his theology less indescribable than has been supposed.

We may perhaps allow Luther himself to remind us of an elementary principle of interpretation. Recalling a passage in Saint Hilary's *De Trinitate*, he says:

He who will understand what is said must see why or for what reasons it is said.[14]

Thus [he comments] there are many sayings in the Scriptures which, if taken literally, are contradictory, but if the causes are shown, everything is right.

And the same is true, he believes, of books on medicine and jurisprudence—and of his own writings also; for he complains of people who collect his 'contradictions' without attempting to understand the reasons for them.[15]

Already in his own lifetime, Luther's works were the happy hunting ground of *Antilogistae*, as he calls them, who sought to bring him into contempt by exposing inconsistencies, real or apparent, in his views. But even the presence of actual contradictions in Luther's voluminous writings does not necessarily discredit his powers of thought; and he himself was not greatly disturbed by these critics, but rather treated them with ironical amusement. After a lapse of some years, during which his thought had materially altered at certain points, he could re-issue an earlier work without revision, in order, as he says,

to put forth a public record of my progress and also to show a kindness to the Contradictionists, that they may have whereon to exercise their malice.[16]

He is, in his own words,

one of those who, as Saint Augustine says of himself, have grown by writing and by teaching others, and not one of those who, starting with nothing, have in a trice become the most exalted and most learned of doctors.[17]

The full implications of his 'profound experience and vivid intuitions' were not always clear to Luther in a moment, but his thought is by no means unrelated to them and its development under their influence is traceable in his writings.

Yet even when the significance of his new religious insights had become clear to him, it was not a simple matter for Luther to express it in terms of the scholastic theology in which he had been trained. The old skins were ill suited to contain the new wine; and when they broke, any receptacle that lay to hand must be pressed into service to receive it. Luther was prepared to use all available means, new or old, in the attempt to make plain what he wished to say. It was not, however, possible for him to dispense entirely with scholastic terminology or, what is more important, scholastic points of view; for he was bound to address his contemporaries in their own language. Much of his writing is controversial, and in it he frequently seeks to meet his opponents on their own ground. He accepts their challenge as they issue it; he allows them to state the question in dispute from their own standpoint. The result is that his own characteristic point of view, which strictly speaking requires a different statement of the problem, sometimes fails to find quite clear and unequivocal

expression.[18] In the *De servo arbitrio*, for example, his real intentions are not a little obscured because he adheres so closely
to Erasmus's statement of the issue. The impression can therefore
be gained, even from some of his maturer works, that his position
has not been fully thought out and is lacking in cohesion and
consistency. Nevertheless, it is a false impression; and it indicates
either a refusal or an inability to grapple with the complexities
of his arguments.

Luther has undoubtedly left problems for theology to solve,
and first among them is clearly that of understanding his own
thought. It is a task of historical theology to try to see, as he
himself has suggested, the reasons for the diversity of his statements and to discover the essential homogeneity of his outlook.
The purpose of our present study is to make some contribution
to this end. In order to do so, we need not concern ourselves with
the development of his ideas, nor is it necessary, even if we had
the space for it, to attempt a full and detailed account of his
mature views.[19] What is rather required is a point of view from
which the heterogeneous appearance of his utterances can be
shown to be merely apparent, as it quite evidently was to himself.
We must seek, amid the vast and varied landscape of his writings,
a coign of vantage from which we may survey the whole and
see how the changing aspects of his thought find their place in one
unbroken scene. Needless to say, such a point of view must be one
that is characteristic of Luther himself, so that we may think his
thoughts after him, and find his meaning in the things he says.
Our purpose is to understand Luther, and that is only possible
as we are able to adopt his standpoint and, as it were, see with his
eyes. Whether we consider his position to be ultimately valid, or
whether we find anything of permanent value in what we see, are
questions which different persons will no doubt answer differently,
according to their various predilections, and they do not concern
us here. *point of view matters!!*

2. LUTHER'S CONCERN WITH DOCTRINE

In seeking such a point of view as we have just described, it is
natural that we should turn to consider the significance of Luther's
reforming work. What was it that impelled him to this work?
What was the specific point of distinction between his outlook

and that generally prevalent in the Church of his day? What was
the fundamental distinguishing feature of his reformation? Different answers have been given to these questions at different times;
and not unnaturally, since a movement of such vast consequence
as he initiated is not easily summed up in a simple formula.
Different aspects of it will appeal in different circumstances.
A glance at some of the various views may assist us, however, in
penetrating to the heart of the matter.

First of all we may dismiss the idea that the primary virtue
of Luther's work lies in his protest against the 'religious and
practical' degradations of medieval Christendom. That is far
too negative a conception, which entirely overlooks, among
other things, the fact that apart from some new and positive
contribution, no mere negative protesting, however vigorous,
could possibly have effected a reformation. Luther was not
simply a Protestant; it is much more important that he was, to use
his own favourite word, an Evangelical. And it was his evangelical
convictions that led him to protest, not only against excrescences
and abuses in the practical piety of his time—for others who
did not share his convictions did that—but also and more especially against the prevailing theological outlook—for that, on
his own testimony, was his primary concern.

Luther deliberately draws a distinction between his own work
and that of earlier reformers, on the ground that they attacked
only the 'life', whereas he is attacking the 'doctrine'.[20] The
same distinction can also be made between Luther and many of
the more serious minds among his contemporaries, who were no
less concerned than he about the condition of the Church and
could speak of it in terms just as severe. Erasmus, for instance,
if he is less violent in speech, is no less ruthless in his castigation
of ecclesiastical abuses, and he gives abundant evidence to
support his complaint that 'corruption under the name of religion
has gone so far as almost to extinguish the Christian Faith'.[21]
But Erasmus and the Catholic reformers saw by no means so
deeply into the situation as Luther, who finds at the root of
all abuses and corruptions corrupt and false doctrine.[22] Against
this, however, he would have fought quite apart from any
mischievous 'practical' consequences it might have, although he
fears he would have had little success 'if the Papacy had the same
holiness and austerity of life which it had in the time of the

ancient fathers'. Moved as he is by the vices and follies that have invaded the Church, he is more deeply stirred by what he considers the perversion, amounting to the virtual suppression of Christian truth.

Wherefore [he says] we ought not so much to consider the wicked life of the Papists, as their abominable doctrine and hypocrisy, against the which we especially fight.[23]

In consequence of his distinction between 'doctrine' and 'life', Luther never descends to that level of argument where the disputants claim that they and theirs are better men than their opponents. He frankly admits that there is ample room for improvement in the 'life' of Evangelicals as well as of Papists.[24] But his charge against the latter is that they maintain a doctrine which contradicts and falsifies the very Word of God.

They themselves [he says] do not defend their wicked life, nay rather they which are best and soundest of them all do detest it; but they fight for the maintenance and defence of the doctrine of devils.[25]

It is for right doctrine, then, that Luther contends, at least according to his own view of the matter. We must therefore inquire with what doctrine or doctrines he is particularly concerned. Or perhaps, since he neither introduced any new doctrine nor wished to do so, we should rather ask what is the nature of his concern with doctrine. Where does he believe the error he is attacking essentially lies, and how does he propose to correct it?

It used to be, and in some quarters still is, a popular idea that the Reformation can be described as nothing more nor less than a return to primitive, biblical Christianity. By his assertion of the authority of the Bible against that of the Church and ecclesiastical tradition, and by his insistence upon justification by faith (or by grace) alone against the Catholic conception of 'work-righteousness' and salvation by merit, Luther—it is said—arrested the centuries-old process of degeneration and restored the original purity of the Christian Faith. The doctrines of the sole sufficiency of Scripture, on the one hand, and of faith on the other, thus furnish what the old Lutheran dogmatics termed the 'material' and the 'formal' principles of the Reformation, and concisely express the whole issue at stake between the Reformers and their opponents. There is much truth in this view; yet it cannot be regarded as doing full justice either to the Evangelical or, indeed, to the Catholic position.

In the first place, the thought of a return to primitive Christianity all too easily suggests that the stream of Christian truth had early been lost in desert sands, never to reappear until it burst forth again in its original freshness and vigour in the sixteenth century. But that is clearly false. The intervening ages had not been barren, and their story is by no means one of unrelieved apostacy. The developments that had taken place, moreover, were of no merely negative significance even for Luther himself. He was a man of the sixteenth century, not of the first, and his understanding of Christianity, with all its original and penetrating insight into the New Testament, clearly bears the marks of his day and generation. In the Reformation we are not transported back through the centuries to the beginning, but we rather see the stream, which had flowed unceasingly on its very varied course from the first, divided into two channels, Evangelical and Roman Catholic. What we are interested to discover is the fundamental point of divergence, which cannot be said to be satisfactorily given in terms of the 'material' and 'formal' principles we have described.

For—in the second place—medieval Catholicism was by no means unfamiliar with the idea of the authority and, indeed, of the plenary inspiration of Scripture; nor must we forget that it also had its very highly developed doctrine of grace. In controversy, the Bible was quoted as authoritative both by the extreme 'Romanists' and the more moderate Catholic reformers. Luther's quarrel with both was not that they did not recognize the authority of Scripture, but that they did not interpret it according to its plain sense. It is all a question of what is to be found in the Bible. His antagonists, he protests, 'treat the Scriptures and make out of them what they like, as if they were a nose of wax, to be pulled about at will'.[26] The question at issue is not so much concerning a doctrine of the Bible as concerning biblical doctrine; and here the doctrine of justification is central. But it is easy to oversimplify the contrast between Luther and his opponents at this point, too. Ever since the time of Saint Augustine the question of sin and grace had been a living issue. His work had not gone for nothing, and it had made a considerable contribution especially to Saint Thomas Aquinas. Luther, trained in Nominalist ways of thought, may not have been very familiar with Aquinas[27]—who did not, in any case, at that time enjoy the authority with which he was later invested—but he well knew the important place accorded to the grace of God in the Catholic scheme of salvation. He never professes, therefore, to be preaching grace where it was not preached before; nor is it the case that his Gospel offers, so to speak, a larger proportion of grace. The question at issue is rather the very meaning of the term 'grace'—and the same may also be said of 'faith'—which Luther regards in a different light and from a different point of view from his opponents.[28]

In the attempt to express this difference, other formulae have been devised in more recent times. It is said, for instance, that the characteristic feature of the Reformation is its concentration of interest upon the inward life, the disposition of the heart, as opposed to all merely external observances. Herein lies the protest of Protestantism against both the 'sacramentalism' and the 'legalism' of Catholic piety. Closely connected with this idea is the conception that Evangelical Christianity means the assertion of subjectivism and individualism in religion against the authoritarian and hierarchical character of the Catholic system. The advantage of these views is that they recognize, at any rate, that Luther's concern is not simply with individual points of doctrine, but that his reforming point of view is one which vitally affects the whole conception of Christianity. Yet even here the contrasts suggested are misleading. We are far from doing justice to Catholicism, if we regard it as merely a matter of external observance and as lacking in appreciation of the inward disposition.[29] And we need only think of the mystics to realize that it is equally an error to suppose that no room could be found for religious subjectivism in the wide bosom of the Catholic Church. Furthermore, a grave injustice is done to Evangelical Christianity as well, if its concern for 'inwardness' is thought to imply a lack of interest either in the Sacraments or in 'good works'; or if from its 'individualism' there is deduced an unlimited 'right of private judgement' which can dispense with all authority in religion and order in the Church.

There could hardly be any more perverse caricature of Luther's whole intention than to say that the main plank in his reforming platform was the assertion of the 'right of private judgement'.

With Luther himself we may protest: 'Shall it be lawful for every
fantastical spirit to teach what himself listeth?'[30] For he is
acutely aware of the problems that are raised when he ventures
to stand, like an Athanasius *contra mundum*, against the massive
tradition and authority of the Papal Church. What assurance
can he have that he is right? Is it possible that Christ should have
permitted His Church to be in error so long, waiting for Luther
to correct it? 'Art thou alone, say they, wiser than so many holy
men, wiser than the whole Church? . . . The Church hath thus
believed and taught, this long time. So have all the doctors of
the primitive Church, holy men, more ancient and better learned
than thou. Who art thou, that darest dissent from all these and
bring unto us a contrary doctrine?'[31] Moreover, in addition
to attacks from the side of the Church, Luther has to meet the
pretensions of sectarians like the Anabaptists, who claim the
superior worth of their doctrines in virtue of special inspiration.
In all this confusion, how can we possibly know who is right?
If we say that we must believe only those who teach the pure
Word of God, we are little the wiser; for all assure us that the
Word is with them. Whom, then, shall we choose to believe?
How are we to distinguish between mere human opinion, public
or private, and the Word of God?

These were serious questions for Luther, which at times gravely
disturbed him;[32] but he has an answer for them—no matter who
opposes him:

whether it be Cyprian Ambrose, Augustine, either Saint Peter, Paul,
or John, yea, or an angel from heaven, that teacheth otherwise, yet
this I know assuredly, that I teach not the things of men, but of God:
that is to say, I attribute all things to God alone, and nothing to man.
My doctrine is such that it setteth forth and preacheth the grace and
glory of God alone, and in the matter of salvation, it condemneth the
righteousness and wisdom of all men. In this I cannot offend, because
I give both to God and man that which properly and truly belongeth
unto them both.[33]

This is for Luther the supreme test of his own and all other
doctrines—whether they set forth in one way or another the glory
of God alone. For him, no less than for Calvin, with whom we
are chiefly accustomed to associate the phrase, the watchword is
soli Deo gloria.[34] This is the ultimate ground on which he bases his

entire criticism of medieval Catholic theology and piety, and proposes to 'alter the whole religion of the Papacy'; for these, in his view, rob God of the glory that is properly His and His alone. In order to understand more precisely what this implies, we shall first consider the transformation that had taken place in Luther himself, so as to make of the monk the reformer.

3. LUTHER'S DISCOVERY OF A 'GRACIOUS GOD'[35]

Whatever may have been the occasion that led to Luther's entry into the monastery of the Augustinian Eremites at Erfurt on 17th July 1505, the ultimate reason for his taking this step cannot be in doubt. He became a monk in order to save his soul. Not that his primary motive was either the hope of heaven or the fear of hell; it was rather an imperious sense of the need for a right personal relationship to God. He wanted to be sure of his standing with God, to 'find a gracious God', to assure himself of God's goodwill toward him; and the monastic vow was the most certain means to that end. By following the evangelical 'counsels of perfection', by ascetic discipline, prayer, and meditation, he would foster that perfect love toward God and man which God's commandment required of him,[36] and without which it was impossible for him to be pleasing to God.

According to his theological preceptors—William of Occam, Pierre D'Ailly, and more especially Gabriel Biel, the masters of Nominalism and the *via moderna* that was taught at Erfurt—the goal Luther had set himself was by no means unattainable. In spite of sin, man's will was free and he could, if he would, fulfil the commandments of God to the letter. By his own native powers (*ex puris naturalibus*) he could rise from all lower affections to a disinterested love for his neighbour and a pure love for God above all things.[37] His fulfilment of the commandments in this way 'according to their substance'[38] did not of itself suffice, it is true, to give effect to the purpose of God in giving them,[39] which was man's attainment of salvation. To this end, Divine grace was essential; for salvation was unattainable without meritorious works, and no works—not even those performed in pure love— were meritorious in themselves, but only as God freely bestowed upon them the 'ornament' of grace. Nevertheless, if a man did what in him lay (*facere quod in se est*), he could at any rate acquire the merit of congruence (*meritum de congruo*) which, although it was not strictly meritorious, God in His mercy would fittingly reward with His grace. Adorned with this grace and so made acceptable to God (*gratia gratum faciens*), a man could then proceed to perform works in the strictest sense meritorious (*meritum de condigno*[40]), in virtue of which he became worthy to claim the eternal life and blessedness which he sought.

Luther threw himself wholeheartedly into the pursuit of his goal; and at times he was able to feel that he was making progress and all was well with him. But such times were neither frequent nor prolonged. He became far more familiar with tormenting doubt and fear, the fruit of constant self-examination which convinced him that he simply did not possess the true and perfect love for his neighbour and, above all, for God, without which he could not be saved. Instead, he was acutely aware of *concupiscentia*, self-love, that would not let him rest.[41] Even though he committed no particular, actual sins and, unlike many monks, was but little troubled by sexual temptations,[42] he found this 'concupiscence' in the form of self-will, pride, anger, and so forth, infecting all he did; and it filled him with doubt and anxiety.

When I was a monk [he says] I thought by and by that I was utterly cast away, if at any time I felt the lust of the flesh; that is to say, if I felt any evil motion, fleshly lust, wrath, hatred, or envy against any brother. I assayed many ways to help to quieten my conscience, but it would not be; for the concupiscence and lust of my flesh did always return, so that I could not rest, but was continually vexed with these thoughts: This or that sin thou hast committed: thou art infected with envy, with impatiency, and such other sins: therefore thou art entered into this holy order in vain, and all thy good works are unprofitable.[43]

The scholastic theologians, it is true, taught that *concupiscentia* was not in itself to be regarded as sin. It was, after the grace of Baptism at any rate, merely a remnant of original sin, a 'tinder', which gave rise to real sin only when the will consented to it. But this again occasioned questionings and apprehension in Luther's mind. Had his will not consented? Had he perfectly performed all the obligations of his Order? Was he fit to say Mass? Was he really in a state of grace—for he could perceive no evidence of its effective working in him? Was not *concupiscentia*, after all, real sin? At any rate it was directly contrary to the commandment of God, according to Romans 77: 'I had not known concupiscentiam, except the law had said, non concupisces.' Desperately Luther applied himself to his disciplines, performing more than was required by the rule of his Order, and doing serious injury to his health.[44] But still he could not find peace; for he could not find in his heart that pure love toward God, which God required of him. It is true that scholastic theology knew how to break the force of the commandment of love, by teaching that the love in question need not be present at every moment of life; it was enough if it were shown from time to time. But Luther could not be satisfied with a compromise where God's command was clear and unequivocal. He took God too seriously for that, and he knew himself under the condemnation of His law. He feared God's righteous judgement and he trembled at the name of Christ, for he was persuaded that Christ, too, was a 'severe judge'.[45]

Nor was Luther helped by the Church's unfailing panacea, the Sacrament of Penance. His sin, he was taught, could be forgiven and his standing with God assured, if in perfect penitence (contritio), marked by a whole-hearted love toward God and a hatred of evil, he made confession of his mortal sins and received absolution from a priest. Indeed, even if he could not show such a perfect penitence, the Sacrament itself would make up what was lacking to the imperfect penitence (attritio) inspired by fear. But none of this contented Luther. He did not find his fearful penitence transformed into the penitence of love, no matter how often he went to confession; and he dared not rely upon mere 'attrition'. For strongly as the Nominalists could assert the power of Divine grace in the Sacrament, Occam and Biel had insisted upon the necessity of a contrition based on pure and selfless love for God, which a man could and should produce ex naturalibus suis; and Luther took them seriously. According to Holl, the term attritio does not occur in his writings before 1517, and afterwards it is named only to be criticized.[46] Contritio was Luther's word, since contrition was what God required; but he failed to attain the contrition he sought.

When I was a monk [he tells us] I was wont to shrive myself with great devotion, and to reckon up all my sins (yet being always very contrite before); and I returned to confession very often, and thoroughly performed the penance that was enjoined unto me: yet for all this my conscience could never be fully certified, but was always in doubt, and said: this or that hast thou not done rightly: thou wast not contrite and sorrowful enough; this sin thou didst omit in thy confession, etc.[47]

It was in vain that his confessor reminded him of the authority of the Church and bade him obediently cast away his anxieties as superfluous. How could he be sure his penitence was sufficient even for that? How could he be certain he had confessed all his mortal sins? Who could exactly distinguish between mortal and venial sins?[48] It is hardly surprising that Luther could find no lasting peace, and that 'penitence' became a 'bitter word' to his ears.[49]

To add to his disquiet, another possibility occurred to Luther, which drove him quite to despair. The Occamist theology of the *via moderna* contained a great antinomy. It not only asserted without reserve man's freedom of will, by which he could do whatever he willed to do, but it also asserted in the most unqualified manner divine predestination. God's will was unconditioned and His power absolute. By an act of sheer 'arbitrary' might He had brought this world into being rather than another; He had arbitrarily determined what should be counted good or evil and had given His law; He had arbitrarily decreed certain means of salvation and just as arbitrarily predestined some to be saved and others not. This God, this irresponsible almighty Will, whose mere whim, as it seemed, had elected one section of mankind to salvation and the other to damnation—for He could have willed both that and all things else quite differently—raised a new question, the most terrifying of all, for Luther. He was endeavouring with all his might to fulfil God's commandments; and his teachers assured him that he could do so, if only he seriously willed it. Did his failure, then, mean that he did not seriously will it? If he did not, was it that he could not, that he had not the power to will it? And if so, must that not be due to God's decree, and was it not a sign that he was numbered among the eternally lost? More than once, he tells us, this thought drove him into the very abyss of despair, and he wished he had never been born.[50] It is true that late medieval Nominalism had devised means for drawing the sting from its doctrine of predestination, just as from its doctrine of *contritio*; but Luther was as incapable of compromise in the one as in the other. At times, he says, he felt the very torments of hell, which neither tongue can tell nor pen describe.[51]

Luther read Augustine; he read the mystics; he tried the mystic way. He sought to follow the directions of the Areopagite and Bonaventura, to 'climb up into the majesty of God' and experience the union of his soul with the Divine. He endeavoured after the manner of Bernard to lose himself in meditation on the Passion of Christ. But the experience the mystics described was denied to him; and the reason for this he could not doubt—he was not pure enough. Through all his tribulations he received some help from members of his Order and especially from the Vicar General, Staupitz. He was surrounded at Erfurt by personally devout and good men who, although they did not properly understand him and could not solve his problems for him, nevertheless pointed the direction in which the solution was to be found. To his wretched cry: 'O my sin, my sin, my sin!' Staupitz replied:

Thou wilt be without sin, and yet hast no real sin: Christ is the forgiveness of real sin. . . . Thou must have a register in which proper sins stand, if Christ is to help thee. . . .[52]

These words and many others of his superior Luther never forgot, nor those of his confessor, who told him: 'Thou art a fool! God is not angry with thee, but thou art angry with Him.'[53] They have left their mark on much of his later thought, but they did not at the time deliver him from his distresses.

Of greatest importance for Luther were three wise counsels of the Vicar General. Staupitz impressed upon him, first, that love for God and righteousness was only the beginning of true penitence, not its end and completion. This made clear to him the vanity of 'making pretences to God' with the 'forced and feigned love' that was all he could himself produce; for if repentance meant a complete change of heart, then only God could effect it by His prevenient grace.[54] Secondly, when he spoke of the distress he felt at the thought of predestination, Staupitz sought to lead him away from such thoughts.

In the wounds of Christ [he said] is predestination understood and found, and nowhere else; for it is written: Him shall ye hear (Matthew 17₅). The Father is too high, therefore He says: I will give a way by which men may come to Me . . . in Christ you shall find what and who I am, and what I will; otherwise you will not find it either in heaven or on earth.[55]

Lastly, Staupitz urged Luther to study his Bible, to know it chapter and verse, and become a good *textualis et localis*; and he helped him to do so, moreover, by overcoming his reluctance to take his Doctorate and inducing him to accept a Professorship in Biblical exegesis.

It was, above all, his study of the Scriptures and in particular of the Epistle to the Romans, that finally brought Luther to deliverance. Early in 1513 he began to lecture on the Psalms; and there, more than anywhere else in the Bible, he found himself confronted with the thought of the righteousness of God. It was this idea that lay at the root of all his distresses, and he was compelled to come to terms with it. If God judged men according to strict justice, who could be saved? Even the Gospel offered no alternative, it seemed; for there also, according to Romans 1.17, it was the righteousness of God that was revealed. 'Day and night' he pondered the phrase, until suddenly, with the force of a revelation, he realized the meaning of the Pauline doctrine of salvation as he read the Old Testament words, quoted and charged with new significance by the Apostle: 'The righteous shall live by faith.' 'That helped me', says Luther; and he explains that it enabled him to distinguish, as he had not done previously, between the Law and the Gospel.[56] If it was by faith that the righteous should live, then it was clearly not by doing 'what in him lay' in order to obtain the 'ornament' of grace and so become worthy of eternal life. And the righteousness of God that was revealed in the Gospel could not mean the same as that revealed in the Law. It must mean, not the retributive righteousness by which He justly visited sinners with His wrath, but a righteousness by which He justified sinners and made them righteous. It must, in fact, be one with His grace.

With his discovery of the difference between the Law and the Gospel, the solution was at hand for the problem that had driven Luther into the monastery. But the answer to his question: 'How can I find a gracious God?'—and this cannot be too strongly emphasized—was not found along the lines on which he had sought it. In his mind the question had meant: 'How can I fulfil the commandments of God and attain such conformity

with His Law as to become pleasing in His sight and be assured
of acceptance with Him?' He had understood it, that is to say,
in legal terms. But the *via moderna*, with its great antinomy—all
things are subject to God's sovereign will, yet the human will is
the decisive factor in the matter of salvation—had led him into a
complete impasse in the problem of *contritio*. To this problem he
received no solution from a legal point of view, although he did
receive the assurance of a 'gracious God' which he sought.
Deliverance came through the Gospel, not because by it he was
enabled to attain perfect contrition and secure the grace that
would make him acceptable to God, but because it revealed to
him that God in His grace freely forgave his inability to do so and
accepted him, unworthy as he was and in spite of his sin. In other
words, Luther gained a new conception of God—or rather, he
entered into a new relationship to God, a relationship established
not on the basis of Luther's righteousness—his fulfilment of the
commandment of love toward God according to the Law—but
on the basis of God's righteousness—God's fulfilment of His
promises of love, according to the Gospel, toward Luther.

The radical change in his own relationship to God changed
much else besides for Luther. A whole series of biblical ideas,
for instance, like 'the righteousness of God', received new meaning. The love of God became no longer primarily our love for
Him, but His for us; the work of God, that which He effects
in us; the wisdom of God, that whereby He makes us wise; and so
forth. Christ, moreover, appeared in a quite different light. He
was no longer a 'severe judge', a second and greater Moses with
more exacting demands, but a Saviour, whose work was to forgive
sinners and deliver them from their sin, for which Moses judged
and condemned them. Not that the reality or seriousness of
Divine judgement and wrath was lessened for a moment; for the
Law still stood, in all its rigour. But its significance was new. It
no longer prescribed the terms and conditions of salvation, but
was the hammer of God to break down man's pride and self-
reliance and drive him to surrender in faith to the forgiveness and
grace revealed in Christ, and supremely in His Cross. By the
fire of this grace, the entire medieval Catholic scheme of salvation,
with every thought of merit and worthiness, was reduced to ashes;
and Luther's own heart, which for all his endeavour had remained
so cold, was kindled with the love of God through the Holy Spirit

c

given unto him. The gift of the Spirit and the gift of love were, indeed, one and the same; and the Spirit became a living reality in Luther's life and thought as never before. He felt, he tells us, that he had become a new man and had entered through an open door into Paradise itself.[57]

For Luther now, all was gift, the undeserved and undeservable gift of Divine grace, which must be received by faith alone. It is the exclusive connexion of grace with faith that marks the main contrast between the Evangelical conception of salvation and the Catholic, in which grace is always more or less linked with the idea of merit. The Evangelical conception represents a different kind of religious relationship, in which God deals with men, not in the necessarily rather impersonal manner of a magistrate assessing their deserts, but in a wholly direct and personal way, as a true Father, who considers not what His children deserve, but what they need and what He can do for their good. Any thought of man's merit or worthiness in such a context is utterly out of place; indeed, it is blasphemy, it is an insult to God Himself.

For God giveth his gifts freely unto all men, and that is the praise and glory of his divinity. But the justiciaries and merit-mongers will not receive grace and everlasting life of him freely, but will deserve the same by their own works. Thus they would utterly take from him the glory of his divinity.[58]

It was this conviction that drove Luther to criticize 'the whole religion of the Papacy' and to seek to build up his reforming conception of Christianity. From the standpoint of his new, evangelical relationship to God, the fault of 'the Papacy' was not primarily nor essentially that it had proved incapable of satisfying the religious needs of Luther's unhappy soul,[59] but that it obscured the glory of the living God, it robbed Him of His divinity, it would not let Him be God.

4. THE THEOLOGICAL CONSEQUENCES OF LUTHER'S DISCOVERY

We may now turn to consider the broad significance of Luther's religious experience for his theological outlook. As early as 1516 he showed himself plainly opposed to the prevailing scholasticism and began to set over against it what he calls 'our theology'.

In the following year he launched an open attack upon it with his theses, *Contra scholasticam theologiam*. Not that he wished to introduce any 'new theology' in its place. 'We teach no new thing,' he insists, 'but we repeat and establish old things, which the apostles and all godly teachers have taught before us.'[60] When he is accused of innovation, he vigorously rebuts the charge and turns it against his accusers. It is not he who is the innovator, but the 'sophists', the Schoolmen, who have introduced a multitude of novelties, both in faith and practice, of which genuine Christianity knows nothing.[61] Of these he is determined to be rid—but not in order to make room for others bearing his own name; for nothing is farther from his mind.[62] All he desires is to allow the true Christian Faith to shine forth in its fullness and purity—the Faith which, although grievously obscured, has never been quite lost from the Church.[63] In view of these facts, there seems to be good ground for the contention that in Luther we have 'no innovation in doctrine, but an immense reduction, a concentration on the one article of saving faith in Christ'.[64]

Concentration there certainly is, in the most literal sense of the word. The whole of Luther's thought is centred in his new understanding of the religious relationship. His dominant interest is in what he terms 'the theological knowledge of man and the theological knowledge of God'. 'For the proper subject of theology', he explains, 'is man as guilty on account of sin, and lost, and God the justifier and saviour of man as a sinner.'[65]

Luther concentrates everything [as Bishop Aulén says in other words] around one single issue: faith and God. . . . In Luther there is at bottom only one question—the question of God. Whatever has no relation to this question has no place in his Christian thinking.[66]

Luther's characteristic standpoint, that is to say, is quite strictly and exclusively *theological*. It is not, for instance, philosophical or psychological; and his thought is inevitably misinterpreted if it is approached from such angles. This does not mean, of course, that he is unable to find a place for other than theological pursuits, or that he regards them as necessarily useless to the theologian. But he holds them distinct from theology and, we may add, also from one another. Each must remain within the limits of its own competence, dealing with the questions appropriate to itself and avoiding encroachment on another's province.

There must be no confusion of the different points of view.[67]
The questions appropriate to theology are those which concern
the relationship of man to God. The theologian must not, like
the lawyer, think of man as the 'lord of his possessions', nor,
like the physician, of man 'sick or in health', but of man as a
sinner. And he must think of God, not as 'majesty' only, but as
the justifier of sinful man.[68] He must seek to comprehend, not
the 'divine essence', but the divine 'will and affection', not God as
He is in Himself, but in His relation to men.[69]

Now it is clear that Luther's conception of the theologian's
task must mean, at least in certain directions, a quite drastic
reduction. He has, for example, notoriously little interest and
even less confidence in rational metaphysics—'speculation' as he
calls it. His theology is not speculative, but dogmatic. His
essential concern is simply to give expression to the religious
significance of the Christian Faith as he has come to understand
it. He does not attempt either to establish its truth on a rational
basis, or to elucidate the metaphysical implications of its dogmas.
He has little or no place for the traditional conception of a
'natural theology', a rational knowledge of God independent of
revelation, though consonant with it as far as it goes, such as
Aquinas expounds at length. Nor does he seek to elaborate a
theoretical explanation of the Person of Christ, for instance, or
of the Persons of the Trinity.

It is no doubt partly for such reasons as these that Luther is so
often alleged to have no contribution to make to theology; yet
it might easily be argued that it is just for such reasons that he is
able to make his most valuable contribution. When he rejects
traditional 'natural theology', that is not because he denies all
knowledge of God apart from the Christian revelation, but
because he has a deeper insight into the nature of that knowledge,
as we shall seek to show. And it certainly does not mean that he
has less to say about the nature of God, or that his conception of
God is less rich and powerful than that of Aquinas and theologians
of his type. Similarly, if he does not further the development of
Christological and Trinitarian theory, that is not because the
great classical dogmas are of little interest to him. On the
contrary, they are all-important. But they are important, not as
metaphysical statements, but as religious affirmations and
expressions of the Faith. That is what in fact the ancient dogmatic

formulations of the Creeds essentially are, and Luther seeks to interpret them as such. His concern is to draw out their specifically religious implications, their relevance to the Christian life, which speculative theories—to say no more—can easily overlook.[70] On this he sheds a flood of light—and thereby illuminates many other things besides.

By contrast with the great Schoolmen, Luther no doubt seems to display a very severe limitation of interest. They had sought to construct what may be described as a system of universal knowledge, a comprehensive world-view and an all-embracing theory of life, in which everything was thought of and thought out. In the work of Aquinas, covering virtually every aspect of contemporary intellectual and religious life, we have an un-rivalled example of what could be achieved in this direction. All manner of questions are raised and answered, and the most diverse materials are fused together with consummate dialectical skill in an apparently flawless synthesis. Long before Luther's time, however, flaws had begun to be discovered; and when he came on the scene, the imposing edifice raised by high Scholasti-cism had already crumbled into the ruins of late medieval Nominalism. Luther, needless to say, did nothing to restore it; nor did he attempt to replace it by another of a similar kind. Yet he had something to put in its place. His work was by no means merely negative, and if he dispensed with much of first im-portance to medieval (and to many modern) theologians, he did so only because he found it irrelevant or actually a hindrance to his central, constructive aim. For he sought to reconstruct Christianity on another than the medieval basis—that is to say, on the basis of his own new and positive insight into its nature. And of this it can be very justly said: 'There is nothing new here, yet it made all things new.'[71]

Luther's 'reduction' is of a kind that limits him to one point of view, yet does not restrict, but rather enlarges his range of vision. From the high vantage ground of his own new standing with God, he can survey the manifold aspects of the world and human life in the light of the knowledge of the glory of God as he now understands it. He seeks to see everything from God's point of view, as it were, and in its relation to God—for all things stand in some relation to God, even though it be a wrong one like that of the devil and wicked men. His outlook therefore lacks nothing of universality, even though there are some questions unasked because they are irrelevant to it, and others unanswered because the answer lies with the sovereign freedom of the living God. His thought, moreover, bears no less than medieval Catholicism the marks of synthesis, although it is a synthesis of a different kind.[72] Viewing things as he does in their relation to God, he is in a position to relate them also to one another in the light of the Divine will and purpose. In a world of life and movement, however, where relationships are not static and can be wrong as well as right, manifold contrasts and oppositions naturally arise; and these Luther seeks neither to conceal nor to minimize. They are reflected especially in his many paradoxes and apparent contradictions. Yet there is no inconsistency in his thought. When, to take but one example, he sharply opposes the Law to the Gospel, yet at the same time insists that it is equally a word of God, there is no real contradiction. Rightly understood, the Law is an expression of the same Divine will revealed in the Gospel; wrongly understood, it runs counter to it and contradicts the true character of God's dealings with men. For Luther, every question must be examined in the light of its relevance to the one ultimate issue of the religious relationship.

It is Luther's 'concentration', in the sense we have described, on the one point of view, that guarantees the fundamental coherence and organic unity of his outlook.

Anyone who is but a little familiar with Luther [says Einar Billing] knows that his different thoughts are not strung together like pearls in a necklace, united only by the bond of a common authority or perhaps by a chain of logical argument, but that they all lie close as the petals of a rose about a common centre, they shine out like the rays of the sun from one glowing source: the forgiveness of sins. We should be in no danger of misleading the would-be student of Luther, if we expressly gave him the rule: Never imagine you have rightly grasped a Lutheran idea until you have succeeded in reducing it to a simple corollary of the forgiveness of sins.[73]

Only, as Billing is careful to point out, we must remember that for Luther the forgiveness of sins means very much more than a doctrine to be 'believed' and much more also than a merely subjective 'experience'. It is a real act of God, the living God, through Christ, the living Christ, by which God Himself, in sheer unmerited love, establishes communion with sinful man.[74] The thought of this 'gracious God', by whom Luther's monastic struggles were brought to an end, became the starting point and dominant theme of all his subsequent thinking and living. The stamp of Divine love is impressed, in one way or another, on every aspect of his theology;[75] and for this reason alone it is no exaggeration to say that, despite all the formal diversity of his utterances, hardly any religious thinker has had so fundamentally unified an outlook as he.[76]

Luther has not bequeathed to us an ordnance survey, so to speak, of his entire theological terrain; yet if a profound insight into the nature and ways of God and a consistent ability to survey wide ranges of ideas in the light of what he sees are any qualifications for a theologian, then Luther has no less a claim to the title than Aquinas or Calvin, not to mention Melanchthon. Only the indolent, who will not submit to the discipline of thinking his thoughts after him, or the prejudiced, who for reasons of their own do not approve of him, will readily allow him to be dismissed as 'no theologian' because he does not display what have been called 'the second-rate virtues of the systematic mind'.

NOTES

1. Holmquist, *Kirkehistorie*, II.631.

2. *Works*, XIII.267.

3. *Works*, I.275.

4. *W.M.L.* V.256.

5. *Tischr.*, 31.nr.43.

6. Cave, *Person of Christ*, 148.

7. If the first edition of the *Loci* (1521) is very close to Luther's position, it does not profess to offer a complete system; and later editions, which aim at completeness, show a progressive departure from Luther on several important issues. Although Melanchthon ranks as the systematic theologian of the Lutheran Reformation, there are points of divergence between his outlook and Luther's which were often unnoticed by either of them, but which have had considerable influence on the subsequent development of Lutheranism—not least because Luther's writings have often been edited and interpreted from a Melanchthonian standpoint. See R. Bring, *Tro och g.*, and F. Hildebrandt, *Melanchthon*.

8. *W.M.L.* I.352; cf. ibid., 351: 'For whosoever keepeth one divine command, keepeth them all, and none can be kept without keeping the others.'

9. *Gal.* E.T. 344 (v.9).

10. ibid. 75.(ii.14).

11. *W.A.* XXXIX.1.205.2ff.

12. *Tischr.* 29.nr.40.

13. It is not possible to deal in detail with these questions within the limits of a single lecture. But it is hoped that the lines along which the answers must be sought will become clear in the following chapters. Their fuller treatment must be reserved for a future volume.

14. *W.M.L.* V.174.

15. ibid. 175.

16. *W.M.L.* I.109.

17. ibid. 11. The quotation is from the Preface to the 1545 edition of Luther's *Collected Works*.

18. It is particularly true of his earlier works that, as Bring, *Tro och g.* 44, says, 'his own theological intention is often as it were hidden under scholastic modes of expression'.

19. It should perhaps be said that the development of his ideas indicates no essential change in Luther's outlook. The suggestion, often used by his critics, that there is a marked divergence between the earlier and the later Luther, has been shown by modern scholarship to be without foundation. The basic principles of his reforming, or rather, evangelical position emerge in the course of his *Lectures on the Psalms*, 1513-15. They are to be seen first possibly in the exposition of Psalm 31, but certainly in that of Psalms 70 and 71—i.e. not later than the beginning of 1514 (cf. Holmquist, *Kirkehistorie*, II.15f.). From that time until his death in 1546 Luther's outlook remains in all essentials the same. There are, of course, important developments within it, due in particular to the pressure of controversy; but they are developments on the basis of, not away from, the position reached in 1513-14 (cf. R. Prenter, *Spiritus Creator*, 15).

20. *Tischr.* 26.nr.35: 'Others, who have lived before me, have attacked the Pope's evil and scandalous life; but I have attacked his doctrine. . . .' ibid. 380.nr.641: '[John Huss] attacked and castigated only the Pope's abuses and scandalous life; but I . . . have attacked the Pope's doctrine and overthrown him'; cf. ibid. 379.nr.639.

21. *Ep.* 848. cf. J. A. Froude, *Erasmus*; L'Estrange, *Colloquies.*

22. cf. Holl, *Ges. Aufs. I.* 301ff.

23. *Gal.* E.T. 320(iv.30)

24. *Tischr.* 31f.nr.44: 'Doctrine and life are to be well and truly distinguished and sundered from one another. The life is bad even with us, as also with the Papists; therefore we contend with the Papists not on account of the life, but about the doctrine. . . . When, however, the Word remains pure, then the life can come and be put right. . . .' *W.M.L.* III.299: 'I am not concerned with the life, but with doctrines. Evil life does no great harm, except to itself, but evil teaching is the greatest evil in the world, for it leads hosts of souls to hell. It does not concern me whether you are good or evil, but I will attack your poisonous and lying teaching that contradicts God's Word.'

25. *Gal.* E.T. 320f.(iv.30).

26. *W.M.L.* I.367.

27. Loofs, *D.G.* 690, says that Luther appears never really to have become acquainted with Aquinas, and comments that many contemporary Catholic theologians would be in the same position. Holl, *Ges. Aufs. I.* 172.n.2, quotes Luther's modern Catholic critic, Denifle, to the effect that a large proportion of the Doctors of Divinity contemporary with Luther in Germany 'knew no other theology than the Scotist-Nominalist'. Holmquist, *Luther,* 44, thinks Luther's theological studies included Aquinas 'to some extent'.

28. cf. Franks, *Work of Christ,* I.356f., though the definitions given there hardly express the fullness of Luther's conception. In particular, it is misleading to identify Luther's 'faith' simply with *fiducia,* confidence or trust.

29. As Luther himself points out (*Gal.* E.T. 170(iii.10)): 'The very sophisters and schoolmen are compelled to confess, and so they teach also, that a moral work outwardly done, if it be not done with a pure heart, a good will, and true intent, it is but hypocrisy.'

30. *Gal.* E.T. 41(i.12).

31. ibid. 40.

32. cf. *Tischr.* 388.nr.653: '[The devil] comes oft and casts it in my teeth that great scandal and much evil have arisen from my doctrine. Then truly at times he puts me hard to it, makes me anxious and afraid. And if I reply that much good has come of it, too, he can twist it for me masterly, etc. He is a quick, crafty talker, who can make a great beam out of a splinter; and the good that comes of the doctrine—of which, praise God, there is a great deal—he can make into sheer sin.'

33. *Gal.* E.T. 40(i.12).

34. cf. Holl, *Ges. Aufs. I.* 106.n.2: 'It is one of the peculiar prejudices of modern scholarship, that the formula "to seek the glory of God" is a "Calvinistic" conception. As if the two passages from which the idea is derived (1 Corinthians 1031 and Colossians 317) had not played a part throughout the whole of Scholasticism. Here also Calvin proves to be only continuing Luther's work.' It might, however, be said that there is a certain difference of emphasis in Calvin. For him, the glory of God is conceived primarily in terms of His sovereignty, whereas for Luther it is essentially His fatherly love—which, incidentally, determines also the nature of His sovereignty.

35. cf. H. Boehmer, *Luther,* 31-81; K. Holl, *Ges. Aufs. I.* 15-35 *et al.*; Holmquist, *Kirkehistorie,* II.1-18, *Luther,* 35-76; J. Köstlin, *Luther,* 33-67; F. Loofs, *D.G.* 685-714; T. M. Lindsay, *Hist. Ref.* I.193-213; J. Mackinnon, *Luther,* I.90-156; A. Nygren, *Agape and Eros,* II.ii.475ff.

36. Mark 12.30f.

37. cf. *Gal.* E.T. 113(ii.20): 'They teach that a man, *ex puris naturalibus*, that is, of his own pure natural strength, is able to do meritorious works before grace, and love God and Christ above all things.'

38. *quoad actus substantiam.*

39. *non ad intentionem precipientis.*

40. i.e. 'the merit of worthiness'.

41. It is of fundamental importance that for Luther *concupiscentia* means essentially self-love, self-seeking, and not primarily sensuality. 'The schoolmen', he says, *Gal.* E.T. 362f. (v.16), 'take the concupiscence of the flesh for carnal lust. . . . I do not deny therefore but that the concupiscence of the flesh comprehendeth carnal lust, but not that only. For concupiscence comprehendeth all other corrupt affections . . . as pride, hatred, covetousness, impatiency, and such like.' The 'flesh', of course, Luther understands in the Pauline sense of the term; and he regards its sensual propensities as by no means the most difficult to deal with, as K. Holl, *Ges. Aufs. I.* 137, points out. cf. *Römerbr.* 26.23: 'There is no better victory over carnal heat (*carnalis ardoris*) than the flight and aversion of the heart through devout prayer. For when the spirit is fervent, the flesh soon cools down and grows cold.' *E.A.*[2] 11.250: 'Thou canst not have such evil thoughts in thy heart, if thou settest before thee something out of the Scripture, and readest, or comest to thy neighbour and speakest of it with him. Then the evil desires are laid to rest and the flesh grows quiet. I have often tried that, and if you try it, you will find the fruit of it.' The cruder and more obvious expressions of self-love are clearly no great problem for Luther. cf. *W.A.* III.451.24: 'First is the lust of the flesh (*concupiscentia carnis*) to be overcome, and it is easier; secondly, and more difficult, the desire of the eyes (*concupiscentia oculorum*) . . .; lastly, and most difficult, the pride of life (*superbia vitae*).' *W.A.* II.584.33: 'No one is able not to feel desire (*non concupiscere*), but we are able not to give way to desires (*non obedire concupiscentiis*).' *W.A.* X.2; 291.30: 'But if thou sayest: Nay, I cannot restrain myself, then thou liest.'

42. cf. Holmquist, *Luther*, 43; Holl, *Ges. Aufs. I.* 20; Boehmer, *Luther*, 210. Luther himself says, *W.A.*, *Tischr.*I.47.15ff.: 'As a monk, I did not feel much passion (*libidinem*). I had *pollutiones* of physical necessity. I did not even look at girls when they came to confession; for I did not want to know the faces of those I heard. At Erfurt I heard none; at Wittenberg three only.' *Tischr.* 14.nr.22: 'I often confessed to Dr. Staupitz, not about women, but real problems.' Luther's sensitive soul had more subtle and serious difficulties to wrestle with than sexual desire. Detractors of his, who invent immoralities to ascribe to him, seem unwilling or unable to understand this; or else they admit it to be true of the earlier Luther, but allege that he degenerated as his reforming views developed. Yet there is not a shred of undistorted evidence that he did so. We may recall that he found it particularly difficult to rid himself of the idea of the religious value of celibacy, which he did not discard before 1521; and it was not until 1525 that he married. Melanchthon, who did not at first approve the marriage, nevertheless wrote of Luther, in a letter otherwise critical of him, that he was 'a noble and upright man', and denounced as a lie a suggestion that he had been guilty of immoral relations with his wife to be (cf. Boehmer, op. cit. 206). Of marriage itself, Luther teaches that it is the next best thing in the world to religion (*Tischr.* 184.nr.296), an ordinance and creation of God (ibid. 180ff.), 'a divine kind of life' (*W.A.* XLII.101.1). Marriage is *opus Dei*, a work of God, and it is the devil's work to destroy it (*Tischr.* 189.nr.305; 182.nr.293; 185.nr.297). It is the devil, Luther holds, that drives men to illicit sexual relations; and he thinks it might not be a bad thing if adultery were made a severely punishable offence (*W.A.* XI.94). It would be strange indeed if a man who held such views, and whose own marriage, as his letters to his wife abundantly testify, was a singularly happy one, should either have committed or countenanced immorality—unless, of course, we are to share Father Denifle's monkish view, that Luther's marriage was really no marriage at all, but a worse offence than the concubinage practised by celibate priests (cf. Boehmer, op. cit. 210).

43. *Gal.* E.T. 367(v.17).

44. ibid. 42(i.14): 'I was so diligent and superstitious in the observance hereof, that I laid more upon my body than, without danger of health, it was able to bear.' *S.W.* I.146: 'For I have learnt this also in my own experience—that, after all my watching, my strivings, my fastings, my prayings, and other laborious exercises, by which, when a Monk, I afflicted myself almost unto death, that doubtfulness still remained in my mind, which left me to think thus: Who knows whether these things be pleasing unto God?'

45. *Gal* E.T. 117(ii.20): 'At the very hearing of the name of Christ my heart hath trembled and quaked for fear: for I was persuaded that He was a severe judge.' ibid. 99(ii.18): 'I thought Christ to be a judge (although I confessed with my mouth, that He suffered and died for man's redemption) and ought to be pacified by the observation of my rule and order.' cf. ibid. 254(iv.4).

46. *Ges. Aufs. I.* 24.n.1.

47. *Gal.* E.T. 330(v.3).

48. Luther's Catholic critics have seen in his attitude here a mark of his spiritual pride. His refusal to content himself with the authority of the Church on these matters is alleged to mean that he blindly opposed his own private judgement to that of the Church. Yet in fact it was no private judgement, but an unequivocal commandment of God, which Catholic theologians had taught him he must fulfil, that he opposed to the methods they used for accommodating it to human frailty.

49. *W.M.L.* I.40; *Letters,* 26.

50. *B.o.W.* 243; *W.A.* XVIII.719.9ff.

51. In the *Resolutions to the Theses* of 1518. cf. Mackinnon, *Luther,* I.113f., where the passage is quoted.

52. *Tischr.* 13.nr.20.

53. ibid. 14f.nr.22.

54. *W.M.L.* I.39ff.

55. *Tischr.* 12.nr.19.

56. ibid. 26.nr.36: 'I was long in error under the Papacy . . . until at last I came upon the saying in Romans 117: "The righteous lives by his faith." That helped me. Then I saw of what righteousness Paul speaks, where there stood in the text *Iustitia,* 'righteousness. Then . . . I became sure of my case, learnt to distinguish the righteousness of the Law from the righteousness of the Gospel. Before, I lacked nothing but that I made no distinction between the Law and the Gospel, held them to be all one, and said that between Christ and Moses there was no difference but in time and perfection. . . .' cf. *W.A. Tischr.* V.210.7ff., where the continuation of this passage reads: 'But when I found the distinction, that the Law was one thing, the Gospel another, then I broke through. Then Doctor Pomeranus: I, too, began to change when I read concerning the love of God, that its meaning was passive, namely, that with which we are loved by God. Before that, I always used to take love in the active sense. Doctor Luther: Aye, it is clear, *charitate* or *dilectione*! I mean, that it is often understood of that with which God loves us.'

57. Mackinnon, *Luther,* I.151, dates Luther's transforming experience between the autumn of 1512 and the summer of 1513, when he began his *Lectures on the Psalms.* Holmquist, *Kirkehistorie,* II.15f., thinks it took place during the course of the *Lectures,* but not later than the beginning of 1514. Since there is no decisive evidence of it before the exposition of Psalm 70, Holmquist's date seems the more likely.

58. *Gal.* E.T. 81(ii.16).

59. For Luther, the Gospel is never an easier way for sinful man to obtain a salvation he desires but cannot attain by his own endeavours. It is essentially the means by which God's will is realized for and in and through man; and it brings with it a different conception of salvation, as we shall see.

60. *Gal.* E.T. 20(i.14). cf. *W.M.L.* III.15: 'I preach nothing new, but I say that all things Christian have gone to wrack and ruin among those who ought to have held them fast, to wit, the bishops and the doctors; yet I have no doubt that the truth has remained even until now in some hearts . . . poor peasants and children understand Christ better than pope, bishops, and doctors.'

61. cf. *W.M.L.* IV.344ff.

62. *W.M.L.* III.218: 'I ask that men make no reference to my name, and call themselves not Lutherans, but Christians. What is Luther? My doctrine, I am sure, is not mine, nor have I been crucified for anyone. . . . How then should I, poor, foul carcase (*Madensack*) that I am, come to have men give to the children of Christ a name derived from my worthless name?'

63. *W.M.L.* V.26: 'Many children and young people have died in Christ: for even under Antichrist, Christ has with might preserved baptism, the bare text of the Gospel in the pulpit, the Lord's Prayer, and the Creed, so as to preserve many of His Christians and thus preserve His Church.' cf. n.60 *supra*.

64. Cave, *Person of Christ*, 139.

65. *S.W.* I.65.

66. Aulén, *Gudsbilden*, 163.

67. cf. *W.A.* XLII.35f., where Luther argues this point at length and also urges that none of the various arts and sciences should regard any of the rest as valueless, but that all should assist one another and co-operate for the common good.

68. *S.W.* I.65.

69. ibid., 187: 'Men describe God, speculatively, by certain similitudes;—that God is the centre which is everywhere, and the sphere which is nowhere. But all that is mathematical and physical, which we leave to other professors. We are seeking the theological definition: that is, not a definition of the divine essence, which is incomprehensible, but of his will and affection,—what pleases him and what does not please him.'

70. Luther himself appears to make an occasional 'speculative' excursion, as when, for instance, he propounds such doctrines as the 'communication of the attributes' or 'consubstantiation'. Yet if these doctrines are understood as metaphysical statements, they are singularly unilluminating. What Luther means to convey by them can only be seen if they are interpreted as religious affirmations and expressions of his fundamental conviction about the nature of the religious relationship.

71. Cave, *Person of Christ*, 139.

72. Aulén describes it as 'dynamic' in contrast to the 'dialectical' synthesis of Aquinas (*Gudsbilden*, 166); Nygren terms it 'organic' (*Etiska grdfr.* 76f.).

73. *V. Kallelse*, 6f.

74. ibid. 10. Billing says: 'When I lie prostrate in deepest spiritual need, He Himself comes—this is not a metaphorical description of a change in my subjective condition, but a full, actual reality—in order to effect that blessed exchange of which Luther speaks in his book on the Liberty of a Christian: He takes all my sin, I receive all His fullness.'

75. Nygren, *Agape and Eros*, II.ii.477: 'It could be shown without difficulty how the Agape motif has set its seal on Luther's thought at every point.'

76. Bring, *Dualismen*, 26.

CHAPTER TWO

THE MOTIF OF LUTHER'S THOUGHT

5. LUTHER'S COPERNICAN REVOLUTION

LUTHER, we have said, believed it to be of the nature of his task to 'alter the whole religion of the Papacy'. Modern Lutheran scholars have spoken of his achievement in this direction as a 'Copernican Revolution'.[1] They have likened the change he effected in the conception of Christianity to that which Copernicus effected in the conception of the physical universe. This comparison has been challenged, and we shall have occasion to consider some of the objections that have been raised against it. But first we must try to see precisely what it implies.

In the Preface to the *Critique of Pure Reason*, Immanuel Kant compares his own work with that of Copernicus. 'In metaphysical speculations', he says, 'it has always been assumed that all our knowledge must conform to objects. . . . The time has now come to ask, whether better progress may not be made by supposing that objects must conform to our knowledge. . . . Our suggestion is similar to that of Copernicus in astronomy. . . .' Now, quite apart from the fact that Kant's epistemological subjectivism, as it is called, is open to more serious criticism, it is clear that the suggested comparison is curiously inapt. Kant seeks to solve the problem of knowledge in exactly the opposite way to that in which Copernicus sought to solve his astronomical problem. In pre-Copernican astronomy it had always been assumed that the earth, the standpoint of the spectator, was the centre of the universe, around which the sun and planets revolved. Copernicus' revolutionary thesis is directly to the contrary. The sun is the centre, the fixed point, by reference to which the place of all else in the solar system is determined. Nothing but an easily explicable optical illusion leads us to imagine that everything moves round the earth and round the spectator. The universe is heliocentric, not geocentric. A Copernican revolution therefore means the transference of the centre of gravity from the subject to the object— exactly the reverse of Kant's procedure when he makes the object of knowledge conform to the knowing subject.

We have far more reason to speak of a Copernican revolution in Luther's case than in that of Kant. For just as Copernicus started with a geocentric, but reached a heliocentric conception of the physical world, Luther began with an anthropocentric or egocentric conception of religion, but came to a theocentric conception. In this sense, Luther is a Copernicus in the realm of religion.

Whatever else religion may be, it is at any rate a relationship; and as such it includes two factors. It is the relationship between man and the eternal, man and God. Hence the possibility is given, broadly speaking, of two main types of religion, according as one or the other of these two factors predominates and becomes the centre of gravity, so to speak, in the relationship. If the religious relationship centres in man—if my relation to God depends essentially upon me—then it can be described as anthropocentric or egocentric; if it centres in the eternal and the divine, then it is theocentric. Now it might well seem as if all religion must, in the nature of the case, be theocentric; for if the word 'God' is to have any meaning at all, it cannot but signify the dominant centre of life and of all existence. And it is true that no religion is entirely lacking in awareness of this fact. All religions display at least some traces of theocentricity.[2] Such traces, however, do not generally suffice to form what may be termed the *leitmotif* of the religion; they are not determinative of its character as a whole, but in one way and another are subordinated to the egocentric tendency. For illusion occurs in religion as easily as in the physical world. Even though I have learnt that the sun is the centre around which my earth moves, and I with it, I still tend to live and think as if the sun moved around my earth and me. Similarly in religion, although I readily admit that God must be the centre of existence, I do not as readily perceive or accept all that this implies; and it is the most natural thing for me still to live and think as if I myself were the centre around which all else, even including God, moved. I find it exceedingly difficult to rid myself of this illusion and allow God really to be the centre, that is, really to be God.

Egocentricity in religion is seen perhaps at its simplest and crudest in that conception of sacrifice which is expressed in the formula *do ut des*. I offer my gift in order to win the Divine favour and so to obtain what I wish from the Divine power. But the same egocentric motive can be exhibited equally, if less obviously, at much more refined levels. It finds characteristic expression in the moralism, or legalism, and the eudemonism which, commonly going hand in hand, are to be observed in many otherwise widely differing forms of religion. Moralism means that my moral and spiritual attainments are regarded as decisive for the establishment and maintenance of the religious relationship. I have to do or become something in order to enable God to regard me with approval and in this way secure my standing with Him. My good and meritorious works, for example, or my personal holiness, however conceived and acquired, are assumed to be the essential basis and guarantee of my acceptance with God. Eudemonism means that my desires and needs, whether temporal or spiritual, are the fundamental inspiration of my quest for acceptance with God. I seek God in pursuit of my own interests. Impelled, for instance, by the fear of hell and hope of heaven, or by a yearning for present peace of heart and mind, I seek God no less for my own satisfaction than if I sought material advantages at His hands. In egocentric religion, fellowship with God depends ultimately on man's achievement and is sought ultimately for man's own ends. God is characteristically conceived in terms of the answer to human problems and needs.

In theocentric religion, on the other hand, God is the sovereign and unquestionable Lord of man's existence. He confronts man with compelling authority; and in His presence there is no place left for egoism in any form. He cannot be regarded here as the One from whom I expect either the fulfilment of my desires or the reward of my deserts. The question of my relationship to Him is not even in the remotest sense optional, dependent on my wishes or sense of need. It is a matter of urgent and imperious necessity. It is also a question to which the answer does not lie finally with me. Nothing that I may do or become can decisively ensure my standing with God. I cannot establish a claim to His favour or control His dealings with me. He is not to be moved by my merits or worthiness or by anything else of mine. On the contrary, I am moved by Him. I am moved both to seek fellowship with Him and to strive to do His will—not for the sake of any benefit I may derive therefrom, but simply and solely because such is His good pleasure and my unconditional obligation.

In egocentric religion, we may say, man is the measure of

all things—even of God. For God Himself is understood in the light of man. In theocentric religion it is God who is the 'disposer supreme', the final arbiter of all things. Here, man is understood in the light of God. Expressing the difference in specifically religious language, we may say: in egocentric religion, man chooses or 'elects' God; in theocentric religion, God chooses or 'elects' man.

There is no single aspect of religion which may not bear the marks of egocentricity or theocentricity, according as the one or the other of these constitutes the fundamental character of the religious relationship. Prayer, for instance, may be simply the means by which I seek to obtain for myself benefits that are otherwise beyond my reach; or it may express—not least in its petitionary form—my utter dependence for all that I have and am on God alone. A belief in Providence may mean that I regard God as existing simply to safeguard my interests and furnish me with a secure basis for the pursuit of my own purposes; or it may mean that I am persuaded of the goodness and wisdom of the Divine purpose, even when this runs counter to my own. Salvation may suggest nothing to me but the idea of my own perfect happiness, if not in this world, at any rate in the next; or it may signify the conformity of my human will with the Divine, so that I am content to play whatever part God may appoint for me in His scheme of things. Again, God Himself may be conceived as the *summum bonum*. As generally interpreted, this means that, although I must not seek God for the sake of anything beyond Himself, yet I may and should seek Him as *my* 'Highest Good', as that which alone can give full and permanent satisfaction to my deepest needs. In sharp contrast with this, there stands the witness of the New Testament that there is none good but God, whose ways are to be acknowledged as righteous even when from my point of view they least seem to be so, and whose holy will is to be sought and obeyed as good even though it in no way ministers to my wishes.

The two types of religion we have described, it is clear, stand in the sharpest opposition to one another. In their purest forms they would be mutually exclusive. But in actual practice they rarely appear in their purity. As we have already said, all religions show at least some traces of the theocentric motif; and we may add that even the most theocentric of all religions has been unable, in the course of its history, to escape the influence of man's natural tendency to adapt everything to his own point of view. The history of Christianity is a story of continuous conflict between the two contrasted tendencies.[3]

In the light of what has been said, it should be clear what is implied by the claim that Luther is a Copernicus in the realm of religion. Religion as he found it in medieval Catholicism was of an essentially egocentric character—despite the presence of certain undeniably theocentric traits in it. His significance in the history of religion is that in him the theocentric tendency fully and unequivocally asserted, or rather reasserted itself. For it had done so at least once before. In primitive Christianity, God was both Alpha and Omega, both the ground and the goal of the religious relationship. Of Him and through Him and unto Him were all things. But this insight early began to be obscured and subordinated to the egocentric tendency that crept in with moralistic and eudemonistic ideas. Such ideas Luther found playing a dominant role in medieval Catholicism. He himself began with an egocentric conception in his quest for a 'gracious God'. His problem was: 'How can I attain such conformity with the Law of God that I may be sure of acceptance with Him and secure peace for my troubled mind and conscience?' He found a gracious God, as we have seen, but not by the way he had sought, not by becoming worthy of God's approval. Indeed, it was rather the gracious God who found him and took him to Himself, despite his unworthiness and sin. Luther did not win God's favour by his merits, but God's unmerited grace overmastered Luther and became the compelling force in his life. To his egocentric question, we might say, Luther received a theocentric answer, which became thenceforward his dominant and all-absorbing theme. We can certainly speak of a Copernican revolution here.

In Luther, the theocentricity of primitive Christianity returns; and it is the determining factor of his whole outlook. His opposition to Catholicism is due ultimately to nothing else but this. In the Catholic conception of Christianity, it is in the last analysis man who occupies the centre of the religious stage; in Luther's reforming conception it is God. Luther seeks to eradicate every vestige of the egocentric or anthropocentric tendency from the religious relationship. There is no place for the slightest degree of human self-assertion or self-interest in the presence of God.

D

Here, man must be content to receive undeserved the gifts God wills to bestow on him, and to obey without thought of reward the commandments God pleases to give him. In other words, he must let God really be God, the centre around which his whole existence moves. This theocentric emphasis can be described as the fundamental motif of Luther's entire thought.[4]

6. THE CONSISTENCY OF LUTHER'S OUTLOOK

The importance to Luther himself of the theocentric point of view, and his consequent opposition to the egocentric tendency, can easily be seen if we consider a number of representative passages. These are not quotations taken at random, or in isolation from their contexts, but are illustrative of the way in which Luther handles quite fundamental themes.

(a) The first passage comes from the *Lectures on the Epistle to the Romans* of 1515-16.[5] At the outset of the *Lectures*, Luther seeks to epitomize the message of the Epistle as he understands it. Knowing the significance that Romans 1 17 had acquired for him only a short time before,[6] we might well expect here a dissertation on justification *sola fide*. And this, in a sense, is what he gives us, although he presents it in a rather unexpected light. 'The sum of this Epistle', he begins, 'is to break down, pluck up and destroy all carnal wisdom and righteousness'—and he makes it clear that he means no mere outward show of wisdom and righteousness, but all wisdom and righteousness of ours, 'be they exercised never so sincerely and from the heart'. Where, then, are such wisdom and righteousness at fault? Simply in that they minister to our self-complacency and confirm us in our self-centredness. Even the best and sincerest of men, who have pursued righteousness 'from a sheer passion for virtue', with never a thought of making a boast of it before others, have not been able to prevent themselves from being inwardly pleased with themselves and glorying in it at least secretly in their hearts. In the Epistle to the Romans we are taught that the precise opposite of this must be done. Not only are we to make no parade of our righteousness, but it is to be rooted out of our hearts. What was said to Jeremiah holds good here:

'To pluck up, break down, destroy and overthrow', namely, everything that is in us (i.e. all that of ourselves and in ourselves pleases us), 'and to build and to plant', everything that is outside of us and in Christ.

When he sets what is 'outside of us' over against that which is 'in us', Luther is simply giving expression to the opposition between the theocentric and the egocentric tendency in religion.

For [he continues] God wills to save us, not by domestic, but by extraneous righteousness and wisdom, not that which comes and springs from us, but that which comes from elsewhere into us, not that which originates in our earth, but that which comes down from heaven. Therefore it behoves us to be instructed in a righteousness altogether external and alien. Wherefore it is first necessary that our own and domestic righteousness should be rooted out.

When the relationship between God and man is under discussion, the question of righteousness is always immediately raised; for without righteousness there can be no fellowship with God. But whose righteousness, what kind of righteousness, is decisive here? Is it 'domestic' or 'extraneous', earthly or heavenly, man's or God's? For Luther, the answer is not in doubt. The religious relationship does not rest on the basis of human righteousness, but of Divine.[7]

For [he explains] if anyone in virtue either of natural or of spiritual gifts is wise, righteous and good in the sight of men, he is not *therefore* accounted such before God, above all if he himself also accounts himself such.[8]

(b) In a little work that goes under the title of '*A short and good Exposition of the Lord's Prayer forwards and backwards*', Luther sets in sharpest contrast the egocentric and the theocentric types of prayer.[9]

The Lord's Prayer can be prayed, says Luther, either 'forwards' or 'backwards'. It is prayed 'forwards' when the order of its clauses is observed and we pray first for the hallowing of God's name, the coming of God's kingdom and the doing of God's will. It is prayed 'backwards' when—in our hearts, if not with our lips—we begin with the seventh clause. Those who pray it in this way 'seek rather their own honour and glory and a name for themselves than the glory of God'. What they want is salvation from all evil, deliverance from all misfortunes, in order that they may live in happiness and please themselves. And when they come to the first three clauses, they still have not forgotten themselves, but 'want and desire above all things their own glory, their own kingdom and power, and their own will'. Even the first three clauses can be prayed selfishly; and in the very order in which they occur, Luther sees a warning against this.

In order that we should not desire the kingdom of God for our own sake, the hallowing of the Divine name is put in the first place; so that we should pray in this sense to be blessed and for the coming of God's kingdom, not in order that it may go well with us, but that the name and honour and glory of God the Lord may be praised and magnified.

It is true that when God's name is hallowed, 'it follows of itself that things go well and blessedly with us'; but we must not pray for it on that account. If we do, then our concern is not for the glory of God, but for ourselves.

Therefore it is to be noted that in the first three clauses the word 'Thy', and in the following ones 'us' and 'our' stand to teach us that we should first seek and desire God's glory, kingdom, and will, and then seek and desire what is our own, but even then only in and with the things that are God's honour, kingdom, and will.

It is of considerable importance that Luther's theocentric interest does not lead him to exclude petitionary prayer, that is, prayer about our own concerns and needs. He does not share the view, frequently expressed, that such prayer has necessarily a selfish taint and is therefore inferior, from a Christian point of view, to praise and adoration.[10] On the contrary, he sets a very high value on petition, precisely as a means of guarding against selfishness and ensuring true theocentricity in prayer. Our prayer for our daily bread can, of course, be egocentric. It is so when we seek to use God as a means to an end, to have Him at our service, ministering to our requirements. Luther will have none of this, as we have just seen above. He excludes all self-seeking from prayer. But egocentricity can take the form, not only of self-seeking, but also of self-reliance and self-assertion; and of this also Luther will be rid. But it is not to be banished by banishing petition. If we omit the request for our daily bread, or for any other of our necessities, from our prayers, does not this imply that we suppose ourselves capable of managing our own affairs and

THE MOTIF OF LUTHER'S THOUGHT

supplying our own needs without God? And is not this an example of extreme self-confidence? The simple fact is that without God we can do nothing; we are utterly dependent on Him for all that we have and are; and it is precisely by petitionary prayer that we can make clearest and fullest acknowledgement of this fact. Rightly understood, petition gives expression to the true relationship between man and God.[11] We do not move God by our requests to fulfil our desires, but, as Luther explains in the *Short Catechism*:

God gives daily bread to all men, even the wicked, without our prayer; but we pray in this prayer that we may recognize this goodness of God and with gratitude receive our daily bread.

In relation to God, we are always recipients, not bestowers, of good. It is this relationship that petition most effectively expresses, and it is hardly too much to say that to exclude petition from our prayers is to exclude God from our lives. For, as Luther says in the *Greater Catechism*,

because He is God, He takes upon Himself the honour of giving far more, and more abundantly than anyone can understand; for He is like an everlasting and inexhaustible spring, which, the more it flows and runs over, the more it gives forth; and He desires nothing more of us than that we should ask many and great things of Him, and is vexed if we do not ask and demand with confidence. Much in the same way as though the richest and mightiest emperor bade a poor beggar ask for whatever he wanted, being ready to bestow great and royal gifts, and the poor fool asked for nothing but a cup of broth; he would justly be esteemed a rogue and a knave thus to make a jest of the royal command, and therefore not worthy to appear before his sovereign. In the same way it is a disgrace and dishonour to God if we, to whom He offers and promises inestimable blessings, despise them or do not confidently accept them, scarcely venturing even to ask for a piece of bread.[12]

If 'the glory of God is, that He bestows blessings with a certain bounty and overflowing abundance',[13] we do Him no honour, indeed we dishonour Him, by despising petition. We cannot 'give unto the Lord the glory due unto His name',[14] unless we gladly and gratefully accept the gifts He has given, and humbly ask Him to give more and yet more.[15] It is just in thankful and confident petition that we most truly acknowledge God to be God.

(c) In a discussion of two kinds of men and the faith they exhibit, Luther describes and contrasts what may very well be characterized as egocentric and theocentric faith.[16]

The main distinction between the two types of faith is that the one is faith pure and simple, founded on God alone, whereas the other is founded on what man himself perceives and experiences of Divine beneficence. Those whose faith is of the latter kind, if they do not experience 'external help and comfort from God', immediately imagine that God has forsaken them. Such men 'seek nothing but their own', they 'do not commit themselves wholly to the goodwill of God'; they praise God and seek to serve Him so long as He bestows perceptible benefits upon them, but as soon as these are withdrawn, then

an unwillingness seizes their minds to serve God any longer, and their love, their praise, the whole of their worship of God, is frozen up together.

Such men love themselves and not God; and they can hardly be said to have any real faith at all. Of those who have genuine faith, on the other hand, Luther says that 'in whatever they do or leave undone' they 'seek the honour of God only, and not their own advantage'. They are content simply to know that God is good, whether they themselves perceive and experience His benefits or not.

They love God and extol His goodness with praises as much when God deprives them of all those external supplies, as they do when He abundantly bestows these things upon them.

Their religious life, in other words, is centred wholly in God; it does not hinge upon their own experience; they 'walk' quite literally 'by faith, not by sight'.[17]

An exactly similar distinction is drawn by Luther in his exposition of the *Magnificat* (1521). Explaining the second clause, 'And my spirit hath rejoiced in God my Saviour', he finds it easy to read into his text an idea which he has very much at heart.

Mary [he says] calls God her Saviour, or her Salvation, even though she neither saw nor felt that this was so, but trusted in sure confidence that He was her Saviour and her Salvation. . . . And, truly, she sets things in their proper order when she calls God her Lord before calling

Him her Saviour, and when she calls Him her Saviour before recounting His works. Whereby she teaches us to love and praise God for Himself alone, and in the right order, and not selfishly to seek anything at His hands. This is done when one praises God because He is good, regards only His bare goodness, and finds one's joy and pleasure in that alone. . . . But the impure and perverted lovers, who are nothing else than parasites and who seek their own advantage in God, neither love nor praise His bare goodness, but have an eye to themselves and consider only how good God is to them, that is, how deeply He makes them feel His goodness and how many good things He does to them. They esteem Him highly, are filled with joy and sing His praises, so long as this feeling continues, but as soon as ever He hides His face and withdraws the rays of His goodness, leaving them bare and in misery, their love and praise are at an end. They are unable to love and praise the bare, unfelt goodness that is hidden in God. . . . They delighted in their salvation much more than in their Saviour, in the gift more than in the Giver. . . . Here apply the words in Psalm 49: 'They will praise thee when thou shalt do well with them.' That is to say, they love not Thee, but themselves.[18]

It is not difficult to see that, when Luther opposes faith to feeling, perception, experience, he is simply giving expression to the opposition between theocentric and egocentric religion. A 'faith' that depends upon my apprehension of God's goodness in the shape either of my prosperous circumstances or of my peace of heart and mind, is simply not faith in *God*. At the same time, it should be pointed out that Luther by no means wishes to depreciate religious feeling and 'experience'. There is ample evidence that he can value them highly and give great weight to them.[19] Only, true religious faith is not founded on religious experience, but rather religious experience springs from faith.

(*d*) A favourite theme of Luther's, to which he returns again and again, is the exposition of the First Commandment. This Commandment is for him the perfect epitome of the entire Law of God—and more; for he even finds the Gospel included in it as well.[20] The right interpretation of the First Commandment, therefore, gives a complete understanding of the true relationship between man and God; and here there can be no doubt about the theocentricity of Luther's view.

In his *Treatise on Good Works*, Luther explains the Commandment, 'Thou shalt have no other gods', to mean:

'Since I alone am God, thou shalt place all thy confidence, trust and faith on Me alone, and on no one else.' For that is not to have a god, if you call him God only with your lips, or worship him with the knees or bodily gestures; but if you trust Him with the heart, and look to Him for all good, grace, and favour, whether in works or sufferings, in life or death, in joy or sorrow.

Expounding this farther, Luther says:

Now you see for yourself that all those who do not at all times trust God and do not in all their works or sufferings, life and death, trust in His favour, grace, and good-will, but seek His favour in other things or in themselves, do not keep this Commandment. . . . Such are all who wish with their many good works, as they say, to make God favourable to themselves, and to buy God's grace from Him, as if He were a huckster or a day-labourer, unwilling to give His grace and favour for nothing. . . . Such too are all who in adversity run hither and thither, and look for counsel and help everywhere except from God, from whom they are most urgently commanded to seek it . . . they do not run to God, but flee from Him, and only think how they may get rid of their trouble through their own efforts or through human help.[21]

Have we not here once more the contrast between the egocentric (or anthropocentric) and the theocentric life? To seek to 'buy God's grace from Him' is to transfer the centre of gravity in religion from God to man, for it makes everything depend on whether man can find the means—the good works and merits— to pay for the favour of God. It is similarly a denial of theocentricity, of the Godhead of God, if we seek to obtain 'counsel and help' or indeed any good thing otherwise than at His hands.

(e) Luther's constant insistence that God is the great Giver, to whom we must look for all good, might well seem to invite us to seek God, not for His own sake, but for ours, in order to obtain the gifts He alone can bestow. But we have only to consider Luther's conception of the meaning of salvation to see how thoroughly he guards against this danger.

There are those, Luther says, who

do not know what it is to be blessed and saved, unless it is to take their pleasure and fare well according to their imagination. Whereas to be blessed means this: to will the will of God and His glory and to desire nothing of one's own either here or hereafter.[22]

The glory of God is to be sought before all and above all and in all things, and all our life eternally is to redound to God's glory alone, not to our advantage, not even to our blessedness or any good thing, whether temporal or eternal.[23]

Those who seek the Kingdom of God, moved by the thought of heavenly joy and delight and by the fear of hell, 'seek only their own, and their own advantage, in heaven'. They do not know that God's kingdom means our being filled with all virtue and grace, when God himself is, lives, and reigns, in us. 'For this it is to be saved [selig], when God reigns in us and we are His kingdom'. Joy and delight, peace and blessedness, and all else that is to be desired, are a natural and necessary accompaniment of this Kingdom of God, 'just as a good wine cannot be drunk without bringing , unsought and of itself, pleasure and delight'; only, we must not seek the Kingdom for the sake of these things.[24] If we do, we are not truly seeking the Kingdom of God, but our own. Luther leaves no place for the selfish quest of either material or spiritual blessings in religion. Salvation consists, not in the satisfaction of our desires and needs, but in the realization of God's will and purpose for us; and those who truly love God, Luther can say,

freely offer themselves to all the will of God, even to hell and death eternally, should God so will, in order that His will may be fully done.[25]

Luther does not deny, it is important to notice, that there are rewards for the faithful service of God—and punishments for disobedience. He does not ignore the many New Testament passages that speak plainly on this matter.[26] But rewards are to be understood as the natural and inevitable consequence of our service of God, and must not constitute the motive for it.[27]

If you speak of the *consequence* [Luther writes in the *De servo arbitrio*] there is nothing either good or evil which has not its reward. And here arises an error, that, in speaking of merits and rewards, we agitate opinions and questions concerning *worthiness*, which has not existence, when we ought to be disputing concerning *consequences*. For there remains, as a necessary consequence, the judgement of God and a hell for the wicked, even though they themselves neither conceive nor think of such a reward for their sins. . . . In the same manner, there remains a kingdom for the just, even though they themselves neither seek it nor think of it. . . . Nay, if they should work good in order to obtain the Kingdom, they would never obtain it, but would be numbered rather with the wicked, who, with an evil and mercenary eye, seek the things of self even in God. Whereas, the sons of God do good with a free-will, seeking no reward, but the glory and will of God only; ready to do good, even if (which is impossible) there were neither a Kingdom nor a hell.[28]

By all the passages of Scripture which speak of rewards,

the *consequence of reward* is proved and nothing else, but by no means the *worthiness of merit*; [for] those who do good, do it not from a servile and mercenary principle in order to obtain eternal life, but . . . they are in that way, in which they shall come unto and find eternal life.[29]

(*f*) Finally, we may consider the significance of Luther's theo-centric emphasis for his conception of ethics. There is a fairly common idea that his intense concentration on the religious issue obscured for him the importance of ethical realities; but nothing could be farther from the truth. He is just as concerned about ethics as about religion. For him, the two are inseparable; they are but distinguishable aspects of his one dominant theme. God is the sovereign centre of all existence—that is Luther's controlling principle. With it he stands opposed to all human egocentricity, wherever it may be found. Just as—indeed, we may say, *because*—he insists that God and not man's self shall be the determining factor in the religious relationship, so also he insists that the good (the will of God) and not man's own interests shall be decisive in the ethical life. As we have seen, he utterly repudiates every thought of merit and reward as a motive for the service of God. I am to serve God for His own sake, simply because He is God; otherwise I do not really serve God, but myself. Now this repudiation of self-interest in religion has immediate and important consequences for ethics. Since it forbids me to regard my ethical attainments as in any way meritorious, it sets me free to pursue the ethical good for its own sake (or for God's sake) alone. It opens the way for a selfless doing of good that is patterned on the Divine goodness itself. God is the great giver of all good freely to all men, and His children resemble Him in their dealings with others. 'No man', says Luther, 'does good for God's sake or for virtue's sake, but all for his own sake. But God and His children do good gratuitously'.[30] Only the good that is done in this way can, in Luther's view, be regarded as in any real sense ethically good.

THE MOTIF OF LUTHER'S THOUGHT

By this [he says] God shows that His goodness is right naturally good, for it does not stand or fall according to another's virtue or vice, as the goodness of men stands on other people's virtue and falls on account of another's vice.[31]

In other words, God does good because it is His nature to do so; He is not moved by the merits or demerits of men, but only by His own essential goodness. It is from this goodness of God that Luther draws his ethical ideal.

But why should I wish to realize the ethical ideal? Why should I seek to do good at all? If, as Luther so tirelessly asserts, my good deeds are no passport to heaven, what need have I to do them? If God's goodwill toward me is independent of my goodness, why may I not sin, that grace may abound? Such questions, raised by Luther's opponents as by those of Saint Paul, reveal at once an egocentric point of view. The questioner cannot conceive of moral obligation except in terms of a *quid pro quo*, and the idea of doing something for nothing makes moral nonsense to him. But from Luther's theocentric standpoint, such questions could never arise. No man who seriously acknowledges God as the sovereign centre of all existence can seek to assert himself and his own interests as central in any part of it. Being in a right relationship to God, he finds the rest of his relationships transformed accordingly; and being moved by the 'gratuitous' goodness of God, by which he himself lives, he finds it quite natural to do good to others without a thought of what they deserve at his hands, or of what he himself may stand to gain or lose by it. From this point of view, the egocentric principle of a *quid pro quo* must be rejected as entirely unethical. But this does not mean that to do good 'gratuitously' is to do it for no reason at all.

Luther knows of a far deeper moral necessity than his critics have envisaged, and when their questions are put to him, he can only regard them as irrelevant and meaningless. Why should a tree bear fruit? Why ought the sun to shine?

It is as absurd and stupid [Luther declares] to say: the righteous ought to do good works, as to say: God ought to do good, the sun ought to shine, the pear-tree ought to bear pears, three and seven ought to be ten; for all this follows of necessity by reason of the cause and the consequence . . . it all follows without commandment or bidding of

any law, naturally and willingly, uncompelled and unconstrained. . . .
The sun shines by nature, unbidden; the pear-tree bears pears of itself,
uncompelled; three and seven ought not to be ten, they are ten already.
There is no need to say to our Lord God that He ought to do good; for
He does it without ceasing, of Himself, willingly and with pleasure.
Just so, we do not have to tell the righteous that he ought to do good
works, for he does so without that, without any commandment or
compulsion, because he is a new creature and a good tree.[32]

Only a person who is not righteous and good, in Luther's view,
needs to be told that he ought to do good works, or can seriously
think of asking why. But such a person can never produce more
than a fair semblance of good works, just as an evil tree can only
produce evil fruit, however deceptively good its appearance may
be. It is to the doer and not to his deeds, therefore, that the ethical
judgement, strictly speaking, must be applied; for, Luther holds,
'good works do not make a good man, but a good man does good
works'. What makes a good man is another question, a religious
question; for everything depends, as we have seen, upon the
relationship in which he stands to God.

The relation of religion to ethics, as Luther understands it,
may perhaps be described as that of cause to effect. Or we may
put it another way, by saying that fellowship with God is the root
out of which the ethical life springs as its fruit. This is in sharp
contrast to the teaching of Catholicism, where the relation between
them is that of end to means. Good works are done in order to
secure acceptance with God—which in turn is not sought as an
end in itself, but as a means of ensuring man's blessedness. Against
this, Luther maintains that fellowship with God is an end in itself
and the ethical good is an end in itself, neither of which may be
treated as a means to any other end whatsoever. Yet they are
inseparably bound up with each other, and both alike are rooted
in the gratuitous goodness of God.

7. LUTHER IN CONTRAST WITH THE SCHOOLMEN

(a) Duns Scotus

The evidence we have given should suffice to show how consistently and thoroughly Luther maintains the theocentric and
repudiates the egocentric point of view. In this respect, the
comparison of his work to that of Copernicus is certainly not

inapt. But the claim that he effected a Copernican revolution in relation to medieval Catholicism has been disputed. In the Hulsean Lectures for 1938, for instance, Mr. John Burnaby asserts:

to claim that Luther found Christianity egocentric and left it theocentric—that is (to say no more) to do scant justice to Luther's scholastic master.[33]

In support of his contention, Burnaby adduces a number of passages from Luther and compares them with views expressed by Duns Scotus and Saint Thomas Aquinas, to show that there is no such radical difference between them as has been claimed.[34] Luther, he holds, is closely akin to Scotus in his view of original sin as essentially self-seeking, self-love; in his conception of blessedness and heaven itself as such perfect union with the Divine will that a man desires nothing of his own either in this world or the next; and in his demand for a pure love for God such as implies the absolute negation of self, even to the abdication of beatitude. Moreover, Burnaby alleges, when Luther distinguishes between God's love, which 'does not find, but creates, its lovable object', and man's love, which 'is caused by its lovable object', he is simply paraphrasing Aquinas, for whose theology the distinction is no less vital than for Luther's own. Mr. Burnaby would not depreciate Luther's protest against the 'practical Pelagianism' and 'taint of works-religion' that had infected medieval Christianity; but he finds in Luther's polemic against *fides caritate formata* and his 'expulsion of love from the faith that justifies', a proof that Luther never understood Saint Thomas.

Now no one who knows anything of the Schoolmen, would wish to assert that Luther learnt nothing from them, or that the lessons they taught him were entirely negative; but it is difficult to think that Scholasticism was as Lutheran in intention as Burnaby's argument would imply. We may readily admit that there are markedly theocentric features in Scholastic thought; but the question must be asked, whether these in fact constitute its fundamental motif, or whether they are not rather subordinated to, or counterbalanced by, the egocentric tendency. With quotations divorced from their contexts, no matter how close their verbal correspondence may be, it cannot be satisfactorily demonstrated that the Schoolmen represent the same point of view as Luther. The decisive issue here is that of the religious relationship and whether the dominant factor in it is, in the last analysis, man or God. Have the Schoolmen fundamentally the same conception of the relationship between man and God as Luther has?

When Burnaby tells us what Luther learnt from Scotus, he conveniently omits a part of the lesson, which throws a rather different light on the subject. Luther may well be said to have learnt from Scotus the necessity of an absolutely selfless love for God; and the demand for such a love is undoubtedly an attempt to exclude egoism, at least in the form of self-seeking, from religion. To that extent it is evidence of a theocentric tendency. But Luther also learnt from Scotus that man himself, by his own natural will, could and should produce this selfless love.[35] Does not this (to say the least) savour of a singularly egoistic self-confidence? Scotus argues to the familiar effect that, if a man can love a lesser good, then he can also love a greater, for the greater the good, the more lovable it is; and the highest and most lovable good, of course, is God. Luther condemns this view, not merely owing to the failure of his own desperate efforts to follow his scholastic master here, but because he cannot admit that a love evoked by the worth of its object is truly disinterested.[36] Scotus, it is true, seeks to show the contrary, for he is acutely aware of the peril of eudemonist egoism in the conception of God as the *summum bonum*. But it would require more than Scotus' argument to prove the case.

Scotus argues, as Burnaby says, that if a pagan, who has no hope of immortality, sacrifices himself for the sake of his community, his heroism is absolutely disinterested, since he chooses self-annihilation for a greater good in which he himself will have no part. But before we could agree that the disinterestedness was really absolute, should we not have to be sure, not only that the pagan did not look for immortality, but that he had no thought of adding lustre or avoiding dishonour to his name, and that he did not feel the slightest sense of pride in his heroism? And even granted the absence of any such self-interest, would there not remain a subtle and deep egocentricity in the fact that the cause for which he devoted himself was one of his own choosing, one which he deemed worthy of *himself*? The only certain proof of an absolutely selfless love would seem to be a willingness to suffer not an heroic, but a shameful death, for the sake not of one's friends, who have some claim to be deemed worthy, but of one's enemies who have not, as Christ suffered on the Cross.

However that may be, Scotus is quite sure that it is consonant with right reason that a statesman should will himself not to be, lest the good of the state perish, and also that right reason teaches us that the Divine good is more to be loved than any other good. Therefore, he concludes, it is in accordance with right reason that a man should will himself not to be, for the sake of the Divine good. But the conception of God as the supreme Good that is supremely worthy to be loved, derives after all from the anthropocentric question of ancient philosophy: What is the good *for man*? —which is only another way of saying: What is the good for me, who am a man? It is exceedingly difficult to rid such a conception of all egocentric traits. Even if it were free from the suspicion of eudemonism, does it not savour of presumption, that I should venture to place God—even though I give Him the highest place—in the category of those things which *I* judge to be good and therefore worthy of *me* and *my* love and devotion? Luther at any rate, cannot accept this view.

Such [he says] is the argument of Scotus: I love the lesser good thing, therefore I love the greater more. I deny the consequence. For my loving is not God's ordinance, but a devilish corruption. Indeed it should be so, that I, loving myself or another creature, should much more love God the Creator; but it is not so. For the love wherewith I love myself is corrupt and against God.[37]

But let us suppose that Scotus is right, and that it is possible for a man to attain a selfless love for God by his own natural powers. Must we not say that, even so, his theocentric tendency is counter-balanced by an egocentric, inasmuch as the attainment of this selfless love is represented as determinative of the religious relationship? If Scotus expels human self-seeking from religion, he opens at the same time a wide door to human self-reliance.

Nevertheless, it must not be forgotten that Scotus, like the rest of the Schoolmen, has his doctrine of grace. Despite his insistence on the freedom and ability of the natural man, he asserts— though he hardly explains—the necessity of Divine grace for salvation.[38] This is, without question, another instance of the theocentric tendency. Yet here again, the opposite tendency

prevents it from finding clear and full expression. Like Scholasticism generally, Scotus understands grace from a legalistic point
of view. Grace is adapted, subordinated, to a legal scheme of
merit and reward. By the merit of congruence,[39] the grace
is obtained whereby man acquires the merit of worthiness,
without which he cannot be acceptable to God.[40] This is
clearly egocentric; the centre of gravity in the religious relationship is once more transferred to man; everything depends on
man's moral and spiritual attainments. Yet even here the
theocentric tendency seeks to reassert itself. Scotus, as is well-
known, gives great weight to the idea of Divine predestination.
Man cannot determine how God must act in any given situation;
God Himself alone decides freely; and what He wills is right
because He wills it. Despite his insistence on merit, therefore,
Scotus can nevertheless declare that God is not bound to accept
man on account of his merits. Everything depends on God's
free acceptation. Here the legalistic conception is partly broken
down—but not altogether. There is no suggestion that when
God does accept a man, He accepts him regardless of his merits,
or that He would ever justify the ungodly and those who have
no merits. Man's worthiness is still an essential condition of his
acceptance with God, and to the extent that it is so, the religious
relationship is still fundamentally egocentric.

In Scotus and the Nominalist theologians who followed him,
an acute and growing tension developed between the egocentric
and the theocentric tendencies. By Luther's time, this had reached
a point at which, for anyone who took the Nominalist doctrines
quite seriously, it was no longer tolerable. The great antinomy
of late Scholasticism—God is all, man nothing; yet man is the
dominant factor in the religious relationship—could not be
maintained without a considerable measure of compromise in
one direction or the other. Luther, however, as we have seen,
could not thus compromise; and in him the theocentric tendency
broke through and freed itself from the egocentric, to which it
had been held uneasily subordinate.

(b) Saint Thomas Aquinas

But, it may be asked, if the late Scholasticism, with which Luther
was familiar, represents a fundamentally egocentric outlook,
despite its theocentric elements, can the same be truly said of the

THE MOTIF OF LUTHER'S THOUGHT

earlier Schoolmen—of Aquinas, for example? Mr. Burnaby
suggests that if Luther had understood Saint Thomas, he would
not have rejected the conception of *fides caritate formata* and insisted
on his *sola fide* instead. In other words, he would not have regarded
justification by 'faith formed by love' as equivalent to justification
by works, against which he felt bound to maintain that justification
is 'by faith alone'. He would not then have fallen into what
Burnaby regards as the error of expelling love from the faith that
justifies.

Charity [Burnaby explains] no more than Faith is in Thomas's
doctrine a 'work' by which man's effort achieves the fellowship with
God. Both belong to that goodness which the love of God 'creates
and infuses'. Charity is the activity of the New Man.[41]

Now Luther may or may not have understood Aquinas, but any
reader of his large *Commentary on Galatians*—not to mention other
works—must know that he was quite familiar with the idea of
'infused faith' and 'infused charity'. He was well aware that
scholastic theology was not pure Pelagianism. Why, then, will he
not allow that we are justified by faith formed by love? Much
might be said in answer to this question, but here it will suffice to
notice how this conception represents an ultimately legalistic, and
therefore anthropocentric, point of view. The thought of faith
formed by love as the ground of justification, rests on the assumption that God cannot receive man into fellowship with Himself
unless man merits it by fulfilling His law. God's law is a law of
love, and man must therefore possess the love it requires, if he is to
be acceptable to the Lawgiver. If he cannot achieve it by his own
natural powers, then he must have the necessary love 'infused'
into him by a supernatural operation of grace. In other words,
man must be sanctified by some means or other, if he is ever to
be justified in the sight of a God who is Himself holy and just.
Such is the principle underlying the doctrine of justification by
fides caritate formata. It cannot be said to differ in any essential
way from the standpoint of 'works-religion', for it is fundamentally
legalistic; and since everything depends finally on man's fulfilment
of the Divine law of charity, the religious relationship may not
unfairly be said to be anthropocentrically conceived.

It is true, of course, that the conception of man's fulfilment of
the Law as due, not to his own endeavours, but to supernatural

E

grace, is an important assertion of the theocentric tendency. In
the case of Saint Thomas, this tendency is very clearly to be
discerned; for if Saint Thomas teaches on the one hand, that there
is no salvation without merit, he also teaches on the other, that
there is no merit without grace. Nevertheless, it cannot be denied
that the theocentric tendency is here subordinated to the anthropocentric point of view. The insistence on the necessity of merit,
however acquired, makes man's worthiness decisive for his
relationship to God; and grace itself is reduced to the level of a
means whereby man may acquire the necessary merit. For Luther,
however, grace is the very antithesis of merit, of which it excludes
even the possibility. It is not conceived by him as a supernatural
gift from God, given to man in order to make him worthy of
acceptance with God, but as the gracious action of God Himself
in Christ, in whom He seeks men out, unworthy as they are, and
takes them into fellowship with Himself in spite of their sin.[42]
Here God acts with sovereign freedom—the freedom of a love
that is not bound by any law, nor moved by any consideration
of what its object may deserve, but only by its own eternal purpose
of good. From Luther's point of view, the objection to the
scholastic doctrine is, that it does not permit God to deal freely
with men; it forbids Him to befriend publicans and sinners and
to justify the ungodly; it does not allow Him, in fact, to be fully
and truly God.

Luther's expulsion of love from the faith that justifies, as
Burnaby calls it, is therefore not a very satisfactory proof that he
never understood Saint Thomas.[43] His insistence, however, that
the ground of our justification is not any love of ours, but God's
own love toward us in Christ (who is the object of faith), is clear
proof of his theocentric interest. It means a refusal to allow the
centre of gravity in the religious relationship to be transferred
from the throne of heavenly grace even to a supernaturally infused
quality in the human soul. Luther's thought moves along other
than Thomistic lines, and we may well pause to consider whether,
even when he appears to be 'merely paraphrasing Aquinas',
his meaning is really the same.

In his *Summa Theologica*, Aquinas raises the question whether
and in what sense we can speak of love in God. In the course of
his answer, he draws a distinction between human love and
Divine. Our love, he says, is called forth by the goodness, real or

imagined, of its object, whereas God's love infuses and creates goodness in things.[44] With this conception we may compare Luther's statement in the twenty-eighth thesis of the Heidelberg *Disputation*. God's love, Luther says, does not 'find' its object, but creates it, whereas man's love is created by its object.[45] If similarity of expression were proof of identical meaning, we might well be satisfied that Luther is making the same point as Aquinas here. But the matter is hardly so simple. There is little difference, it is true, between the two in their conception of natural, human love; but their attitude to it cannot be said to be the same, nor do they distinguish Divine love from it on the same grounds or with the same effect.

It is characteristic of human love, according to both Luther and Saint Thomas, that it is 'caused' by its object. Saint Thomas's explanation of this is that the 'goodness' of the object evokes the love. For according to his way of thinking, 'the essence of goodness consists in this, that it is in some way desirable'.[46] Our loving, therefore, means that we set our desire upon an object which we regard as a 'good' for us. The object's goodness is the only reason why it can be loved at all. Love thus corresponds to the acquisitive will,[47] which is the expression of man's natural quest for happiness. In other words, Aquinas assumes with Aristotle that all love is reducible to self-love.[48] Luther takes a similar view of human love, holding that in all things it 'seeketh its own'. It seeks rather to receive than to confer good; its concern is to find a good that it can itself enjoy. It is thus called forth by the desirable qualities of its object. In support of this view, Luther believes he can invoke the testimony, not only of Aristotle, but of all philosophers and theologians. Natural, human love is self-centred love; it is, in the language of classical philosophy, Eros.[49]

Now neither Luther nor Saint Thomas can allow the love just described to be predicated of God. For Saint Thomas the reason is that such love is inevitably associated with a sense of need and want in the lover. It suggests that he lacks some 'good'. But God lacks nothing. He is in Himself, not only good, but the all-inclusive and supremely desirable good, the *summum bonum*. Hence, if we are to speak of love in God, as with the New Testament we must, then the word must have another meaning than that described above. With this last statement Luther agrees, but for a different reason. His thought of love does not begin either with the theories of philosophers or with common human experience. It begins with the revelation of God in Christ.[50] In Christ, who came not to call the righteous, but sinners, he sees a love that does not turn to the good and worthy in order to enjoy them for itself, but to the unworthy and the lost in order to help and save them. This love is revealed above all in the Cross of Christ. It is *amor crucis*, the Divine Agape that seeketh not its own.

In view of his conception of their nature, it is hardly surprising that Luther finds Divine and human love as opposed to one another as light and darkness. Anyone who takes seriously such injunctions as: 'Be ye therefore imitators of God', and: 'Ye therefore shall be perfect as your heavenly Father is perfect', cannot help but regard a love that seeketh its own, as sinful and the very essence of sin. Aquinas, on the other hand, nowhere finds himself obliged to repudiate human self-love. For him, indeed, it can be said to form an indispensable foundation of religion. 'For,' he says, 'assuming what is impossible, that God were not man's good, then there would be no reason for man to love Him.'[51] To this Luther would most surely reply that such a love seeks even in God the things of itself and not God.

It is not, of course, that Saint Thomas lacks all appreciation of New Testament Agape. Indeed, he is aware of the tension between it and the philosophic Eros. This tension he seeks to resolve by means of the doctrine of *amor amicitiae*, the love of friendship,[52] in which, he explains, 'to love means to will good to someone', as Aristotle says.[53] But friendship, it must be observed, is founded in the Aristotelian manner on a 'likeness' between the friends; and even the love of friendship is ultimately reducible to self-love, since the friend is 'another self'.[54] This is hardly a successful attempt to make room for the Agape motif in Aquinas's scheme of thought, as even Burnaby admits.

Here [he says] we encounter just that feature in the Aristotelian account of Philia which seems most incompatible with the character of Agape in the Christian sense—the love which is so little dependent on likeness as to show its nature most fully in forgiveness.[55]

The egocentric tendency clearly predominates in Aquinas's conception of human love in all its aspects. It intrudes even into the religious relationship—quite obviously, when God is regarded as man's *summum bonum*; more subtly, when the Charity of *fides caritate formata* is interpreted in terms of *amor amicitiae* and of a friendship between man and God.[56] Nevertheless, Burnaby maintains that Saint Thomas does succeed in giving expression to the Agape motif—in his conception of the love of God, the Divine love itself.[57]

What, then, is the precise meaning that Aquinas attaches to 'the love of God'? In order to answer this question, we need only consider the significance of his statement that the love of God 'infuses and creates goodness in things'.

First of all, it can be said that 'goodness' in the present context has essentially nothing to do with moral excellence. It is in fact virtually synonymous with existence.

Goodness and being [Saint Thomas explains] are really the same, and differ only in idea. . . . The essence of goodness consists in this, that it is in some way desirable. . . . Now it is clear that a thing is desirable only in so far as it is perfect. . . . But everything is perfect so far as it is actual. Therefore it is clear that a thing is perfect so far as it exists. . . . Hence it is clear that goodness and being are the same really. But goodness presents the aspect of desirableness, which being does not present.[58]

'Goodness' thus signifies for Saint Thomas the desirability of existence; and when he says that the love of God infuses and creates goodness in things, he simply means that God imparts to them a certain degree of being or reality. 'To love anything', he says, 'is nothing else than to will good to that thing', and to will good here means to will its existence. For all existing things are good in so far as they exist, and God is the cause of their existence and goodness; from which it follows that God wills the good of every existing thing; and that is equivalent to saying that God loves everything that exists.[59] In other words, the love of God is simply synonymous with the Divine causality.

It is not without significance that Saint Thomas 'proves' that there is love in God, without a single reference to the revelation of God in Christ. In the whole discussion of this subject, there is not a word about the Incarnation or the Cross or the forgiveness of sins. It is true that he raises the question whether God loves sinners, and that he answers it in the affirmative.

God loves sinners [he says] in so far as they are existing natures; for they have existence, and have it from Him. In so far as they are sinners, they have not existence at all, but fall short of it. . . .[60]

God loves sinners, that is to say, in so far as they are not sinners, but good and like Himself; for, as we have seen, existence and goodness are virtually synonymous for Saint Thomas. But is this the love which is so little dependent on likeness as to show its nature most fully in forgiveness? Is this the love of the Cross, born of the Cross, which betakes itself, not where it finds a good to enjoy, but where it may confer good upon the evil and the needy? How, then, can Burnaby assert that in his conception of the love of God Saint Thomas succeeds in giving expression to the Agape motif?

The fact is that Aquinas's entire argument moves essentially within the circle of ideas belonging to the great Eros-tradition of ancient philosophy as represented by Pseudo-Dionysius and Proclus. It is from these he has learnt that God is absolute causality[61] and therefore love (*eros*);[62] from these he has learnt to identify goodness and being;[63] and from these he has learnt that love is a *virtus unitiva*, a unitive force.[64] His doctrine of God as the efficient and final cause of all existence, moreover, bears no slight resemblance to Pseudo-Dionysius's conception of 'ecstatic' love.[65] According to this conception, God's loving means simply that He lets some measure of His own fullness of being and reality overflow to the creaturely existences.[66] The whole cosmic process can thus be regarded as an expression of God's love and, in the last analysis, of His self-love, which 'ecstatically' proceeds from Him, but also causes all things to return to Him.[67] It is against the background of such ideas as these that we must set Aquinas's doctrine of the love of God, if we are to see how he really understands it.

Now, what connexion is there between Aquinas's equation of the love of God with a Divine causality that imparts reality to things, and Luther's thought of the Divine love revealed in the Cross of Christ, the love which in fathomless compassion seeks and saves the lost? To this question there can be but one answer. Although both Luther and Saint Thomas say that God's love creates its object and imparts good to it, neither the love, nor its object, nor the goodness imparted has anything like the same meaning for the two men. Luther does not think in terms of causality and being, but in thoroughly personal and ethical terms. He is not the metaphysician, questing for man's *summum bonum* which is the *summum ens*, but the Christian theologian, for whom the will of God made known in Christ is all-determining. He can find no room in the religious relationship for the philos-opher's Eros, since he finds it quite irreconcilable with the Agape of the New Testament.

We have no wish, of course, to deny that the idea of Agape has quite deeply influenced Aquinas's outlook—it may even have influenced the Neoplatonist Proclus.[68] Perhaps it should also be said that we do not wish to suggest that Aquinas was not a Christian—we have been discussing his ideas, not passing judgement on his soul.[69] Yet great thinker and saint as he was, it cannot be said that the specifically Christian conception of love, the New Testament Agape, forms the dominant and constitutive motif of his thought. He feels, as we have said, the tension between it and the philosophic Eros, a tension such as imperils the unity of his thought; and it can hardly be denied that if the unity is preserved, that is only because the Agape motif is constantly subordinated to the Eros motif in ways such as we have discussed.

The conflict between the egocentric and the theocentric tendencies, therefore, is as real, if not as obvious, in Aquinas as in the later Schoolmen, and in him, no less than in them, the egocentric tendency proves the stronger force. Luther, on the other hand, decisively repudiates the egocentric tendency and his thought is theocentric at every point. It is this difference between the Reformer and the Schoolmen that makes all the difference, and we may never assume that when they use similar, or even identical expressions, they therefore must mean precisely the same thing.

8. LUTHER'S WATCHWORD: *Soli Deo Gloria*

The watchword of Luther, we have said, no less than of Calvin, was *soli Deo gloria*. But the Schoolmen might also claim that it was no less theirs, and that it was from them the Reformers had it. For what else had they in view but the glory of God, when they proclaimed Him the *summum bonum*, in whom alone lay man's true blessedness, and insisted that He must be sought, not for the sake of any ulterior blessings, but for His own sake alone? And what else had they in view, when they asserted that men must serve God with good works and in conformity with His law, if they would become acceptable to Him and merit the fruition

of their eternal Good? The intention of the Schoolmen is clear;
and it doubtless had no little influence on the Reformers. Luther
himself, speaking of his life as a monk, before ever he had a thought
of his reforming views, tells us that whatsoever he did, he did it
'with a single heart, of a good zeal, and for the glory of God'.[70]
But the zeal he then showed, he says, was like that of Saul of
Tarsus, before he met Christ on the Damascus road; and for all
his sincere intention of serving God, he afterwards discovered,
like Saint Paul, that he had in fact been doing nothing of the kind.
Soli Deo gloria has another meaning for Luther the Reformer than
it had for Luther the monk.

   Just because he was so utterly in earnest for the glory of God,
Luther was led to discover the great, fundamental problem of
religion, and to see that Scholasticism could provide no answer to
it. He was also led to understand how Christianity furnishes the
unique and final solution of it.

   The problem can be stated as follows. How is it possible for
God to be God, really God, in a world where man finds it quite
natural to live and think as if he himself stood at the centre of
things? It is, of course, a fact that God and not man is the
sovereign centre of existence, and no religious person would think
of denying it, at any rate theoretically. But the full implications of
this fact are not always readily conceded even in theory, much less
translated into terms of practical life such as religion requires—
for religion, after all, is not theory, but an existential relationship.
Human egocentricity, however, will sooner rationalize or sublimate itself than yield its place; and it can assert itself in the
most refined and subtle forms, which may deceive even those
sincerely anxious to be rid of it. Sincerity, like patriotism, is
not enough; for men can be sincerely wrong.[71] Such error Luther
detected in Scholastic theology, with its doctrine of God as man's
summum bonum and its insistence on the necessity of human merit.

   The conception of the *summum bonum* is bound up with the
thought of human need, which drives man to seek a 'good' that
will satisfy it. God is identified with the 'highest good' that alone
can satisfy man's deepest need. That I am to seek Him 'for His
own sake alone' means that I am to have no other object of desire
but this all-inclusive *bonum*. 'For His own sake' only conceals the
fact that I still seek Him for my own satisfaction, 'for *my* own sake'.
It does not cancel Aquinas's assertion, that if God were not man's

bonum there would be no reason for man to love Him. But such love, Luther sees, is not true love at all. It is not love for God, but deceptive self-love. For what kind of love is it, that will not let God be God, but wishes to have Him at its own service? The Schoolmen, of course, could protest that, so far from making God into man's servant, they clearly meant man to be His, for they taught the necessity of obedience to God's Law and Commandment, if man would merit his desired 'good'. But Luther can only reply that that makes matters worse. In the first place, even our best works are tainted with sin, the subtle egocentricity of the natural man—above all, when they are done with an eye to a reward and our own blessedness. In the second place, the mere mention of human merit in the presence of God is nothing short of blasphemy. We owe to God all that we have and are, and even if we perfectly fulfilled all His commandments, we could still only say: 'We are unprofitable servants; we have done that which it was our duty to do.'[72] How dare we then seek to trade our 'merits' for His favour 'as if He were a huckster'? That is to rob Him of His glory, to deny that He is God.

What, then, does it mean, in Luther's view, to give glory to God and to let God be really God? His answer to this question will be discussed at greater length in the following chapters. It can be summarily stated in what he calls 'the article of justification', the doctrine of salvation *sola fide* or *sola gratia*—for the two are the same. The glory of God is His grace, the unmerited and unmeritable love that meets us with absolute judgement and fathomless mercy in Jesus Christ. In the Cross of Christ, above all, Luther finds the full depth and majesty of Godhead revealed—to faith, for it is not evident to 'sight' that 'God was in Christ reconciling the world to Himself'. Here, the Divine love that 'seeketh not its own', stands in utter condemnation over against all human egocentricity, exposing it as sin, no matter how refined and religious it may be; and here that selfsame love, by which 'while we were yet sinners Christ died for us', even in the act of judging us, forgives. There is nothing here that we can do to give God the glory due unto His name, except acknowledge the glory that is revealed; and this we do only as we accept in faith both the judgement and the mercy and are reconciled to God. The only way to let God be truly God for us is to let Him have His way with us in Christ, to let Him, as Luther puts it, 'do His work'.[73] This the eudemonistic and moralistic doctrines of scholastic theology preclude; for they do not admit the absoluteness of His judgement on us, which is merited, and they require us to merit His mercy, which is free.

Luther knows, of course, what every Christian and every religious person knows, that man cannot live without God. But he will not allow the interpretation of this fact, common in our day as in his, which takes it to mean: Man *needs* God, therefore man seeks God. This is often assumed to be the basic principle in the light of which all religion is to be understood. Yet there is something very precarious about religion when it is construed in terms of human need, as its antagonists have been quick to see. From Ludwig Feuerbach in the last century to the latest dabblers in psychology who prattle about 'wish-fulfilment', 'projection', and the like, they have found it easy to dismiss religion as a phantasy, a mere illusion, begotten of man's deep and clamant desire. And no doubt much that passes as religion deserves to be so dismissed. Long before Feuerbach, however, Luther directed a similar, though far profounder and more penetrating, criticism against such religion. It was false religion, and he attacked it for the glory of God. God does not exist to serve man's ends, but stands over against man with sovereign, commanding authority. He is the Lord, whose commandments are to be obeyed unconditionally and without a thought of reward. Modern critics of religion sometimes seek to discredit it by alleging the mercenary motives of the devout, who, they say, are inhibited only by fear from doing things that other men unashamedly enjoy. Again we may say that much that passes as religion deserves to be so discredited. Luther attacked it, however, with better arguments and to better purpose, long ago. With his *sola fide, sola gratia*, he sought to deliver men from the 'inhibitions' of their self-centred fears and hopes, not in order that they might indulge themselves, but in order that they might freely devote themselves to the sole glory of God.

For centuries, men had lived and thought on the basis of a given tradition. That is what men generally do. They build on a foundation of inherited assumptions, which they take for granted, hardly recognizing them as assumptions. They may effect alterations and improvements to the superstructure raised on these assumptions by earlier generations; they may even demolish it and rebuild to a fresh plan; but the new building still stands on the same ground. So medieval theology and piety took it for granted, on the authority in particular of ancient philosophy, that religion is grounded in human need, and that human worthiness is the essential condition of attaining the religious goal. If, under the influence of the Scriptural tradition, the peril of human egocentricity in this conception was perceived, it was thought sufficient to refine and sublimate it, or to counterbalance it by expressions of the theocentric tendency such as we have pointed out in Aquinas and Scotus. But human desire and desert remained the essential ground of religion, and this fundamental assumption was never called in question.

It is rarely in human history that anyone appears who will dig down to examine the foundations on which men build, and test their soundness. But that is what Luther has done—and more. For, having discovered the traditional foundations to be insecure, he has gone on to lay bare the living rock on which Christianity stands, and to demand a reconstruction of the entire spiritual life on this basis. He cannot, in the nature of the case, be content with any modifications of its existing structure, however far-reaching they may be, so long as it remains standing on the old ground. In other words, no reformation of ecclesiastical institutions, rites and ceremonies, manners and morals, will suffice, if their doctrinal basis is left unreformed. 'More depends on the doctrine than on the life', Luther maintains;[74] and it is this 'more' that explains his intransigent insistence on the reforming *sola fide*.

Our adversaries [says Luther] object against us that we are contentious, obstinate, and intractable in defending our doctrine, and even in matters of no great importance.

But he reminds them that, as 'a little leaven leaveneth the whole lump', 'so in divinity, one little error overthroweth the whole doctrine'.

Wherefore [he continues] we must separate life and doctrine far asunder.[75] The doctrine is not ours, but God's, whose ministers we are called; therefore we may not change nor diminish one tittle thereof. The life is ours: therefore, as touching that, we are ready to do, to suffer, to forgive, etc., whatsoever our adversaries shall require of us, so that faith and doctrine may remain sound and uncorrupt.[76]

Christians must expect to suffer, and must suffer patiently, hostility toward themselves;

but if the doctrine, when it is preached, is condemned, that concerns the glory of God and the salvation of the world. Here we must be froward and not patient. [77]

Luther is not to be moved by those 'cavillers which say, that we break charity to the great hurt and damage of the Churches'. He desires nothing more than to be at unity with all men; but not at the price of compromising the doctrine of faith. They may 'extol charity and concord as much as they list'; but 'when men teach lies and errors under the colour of the truth, and seduce many, here hath charity no place'.[78] The corrupting 'leaven of doctrine' may be never so little, yet if it is tolerated, it will mean that 'little by little the truth and our salvation shall be lost, and *God himself be denied*'.[79]

Let God be God!—that is the whole purport of Luther's reforming work.[80] It cannot, however, be said to have met with more than partial comprehension, still less to have evoked a wholehearted response. Human egocentricity has known how to assert itself even in the expositions of his own doctrine by his spiritual successors. 'Justification', which for Luther means the way in which God's will is done and His purposes of love are realized for and in and through man, has been reduced to the level of a sedative for man's troubled conscience, a revised version of the answer to man's sense of need. 'Faith', which for Luther describes the human aspect of a relationship between man and God, where God is the all-determining factor, has been transformed into a disposition I must produce, or a faculty I must exercise, in order to obtain the desired justifying grace. The *sola fide* has been dogmatized into a shibboleth of orthodoxy that demands assent; or it has been psychologized into a pietistic mood of heartfelt trust. In consequence, the organic unity, implicit in Luther's view, between faith and regeneration, forgiveness and newness of life, has been broken, and the high doctrine of sanctification, which he is often alleged not to possess, has been replaced by quite inadequate moralizing substitutes. The form of his sound words may have been retained; but their meaning has been altered. In turning to the study of Luther, therefore, we are not going back to a stage of history long superseded, but forward to something that has not yet been reached. It is the measure of his greatness that he has penetrated to the very heart of the deepest problem of humanity, and has given us an answer that four subsequent centuries have not mastered and made fully their own.[81]

NOTES

1. Boehmer, *Luther*, 80; Nygren, *Agape and Eros*, II.ii.463ff., *Urkristendom*, 116ff.

2. There is presumably no religion from which all suggestion of a *divine initiative* is absent. The eternal and divine with which man seeks communion, however it may be conceived, is not thought of purely and simply as a human discovery, but rather as something in some measure *revealed* to man, who would otherwise have no occasion to seek it.

3. cf. Nygren, *Agape and Eros*, II. *passim*. We shall have occasion to notice certain aspects of the conflict in a later section of this chapter, with reference to the thought of Duns Scotus and Aquinas.

4. Nygren, *Urkristendom*, 123 and 128. cf. E. Hirsch, *Luthers Gottesanschauung*, 7: 'God is not only the first, but also the last word in Luther's faith.' cf. Holl, *Ges. Aufs. I.* 20: 'Luther's thinking begins with God'; 37f.: '. . . in the order of thought, the conception of God was dominant. . . . Luther's thought is strictly theocentric. God is not for him as for the philosopher the limiting concept (*Grenzbegriff*), which he reaches as the ultimate behind the world and man, but on the contrary the starting-point from which alone he ever observes the world and man.'

5. *Römerbr.* 1ff.

6. See p. 20 *supra*.

7. It is not legal righteousness, the righteousness of the scribes and Pharisees (Matthew 5₂₀), but the righteousness of the Kingdom, God's righteousness (Matthew 6₃₃). The contrast is most clearly and sharply expressed in Romans 10₃ and Philippians 3₉, for instance, where man's righteousness and God's are represented as mutually exclusive, and the latter alone is able to form the basis of the religious relationship.

8. Luther's talk of an 'alien' righteousness that 'comes from elsewhere into us' may seem to suggest that he is ignoring ethical realities. Righteousness really cannot be transferred like a commodity from one person to another. But we should misconstrue Luther's intention if we supposed he imagined it could. We shall have occasion in a later chapter to discuss what he means by 'the righteousness of God'; but here it may be remarked that if he recognizes only an alien righteousness as true righteousness, that is just as much an indication of his concern for ethics as for religion. He wishes to get rid of ethical no less than of religious egocentricity. (See pp. 46ff.)

9. *W.A.* VI.20-2.

10. It is strange how persistent this notion is, especially in view of the fact that almost all our Lord's teaching about prayer has to do with petition. He continually urges us to 'ask', with never a suggestion that asking represents a lower level of prayer which, as we advance in spirituality, we are to outgrow.

11. Praise and adoration can just as well give expression to it, of course, when they are inspired by the grateful recognition that everything comes to us as a gift from God. Then they are theocentric. But if we regard them as 'higher' than petition, we are in danger of reversing the relationship and putting God in the position of one on whom we bestow our favours.

12. *W.B.* 117.

13. *S.W.* 447.

14. Psalm 29₂.

15. cf. Charles Wesley's lines, *M.H.B.* 399:
> *What shall I render to my God*
> *For all His mercy's store?*
> *I'll take the gifts He hath bestowed,*
> *And humbly ask for more.*

THE MOTIF OF LUTHER'S THOUGHT

cf. *M.H.B.* 383:

The sole return Thy love requires
Is that we ask for more.

16. *W.A.* XI.462ff.—*Von zweierlei Menschen, wie sie sich in dem Glauben halten sollen und was der sei,* 1523. *S.W.* 417f.—'Concerning two sorts of men in respect of faith: and what true faith is.'

17. 2 Corinthians 57.

18. *W.M.L.* III.139f.; *W.A.* VII.556; *E.A.* xlv.228f.

19. cf. Köberle, *Rechtf. u. Heilig.* 108.

20. See p. 159f. *infra.*

21. *W.M.L.* I.194ff. The exposition of the First Commandment in the *Greater Catechism* is on exactly similar lines. Its meaning is quite simply: 'Thou shalt fear, love, and trust Me as thy one, true God. For where a heart feels this toward God, it has fulfilled this and all the other commandments; moreover, he who loves and fears anything else in heaven or on earth cannot keep this or any one of the commandments' (*W.B.* 92).

22. *Römerbr.* 217.23ff.

23. *W.A.* II.94.13ff.

24. ibid 98.29ff.

25. *Römerbr.* 217.27ff. The passage continues: 'But inasmuch as they thus purely conform themselves to the will of God, it is impossible that they should abide in hell. For it is impossible that he should abide outside God, who has so entirely given himself up to the will of God.'

26. cf. *B.o.W.* 191; cf. Holl, *Ges. Aufs. I.* 56.

27. *W.A.* X.1.1; 304.7ff.; cf. X.3; 400.19ff.; ibid. 401.16ff.; VII.559.18ff.

28. *B.o.W.* 190f.; cf. *S.W.* I.419. cf. *E.A.* xxii.133f.: 'Those who are not pleasure-seekers, serve God for His own sake alone and not for the sake of heaven nor of any temporal thing. And even though they knew that there were no heaven, nor hell, nor any reward, they would nevertheless serve God for His own sake.'

29. *B.o.W.* 192. cf. *S.W.* I.426: 'Be not thou concerned about the reward; that thou shalt have in due time, even if thou be not so eager after it. For although it is impossible that the reward should not come to them, who worship God . . . without any consideration of gain or wages; yet, certain it is, that God hates those mercenary characters, who seek themselves and not God, and will never give them any reward at all. . . . God is not the rewarder of our works according to our merit, but according to His own promises; wherein He hath promised that He will reward our works, but, of mere grace.'

30. *E.A.* xli.90f.

31. ibid.

32. *E.A.* lviii.355.

33. *Amor Dei,* 275. Burnaby is criticizing Nygren's interpretation of Luther in *Agape and Eros,* II.ii; but it is difficult to avoid the suspicion that he has quite failed to grasp, not only Nygren's intention here, but the principles of his thesis as a whole. The account he gives of Nygren's general position reveals less of the latter's thought than of his own disapproval of it. He seriously misinterprets it, if he classes Nygren, as he appears to do, with the 'dialectical theologians' (p.15); and his complaint that 'Nygren is not to be disturbed by criticism of his analysis on psychological or ethical grounds' is curiously irrelevant in view of the nature of Nygren's thesis.

34. ibid. 275f.

35. *Gal.* E.T. 82(ii.16): ' " . . . that a man even by his own natural strength, may procure this charity above all things". For so reasoneth Scotus: if a man may love a creature, a young man a maiden, a covetous man money, which are the less good, he may also love God, which is the greater good. If he have a love of the creature through his natural strength, much more hath he a love of the Creator.' cf. Duns Scotus, *Comment. Oxon. in Sent. III, dist. 27 qu. unica*, n.13f.: 'Natural reason shows to the natural understanding that there is something to be supremely loved . . . and by consequence the will can do this by its own natural powers (*puris naturalibus*); for the understanding can rightly dictate nothing toward which the natural will cannot naturally turn. . . .'

36. cf. Nygren, *Agape and Eros*, II.ii.505, esp. n.2. For Luther, a love that is evoked by the worth of its object is not love in the true sense of the term; cf. op. cit. 511f.

37. *Gal.* E.T. 199(iii.15).

38. Loofs, *D.G.* 597; cf. Burnaby, op. cit. 273.

39. Very little is required to achieve the merit of congruence, according to Scotus. A man need only be *parum attritus*, or *aliqualiter attritus*; a bare minimum of penitence was sufficient.

40. See pp. 15f. *supra*.

41. *Amor Dei*, 277.

42. *W.M.L.* VI.450: 'Between grace and gift there is this difference. Grace means properly God's favour, or the goodwill God bears us, by which He is disposed to give us Christ and to pour into us the Holy Ghost, with His gifts.' *W.M.L.* III.159: 'In giving us the gifts He gives but what is His, but in His grace and His regard of us He gives His very self. In the gifts we touch His hand, but in His gracious regard we receive His heart, spirit, mind, and will.'

43. It is also a somewhat misleading phrase. If Luther denies that love in us is the *ground* of our justification, he no less strongly asserts that it is its natural and inevitable *fruit*; only, the very word 'love' has another significance for him than for Saint Thomas, as we shall see. In place of *caritas infusa* as the ground of justification, Luther puts Christ Himself, who is given to believers and dwells in their hearts— and is of course the source and creator of true love in them. The difference between the scholastic view and Luther's might be expressed, perhaps rather crudely, as follows. According to the former, God must be regarded as something like a doctor who refuses to come into contact with his patients so long as they are ill, but is sufficiently well-disposed toward them to send them medicine through the post (sacramental grace!) with a promise that he will see them when they are recovered. According to Luther, on the other hand, we must think of God in Christ as a true physician, who without a thought for Himself enters the plague-stricken dwelling to tend the sick with His own hands and nurse them back to health.

44. *S.T.* I. q.20. a.2: 'God loves everything that exists. Yet not as we love. Because since our will is not the cause of the goodness of things, but is moved by it as its object, our love, whereby we will good to anything, is not the cause of the goodness; but conversely, its goodness, whether real or imaginary, calls forth our love . . . whereas the love of God infuses and creates goodness in things.'

45. *W.A.* I.365.1ff.: 'God's love does not find, but creates, its lovable object; man's love is caused by its lovable object. The second clause is evident and it is agreed by all philosophers and theologians that the object is the cause of the love. They assume with Aristotle that every power of the soul is passive and . . . acts by receiving— whereby he also testifies that his philosophy is contrary to theology, inasmuch as in all things it seeks its own . . . the first clause is evident, since God's love living in man loves sinners, the evil, the foolish, the weak, that it may make them righteous, good, wise, and strong, and so it rather flows forth and confers good.'

46. *S.T.* I. q.5. a.1.

47. *S.T.* II.i. q.26. a.1: 'Love is something pertaining to the appetite; since good is the object of both.' Aquinas agrees with 'the Philosopher' (Aristotle) that 'love belongs to the concupiscible faculty'—ibid.

48. cf. Burnaby, *Amor Dei*, 265; Nygren, *Agape and Eros*, II.ii.424.

49. Whether classical philosophy is entirely right in its conception of natural, human love, is another question, with which we are not here concerned. Our interest is in the *ideas* of love represented by Luther and Aquinas.

50. cf. *W.A.* I.365: 'For sinners are lovely because they are loved; they are not loved because they are lovely. So man's love shuns sinners and evil men. But thus Christ: I came not to call the righteous, but sinners. And this is the love of the Cross (*amor crucis*) born of the Cross, which betakes itself not where it finds a good to enjoy, but where it may confer good upon the evil and the needy. For it is more blessed to give than to receive, says the Apostle.'

51. *S.T.* II.ii. q.26. a.8.

52. cf. Nygren, *Agape and Eros*, II.ii.426f.; Burnaby, *Amor Dei*, 266f.

53. *S.T.* II.i. q.26. a.4.

54. cf. Nygren, op. cit. 427; Burnaby, op. cit. 265.

55. op. cit. 267.

56. It is significant that Luther does not use the expression 'friendship with God', although it originated with Saint Augustine, who greatly influenced him, and was further developed in the Scholasticism with which he was familiar—cf. Holl, *Ges. Aufs. I.* 81.

57. Burnaby, op. cit. 264f.

58. *S.T.* I. q.5. a.1.

59. ibid. q.20. a.1.

60. ibid. q.20. a.2. ad.4.

61. Nygren, *Agape and Eros*, II.ii.361.

62. op. cit. 363.

63. ibid.

64. Nygren, op. cit. 357; Burnaby, op. cit. 269.

65. Nygren, op. cit. 365.

66. cf. *S.T.* I. q.20, a.2. ad.1, where Aquinas quotes Dionysius on this theme.

67. cf. R. L. Patterson, *The Conception of God*, 331f., where Aquinas's argument is summarized as follows (*italics* mine): According to Aquinas, the object of the Divine will is the Divine essence, and 'in willing his own essence, God likewise wills all things. For, since he is both the efficient and the final cause of all beings, in *willing himself* God wills all created things both as his effects and also as directed toward himself as their ultimate end. Furthermore, God *loves himself*, as in due course is to be proved. All of us, however, desire the perfection of that which we love; in other words, we wish it to be improved and multiplied. But the divine essence cannot be improved and multiplied in itself. Yet its perfection can be imitated by the creatures in manifold ways; hence their existence is willed by the Deity. Moreover, anyone who loves something for itself loves all things in which it is found. Consequently, since God *wills and loves his being for itself*, and since everything that exists is a participation in his being through likeness (*est quaedam sui esse secundum similitudinem participatio*), God wills and loves all things that exist.' It could not be more clearly shown than by this summary of Aquinas's argument in *Contra Gentiles*, lib.1, cap.74,75, how close he stands to the Areopagite, and how far he can be removed from the New Testament conception of the Divine Agape.

F

68. Nygren, *Agape and Eros,* II.ii.351.

69. *M.H.B.* 768, a translation of his hymn, *O esca viatorum,* while not unaffected by some of the ideas we have examined, shows much more clearly how the Divine Agape had in fact touched his soul.

70. *Gal.* E.T. 42(i.14).

71. cf. Romans 102f.; John 162; Acts 269.

72. Luke 1710; cf. p. 100 n. 80. *infra.*

73. cf. Hildebrandt, *Melanchthon,* 84: 'In defining heresy Luther counts besides those who err either about the Godhead or the manhood of Christ a third class of those who do not let Him do His work. [*W.A.* L.269.1 et seq. In the context the Papacy is accused of promoting the third heresy.] To deny the justifying grace of Christ is to deprive Christ of His glory and, in fact, to have another God; the controversy about the "sola fide" must needs be Christological too, though in Luther's times it was not always stated in such terms.'

74. *W.A.* XI.67.30.

75. cf. *W.A.* XI.69.21ff.

76. *Gal.* E.T. 344f.(v.9).

77. *W.A.* XI. 69.11ff. cf. *Gal.* E.T. 63,66(ii.6.8).

78. *Gal.* E.T. 345(v.9).

79. ibid. 350(v.12).

80. The phrase also is Luther's; cf. *W.A.* X.1; 25.5, where he says it is sin 'not to glorify God, that is, not to believe, trust, fear Him, not to give Him glory, not *to let Him* rule and *be a God;* in which sin the crude, outward sinners are doubtless sunk deep, but much deeper the wise, holy, learned and religious, who in the sight of the world and themselves are godly and build upon their works—in a word, all who do not commit themselves to the mere goodness and grace of God and live thereby, are all *impii,* ungodly'.

81. It should perhaps be said here, in order to forestall possible erroneous conclusions, that when we contrast Luther's teaching with mistaken interpretations of it, or even with the doctrines of Luther's opponents, we are not passing any judgement on the *persons* concerned. We are contrasting different conceptions of the nature of the religious relationship, not discussing the actual relationship in which those who held them personally stood to God. It would ill become us to do so, when Luther himself holds that true faith is not necessarily excluded by erroneous opinions, and when he ventures to hope that even the heathen Cicero may be saved. But in the nature of the case, only God Himself can be judge of that, and we will let Him be God.

Part Two

The Major Themes of Luther's Theology

CHAPTER THREE

THE REVELATION OF GOD

9. THE TWOFOLD KNOWLEDGE OF GOD

THERE ARE, according to Luther, two kinds of knowledge of God—*duplex est cognitio Dei*. One of these he describes as 'general' and claims it as a natural possession of all men. The other, which he terms 'particular' or 'proper' (*propria*), is that given in and through Christ. It is hardly too much to say that the problem of reconciling the contents of these two kinds of knowledge sets its mark, in one way or another, on the whole of Luther's thought. An understanding of the relationship between them, as he conceives it, is consequently of no little importance for the interpretation of his theology. Here, however, an initial difficulty arises from the fact that Luther often speaks as if Christ were the one and only source of our knowledge of God.[1] Yet he does not mean to deny either the reality or the relevance of the general knowledge, since even after speaking in this way he is still able to affirm that all men possess it.[2] Moreover, the comparative frequency of his references to it would justify the assumption that it is integral to his thought.

At first sight, Luther appears to hold contradictory views of the relation between the two kinds of knowledge. He represents the particular knowledge now as if it were complementary to the general, now as if it were its antithesis. Commenting on Galatians 48, for instance, he says:

If all men knew God, wherefore doth Paul say, that the Galatians knew not God before the preaching of the Gospel? I answer, there is a double knowledge of God, general and particular. All men have the general knowledge, namely, that there is a God, that He created heaven and earth, that He is just, that He punisheth the wicked. But what God thinketh of us, what His will is toward us, what He will give or what He will do to the end we may be delivered from sin and death, and be saved (which is the true knowledge of God indeed), this they know not. As it may be that I know some man by sight, whom indeed I know not thoroughly, because I understand not what affection he beareth towards me.[3]

From this it would appear as if the general knowledge were simply an imperfect kind of knowledge, true and valid as far as it goes, but requiring completion by the particular.

But the position proves to be not quite so simple when we read the sequel of the passage just quoted.

For [Luther proceeds to assert] upon this proposition which all men do naturally hold, namely, that there is a God, hath sprung all idolatry, which without the knowledge of the Divinity, could never have come into the world. But because men had this natural knowledge of God, they conceived vain and wicked imaginations of God . . . and so dreamed that God is such a one, as by nature He is not. So the monk imagineth Him to be such a God as forgiveth sins, giveth grace and everlasting life for the keeping of his rule. This God is nowhere to be found. Therefore he serveth not the true God, but that which by nature is no God; to wit, the imagination and idol of his own heart; that is to say, his own false and vain opinion of God, which he dreameth to be an undoubted truth.[4]

Here the argument appears to have veered round so far as to repudiate the original affirmation of a general knowledge of God, or at least to represent it as virtually no knowledge at all. Yet we should misconstrue Luther's intention if we assumed without more ado that he simply dismisses the general knowledge as either false or irrelevant.

It will help us to understand, in principle at any rate, the relation between the two kinds of knowledge, if we develop Luther's own brief but illuminating simile. When we possess only the general, natural knowledge, he suggests, we are much in the same position as when we know some man 'by sight', but are unaware of his 'affection' toward us.

Now we know from experience that it is possible, not merely to be distantly acquainted, but even to have a good deal to do with a man, and still to be in ignorance of his personal attitude to us, his thoughts and feelings about us. In such circumstances, it easily happens that we construct our own picture of his character and disposition, on the basis of whatever knowledge we possess of him. This picture, moreover, can vitally affect our personal attitude to the man, our thoughts and feelings about him; and in this way it can influence our whole approach to him. Yet our picture may be quite remote from the reality. It may be so remote that such a person can be said to exist only in our own imagination, as we might well discover if we came to make the closer, personal acquaintance of the man himself through circumstances which led him to disclose his real attitude to us. This could alter our whole relationship to him, and it would not then be surprising if we felt bound to say that our previous knowledge of him was false, or that we never really knew him at all. The facts upon which we based our former conception of him might be true enough in themselves, but by themselves they proved misleading, or at best inadequate for a valid estimate of him, because their significance was not properly understood. Their real meaning was obscure until they were seen in the light of his personal character and disposition.

Thus interpreted, Luther's simile illustrates directly and in detail his conception of the knowledge of God. 'Men naturally know', he says, 'that there is a God, but what His will is, or what is not His will, they do not know.'[5] They have, that is to say, the general, but not the particular, knowledge of God. On the basis of what they know, however—and they know considerably more than the bare fact of His existence, as we shall see—they form their own ideas of His character and shape their own attitude toward Him.[6] But here they 'are deceived, and become vain in their cogitations, as Paul saith, (Romans 1), not knowing what pleaseth or displeaseth God. Therefore, instead of the true and natural God, they worship the dreams and imaginations of their own heart.'[7] For want of the particular knowledge, the true significance of the general knowledge they possess is lost upon them. From this point of view, it is hardly an exaggeration to say that without the particular knowledge, 'which is the true knowledge of God indeed', men do not really know God at all—just as 'that man does not know a prince who knows his power and his wealth, but he who understands the affections and all the counsels of the prince'.[8] 'Wherefore', Luther can say without inconsistency, 'Christ is the only mean, and as ye would say, the glass by the which we see God, that is to say, we know His will.'[9]

It should now be clear that the apparent contradictions in Luther's view of the knowledge of God are only apparent. The diversity of his statements is simply due to the different points of view from which the subject can be regarded. This fact, however, does not solve the problem set for Luther himself by the two kinds of knowledge which he postulates. There is a deeper distinction between them than those we have so far observed. They are both possessed of a definite content, in respect of which they differ to such an extent that they might well seem to be mutually exclusive. Luther's endeavour to reconcile them, in which he has a remarkable measure of success, is reflected in one way or another throughout his thought. In order to understand the problem at issue, we must turn first to consider the source and character of the general knowledge of God as he conceives it. Although he had neither occasion nor inclination to elaborate a detailed theory of it, he furnishes sufficient evidence for a clear view of what we might almost describe as his 'natural theology'.

10. MAN'S GENERAL OR NATURAL KNOWLEDGE OF GOD

(a) The Creatures as 'Veils' of God

The suggestion that anything like natural theology is to be found in Luther, no doubt calls for explanation. The Reformers have been credited with the rejection of all natural theology. They are supposed to have 'pressed the doctrine of the Fall of Man to a point where the human reason is regarded as incapable of apprehending any divine truth'.[10] Considerable evidence might well be adduced in support of this view; but it must be said that everything depends on what is meant by natural theology.

Luther, it is certain, has little if any place for the conception which finds classical expression in Aquinas and has been traditionally maintained by both Roman and Protestant theologians, that a certain definite knowledge of God can be attained by rational inference from the world of nature. This type of natural theology, deriving ultimately from the theistic argumentation of Plato and Aristotle, treats the existence and, in large measure, the nature and attributes of God as conclusions to be established by means of argument. The 'natural' knowledge thus gained by the exercise of 'reason' is not claimed, it is true, as a complete knowledge of God; but what is lacking in it can be made up by supernatural 'revelation'. There is a 'revealed' knowledge, given in the Scriptures, of truths which, although they may be shown to be not contrary to 'reason', cannot be discovered or demonstrated by it, and must therefore be received by 'faith'. The question, how much of man's total knowledge of God 'reason' is competent to discover, and how much must be sought from 'revelation', has been long and warmly debated. Some would attribute more, some less to 'reason', while others would deny its competence entirely. Among these last the Reformers are generally reckoned.

It was not, however, simply his doctrine of the Fall and its effects upon human reason that made it impossible for Luther to accept the type of natural theology we have just described.[11] The Nominalist theology of late Scholasticism, developing the ideas of Duns Scotus and, more especially, of William of Occam, had already had its solvent effect on the whole discursive knowledge of God, and Luther had learnt too much of that theology to be able to retain any great confidence in the ability of reason to apprehend divine truth.[12] Yet not even his Nominalist training can be said to be the fundamental cause of Luther's rejection of the Thomistic type of natural theology. Nominalism, despite the divergence of its answer, was still dealing with essentially the same question as Aquinas, the question of the relative contributions, so to speak, of 'reason' and 'faith' to our knowledge of God.

But Luther, although he may discuss the Scholastic question, has actually abandoned in his own thinking the whole Scholastic approach to the problem. When the question of our knowledge of God is stated in terms of 'natural theology' and 'revelation', he is bound to exclude the former; but that is not to say that he accepts the latter in the sense given to it here. His own conception of a 'general' or 'natural' knowledge of God has virtually nothing in common with the 'natural' and 'revealed' knowledge of traditional theological thought.

The fact is that Luther has divined a deeper truth than the scholastic doctrine perceives. The latter presupposes what may be termed a 'deistic' conception of God. The Creator is regarded as concealed by His creation, and must be sought behind His works. The knowledge of God is derived from a knowledge of other things than God. From Luther's point of view, such knowledge could never be more substantial than a dream. Even if its 'rational' foundations were secure, it is too abstract, theoretical, impersonal. There is, as Dr. John Baillie has observed, 'an immediacy about Luther's knowledge of God which is lacking in that of St. Thomas'.[13] True, the Thomistic natural knowledge is supplemented by the revealed, but even this tends to be conceived in a somewhat cold and abstract manner as yielding certain

'truths' about God. For Luther, on the other hand, to know God
is something other than reaching conclusions or receiving in-
formation about Him.[14] A God who waits to be discovered as the
result of a speculative argument, the shortcomings of which are
then made up by means of a revelation He has conveniently
supplied, is not the living God with whom we have to do. But
with the living God all men have, in fact, to do; or rather, the
living God has to do with them, and that directly.[15]

Luther would entirely approve the view 'that our knowledge of
God is not inferential in character and that the attempt to reach
God by means of argument is therefore wrong in principle'.[16] He
condemns the inferential method in scores of passages, where he
warns us against trying to find God in the scholastic manner by
means of 'reason' and 'speculation'. He regards it as a vain
endeavour to 'comprehend God in His majesty' and he describes
it as a 'theology of glory', to which he opposes his own 'theology
of the Cross'.[17] The latter, of course, corresponds to what we have
already noticed as his 'particular' knowledge of God. From one
point of view, however, he might equally well have opposed to the
theology of glory his general or natural knowledge. Why he did
not, we shall understand when we examine its content and
effects; but it is plain that it is, in its own way, scarcely less
contrary to the scholastic conception. For Luther, God is not to
be sought behind His creation by inference from it, but is rather
to be apprehended in and through it.

Here it must be observed that, although we have spoken of
God as having to do 'directly' with men, Luther admits no
unmediated relationship between them. The biblical principle
holds good, that man cannot see God, in His naked transcendence,
and live.[18] God, therefore, must wear as it were a 'mask' or
'veil' (*larva, involucrum*) in all His dealings with men, to shield
them from the unapproachable light of His majesty. Luther
specially emphasizes this when he is pointing seekers after salvation to Christ. 'The incarnate Son of God', he says, 'is that veil
(*involucrum*) in which the Divine Majesty with all His gifts presents
Himself unto us'; and it is 'the first step of error, when men leave
the veiled (*involuto*) and incarnate God to pursue the naked God'.[19]
The pursuit of the 'naked God' is, of course, the same as the
theology of glory to which we have already referred. But the
error of such theology is not merely that it ignores the mediation

of Christ. It is equally at fault in its treatment of the created world. If it begins with 'the things that are made', it argues all too literally *from* them, for it seeks in fact to pass *beyond* them, so that they are left behind as knowledge of their Maker is gained.

Luther refuses to regard the creatures as a mere starting-point in the quest for God. He does so, moreover, not simply because he has no confidence in man's ability to find God by that method, but even more because he sets a different value on 'the things that are made'. These also he interprets as 'masks' of God, asserting that 'every creature is His mask *(larva)*',[20] and in-sisting that, in this life at any rate, the mask can never be re-moved for us to see God 'face to face'.[21] In a certain sense, therefore, the Creator is concealed by His works. Yet the *larvae Dei* have another and more positive significance than that of mere concealment. Rightly understood, they are media of Divine revelation. 'All created ordinances', Luther says, 'are masks or allegories wherewith God depicts His theology; they are meant, as it were, to contain Christ.'[22] They 'contain Christ', of course, inasmuch as the God whose 'masks' they are, is none other than He who reveals Himself—albeit in a special way—in Jesus Christ. For Luther, there is no other God.[23]

The whole created world, then, as Luther sees it, occupies a kind of mediatorial position between God and man. Its manifold orders of life—'the prince, the magistrate, the preacher, the school-master, the scholar, the father, the mother, the children, the master, the servant'—can be described as 'persons and outward veils *(larvae)*', which serve God as 'His instruments by whom He governeth and preserveth the world'.[24] The creatures, therefore, are not to be set aside in a quest for God, so to say, behind the scenes, for they may rather be said to represent Him on the stage, where He Himself in fact plays the principal part. All the good that is done to us by men, for instance, according to Luther, we receive in the last resort 'not from them, but from God through them. For His creatures are only the hand, the channel, the in-struments, the means by which God bestows all things on us'.[25]

The instrumentality of the creatures is vividly illustrated by Luther's exposition of Jonah 23: 'For thou didst cast me into the depth. . . . All thy waves and thy billows passed over me.'[26] Here he attaches great importance to the fact that God, and not simply the crew of the ship, is said to have cast the prophet overboard, and that it is not simply the waves of the sea, but God's waves, that are said to have passed over him. To the disobedient Jonah, who was seeking to escape from God and from doing His will, the sailors and the storm were instruments of Divine wrath, the means by which God struck at his conscience. For it is typical of the uneasy conscience to feel that the very forces of nature and all the creatures are leagued with a wrathful God against it, so that it can be terrified even at the rustling of a leaf. This does not represent for Luther a purely subjective and imaginary experience, but an apprehension of the fundamental fact that man is confronted by the living God in all the circumstances of his concrete existence, in all that happens to him and around him.[27]

Clearly, if there is no unmediated knowledge of God, Luther's mediation is of a very different type from that of the Thomistic natural theology. The *larvae Dei* are the means of a Divine confrontation of man, which can hardly be described otherwise than as direct. In order to do justice, therefore, to both aspects of Luther's conception, we could not do better than borrow an apt and striking expression used by Dr. Baillie, and speak of a 'mediated immediacy'.[28] We do not reach God by inferring His existence, nature, and attributes from His masks and veils, but God Himself comes to meet us in them—none other than the God who meets us in Christ. The 'natural man', who has not seen God in Christ, does not rightly recognize Him, it is true, for he lacks the wisdom to distinguish between the veils of God and God Himself, and he is ever prone to worship the creature instead of the Creator.[29] Yet all men have at least some awareness of the God who confronts them in the midst of their creaturely environment, and even though they misapprehend it, they have some knowledge of His nature.

What Luther calls the general knowledge of God, then, is not the result of any human quest for God, but is prior to all man's seeking and is given by God Himself.

Even the heathen [Luther says] have this awareness (*sensum*) by a natural instinct, that there is some supreme deity (*numen*) . . . as Paul says in Romans 1, that the Gentiles knew God by nature. For this knowledge is divinely implanted in the minds of all men . . . even if they afterwards err in this, who that God is and how He wills to be worshipped.[30]

THE REVELATION OF GOD

In his comment on Romans 1 19 Luther declares:

> . . . it most certainly follows that they had a conception or notion of divinity, which without doubt is in them from God, as he here says. . . . They knew that it is the mark of divinity, or of Him who is God, to be mighty, invisible, just, immortal, good; therefore they knew the invisible things of God and His eternal power and divinity. This major of the practical syllogism, this theological conscience (*syntheresis theologica*), is inobscurable in all men. But in the minor they erred.[31]

Clear evidence of the reality of this 'theological conscience' is to be found in the fact of religion itself, since without it there could be no such thing as religion. 'The ceremonies and religions which were, and always remained among all nations, sufficiently witness that all men have had a certain general knowledge of God.'[32] 'Nature teaches that there is one God, who gives all good, and helps against all evil, as even the heathen show by their worshipping of idols.'[33] 'For how could they call an image or any other creature "God", if they knew nothing of what God was, and what it pertained to Him to do?'[34]

(b) The God of Power and of Law

What, then, we may now ask, is the more precise content of Luther's general or natural knowledge of God? From the passages already quoted, it is clear that considerably more is given in it than the bare fact of God's existence. Quite a number of the characteristic attributes of divinity have been named as familiar even to the heathen. Of such attributes, however, there are two that can be regarded as of outstanding importance in Luther's view, and they may perhaps best be described as Sovereignty and Righteousness.

The essence of the general knowledge, according to Luther's own definition of it, is 'that there is a God, that He created heaven and earth, that He is just, that He punisheth the wicked'.[35] There is a remarkable similarity between this idea and the conception presented by Dr. Niebuhr in his Gifford Lectures of a 'general revelation', which is defined as 'the sense of being confronted with a "wholly other" at the edge of human consciousness'. Of the elements included in this awareness, in its most rudimentary form, the first is described as 'the sense of reverence for a majesty and of dependence upon an ultimate source of being'; and the second is 'the sense of moral obligation laid upon one from beyond oneself and of moral unworthiness before a judge'. Those two elements are not sharply defined at first, Dr. Niebuhr says, but they gain in clarity as they are supported by the biblical conception of God as the Maker of all things and the Judge of all men.[36] This biblical conception has doubtless influenced Luther's statement which we have just quoted; for the thought of deity among the heathen, as Luther was aware, is by no means always quite so clearly defined. But be that as it may, it is the sense of Divine sovereignty and righteousness, or the awareness of God as a God of power and of law, that is of chief importance for Luther in his thought of the general knowledge of God.[37]

As evidence of the universal awareness of Divine sovereignty, Luther can cite the prevalence of the idea of Fate among the heathen.

How often [he asks] does Virgil alone make mention of Fate? . . . He makes even their immortal gods subject to Fate. . . . Hence that common saying was on every one's tongue, 'God's will be done'. Again, 'If God will, we will do it'. Again, 'Such was the will of God'. 'Such was the will of those above.'

From this, Luther concludes: 'we may see that the knowledge of predestination and the prescience of God was no less left in the world than the notion of the divinity itself.'[38] Poets and common people alike, he says, thus testified to the supreme power of God; and although some, who 'wished to appear wise', denied it, or pretended not to know it, yet their own conscience bore witness to it. It is one of the sentiments that are written on all men's hearts, which they cannot help acknowledging whenever it is put to them, 'that God is omnipotent, not only in power but in action, and that if it were not so, He would be a ridiculous God'.[39]

If God is thus known as supreme in power, He is not less known as just; for His law is written on all men's hearts.

God wishes the law to be taught [Luther asserts] and He reveals it divinely, nay He inscribes it on the minds of all men, as Paul proves in Romans 2. And from just this natural knowledge all the books of the sounder philosophers have been born, as of Aesop, Aristotle, Plato, Xenophon, Cicero, Cato.[40]

Although the Gentiles did not receive the written law of Moses, 'yet they received the spiritual law . . . which is impressed upon all, both Jews and Gentiles, to which also all are under obligation'.[41] The essence of this law is contained in the Golden Rule (Matthew 712); for men 'naturally judge that a man ought to do unto another as he would another should do unto him'.[42] Here the entire meaning of the traditional law (*lex tradita*) is summed up; it is nothing else but 'this natural law (*lex naturalis*) of which none can be ignorant'.[43] Hence Luther can claim that the Ten Commandments themselves, at least in their essential significance, are written on the hearts of all men, and that Moses was not the author, but only the interpreter of these natural laws.[44]

Man's natural knowledge of the Law of God, it is true, is very weak, for it is obscured by sin. That is why the law has had to be given and taught in the Commandments.[45] Yet some measure of the natural knowledge must exist, Luther maintains, or no amount of teaching and commanding would be of any avail.

It is certain [he says] that the law might be preached to us for a hundred years in vain, as to some ass, if it were not written on our hearts so that when we are admonished we instantly say: Yes, that is so.[46]

It may now be judged with what justification we have ventured to speak of a natural theology of Luther. Unless we are to insist on a Thomistic interpretation of the words, it is plain that to accuse him of the rejection of all natural theology is unjust, or at least that it is liable to be singularly misleading. The same might also be said of Calvin, who maintains a position in many respects similar to Luther's, and frequently expresses himself in identical terms.[47] It may well be, as Brunner says, that 'Luther makes much greater concessions to the *theologia naturalis* than Calvin';[48] but 'concessions' is hardly the term we should use, except in so far as the Thomistic type of natural theology is meant. Luther undoubtedly grants on occasion a certain usefulness to the discursive method. If he denies all value to it 'in the matter of justification', that is, as a means to the establishment of our personal relationship to God, yet 'out of the matter of justification', he says,

when thou must dispute with Jews, Turks, Papists, Heretics, etc., concerning the power, wisdom, and majesty of God, then employ all thy wit and industry to that end, and be as profound and as subtle a disputer as thou canst: for then thou art in another vein.[49]

He quotes with high approval, moreover, an example from Cicero of the teleological argument for the existence of God, which he says he finds deeply moving;[50] and in his comment on Galatians 3 15, he actually warns us against the view that analogies from human experience are necessarily valueless with reference to things spiritual and divine. 'Such manner of arguments are good', he says, 'when they are grounded upon the ordinance of God. But when they be taken from men's corrupt affections they are naught.'[51]

Even apart from such 'concessions to the *theologia naturalis*', however, it would still be misleading to assert that Luther had no natural theology. He had, after all, read his New Testament; and the first two chapters of the Epistle to the Romans, along with other passages dear to the natural theologians, could not escape his notice. He had, furthermore, too much reverence for the sacred text to ignore such passages, or to dismiss them as unimportant. But he was not obliged to give them the same interpretation as had been traditionally read into them. Instead, he expounded them in a manner much nearer to the original intention of their authors, as is shown by his references to them in quotations we have already given. Romans 1 20, for instance, is not, as Aquinas thought, an example of the argument from design; for what is said is not that God's existence can be proved from His works, but that in and through them certain aspects of His nature—'His eternal power and divinity'—are revealed. That is precisely Luther's teaching; and with it he anticipates some of the best modern thought on the subject.

We shall hardly be wrong if we suggest that it was Luther's theocentric interest that led him to this insight into the character of our knowledge of God. It is at any rate entirely in line with his dominant theocentric emphasis. He will have nothing to do with any natural theology that assumes the capacity of the natural man to make his own way to God, or to discover God for himself. The natural knowledge of God which Luther teaches, is wholly God-given. Even his 'concessions' to the traditional *theologia naturalis* actually assume the priority of this natural knowledge; for if, as he says, there could be no religion without it, neither could there be any argument about God Himself.

At the same time, we must beware of exaggerating the value Luther attaches to man's natural knowledge of God. The possession of it may undoubtedly be conceived as furnishing a necessary point of contact in man for the Christian message.[52] Since both come from the same God, there is naturally no essential disharmony between them. But this by no means necessarily indicates that the possessors of the natural knowledge are themselves in harmony with its Giver, or that they are able to achieve a right relationship to Him on the basis of it. On the contrary, Luther holds with St. Paul that inasmuch as God's 'eternal power and divinity' are manifest, men are 'without excuse', because in spite of their knowledge of God they have not rightly worshipped and served Him. He emphasizes this same point in his comment on Romans 2 15, where he speaks of 'this natural law, which cannot be unknown to anyone, and therefore no one has any excuse'. In the hands of the natural man, the natural knowledge of God gives rise, not to true religion, but to 'all idolatry, which without the knowledge of the Divinity, could never have come into the world'.[53] The fault, of course, lies not with the knowledge, but with the man, who invariably misinterprets and misuses it, Luther maintains, in such a way that, without the 'proper' knowledge of God given in Christ, he can never avoid idolatry.[54]

II. THE FALSE RELIGION OF THE NATURAL MAN

It is not difficult to see how the natural or general knowledge of God gives rise to idolatry if we recall Luther's comparison of it to the knowledge we may have of a person by sight. On the basis of such knowledge, we can develop imaginative, and often quite erroneous, ideas of our own about the person concerned, which will largely determine the attitude we adopt in practice toward him. In some such way, men have dealt with their knowledge of the Divine majesty, the sovereignty and righteousness of God. They have drawn conclusions from it that are entirely unjustified, so that they cherish false conceptions of God's will and purpose, and put themselves into a wrong relation to Him. That may be said to be the essential meaning of idolatry as Luther understands it. It is not simply, nor primarily, a question of bowing down to graven images; for mental images can at least equally misrepresent God, and false doctrine is no less an idol than a heathen stock or stone.[55] Indeed, both graven images and false doctrine alike only give expression and embodiment to what is first in the idolatrous mind.

G

Real idolatry, then, is not a matter of outward observance, but of the heart and mind; and Luther's constant complaint is, that instead of the true God, men worship figments of their own imagination. Although they may not outwardly worship the creature instead of the Creator, yet they do so inwardly in their hearts.[56] They attribute to God a character that is not His; they give to something other than God the place that is rightly His alone; they substitute for Him a creature of their own fancy, their own conception of God.[57] Whether they conceive of Him in more or less crudely anthropomorphic terms, or as a 'wholly other' that is the negation of all anthropomorphism, makes no essential difference. An abstract god is as much an idol as a concrete god, and a god produced by human ratiocination as a god fashioned by human hands.[58]

From one point of view, all idolatry can be attributed to *ratio*, 'reason'; for it is by the use of their reason that men both construct and seek to justify their conceptions of God. That is why Luther so often speaks of 'reason' in terms of contempt and condemnation that shock his less discerning readers. 'How does he . . . decry reason, right or wrong, as an irreconcilable enemy to the Gospel of Christ!' John Wesley exclaims after turning the pages of Luther's *Galatians*. 'Whereas,' he continues, 'what is reason (the faculty so called) but the power of apprehending, judging, and discoursing? Which power is no more to be condemned in the gross, than seeing, hearing, or feeling'.[59] With this last statement Luther would whole-heartedly agree; but he would strongly and rightly protest that he has never decried reason 'right or wrong', nor condemned it 'in the gross'. In fact, as 'the power of apprehending, judging, and discoursing', he never condemns it at all, but praises it most highly as one of the best of all God's gifts to men. It is in virtue of his reason, Luther holds, that a man is worthy to be called, and is, a man.[60] Reason is a 'natural light' that is kindled from the 'divine light',[61] and 'above all other things of this life, it is something excellent and divine'. It is the discoverer and governor of all arts and sciences and 'whatever of wisdom, power, virtue, and glory is possessed by men in this life'.[62] About reason in this sense of the term, Luther can wax almost lyrical. What he condemns is the use men commonly make of their reason, when they apprehend, judge, and discourse about matters pertaining to God and their own relationships with Him.

Man, with all his powers, including reason, Luther holds, is a creature of God and has some knowledge of God.[63] Reason, therefore, is naturally aware of God's law, and knows that we ought to do good and to worship and serve God. What it does not understand, however, is how and why we ought to do these things. It is with reason as with the rest of our powers, for they are all corrupted by sin. The flesh, for instance, is a creature of God, yet it is not inclined to chastity, but to unchastity; and the heart is a creature of God, yet it is not inclined to humility and the service of its neighbours, but to pride and self-love. In a similar way, reason, knowing that good is to be done and God is to be served, imagines the good to be that which pleases itself, and thinks to serve God by rites, ceremonies and observances, which it elects to regard as 'good works'. Now when Christ comes, bringing the 'light of grace', He does not extinguish the 'natural light' of reason, for He too teaches that we ought to serve God. But He attacks the ways and means of doing so, which reason has devised. Then, says Luther, there takes place a battle royal, because reason is angry with grace and accuses it of forbidding good works; whereas grace in fact teaches what alone are truly good works, and how alone they can truly be done. But reason does not want to be taught these things, for it thinks it knows them already; and that is why all idolatry, heresy, hypocrisy, and error can be traced back to the stiff-necked, self-willed opinions of natural reason.

It is of interest at this point to refer to what some of his critics have been pleased to regard as Luther's most infamous words— his well-known, but little understood, description of reason as 'the devil's whore'. In the light of what has just been said, his meaning is not very difficult to perceive. If reason opposes Christ with His message of grace, then it espouses the cause of His adversary, it prostitutes itself to the service of the enemy of God. Luther's language is undeniably strong, but its strength is the measure of his indignation at the abuse and perversion of what he regards as one of the Creator's best gifts to His creatures. The choice of metaphor may appear to us to be in exceedingly bad taste, but at least he had biblical precedent for it. The prophets of Israel denounced the idolatries of the Chosen People as whoredoms, and our Lord Himself branded as adulterous the faithless generation that demanded a sign. What is more important, however, than any harsh words that Luther may have used about reason, is the fact that he does not regard it as beyond redemption. If it is put to pernicious uses by the ungodly, so that it becomes an enemy of the Gospel, of faith, and of God Himself, yet in the hands of believers, who are enlightened by the Gospel, it becomes a most excellent instrument.[64]

It should now be clear that when Luther decries reason, he is not attacking the faculty of logical thought, or 'the power of apprehending, judging, and discoursing', as such. He is attacking the use men make of this faculty in matters pertaining to religion, or as he would say, 'in the matter of justification'; and he is particularly concerned, of course, with the reasonings of scholastic theology and popular catholic piety about God and His dealings with men. Outside the sphere of religion, he has nothing derogatory to say of reason, but quite the reverse; and within that sphere he criticizes it only as it is used to maintain doctrines and practices that from his theocentric standpoint must be condemned as idolatrous. Luther is no irrationalist, except to those who either have not grasped, or refuse to share, his fundamental point of view.[65] Rightly understood, all his denunciations of *ratio* are nothing more or less than a part of his campaign against religious egocentricity or anthropocentricity. For it is characteristic of *ratio*, as he sees it, that even in God it seeks only itself and the things of itself, instead of God and the things of God.[66]

The burden of Luther's complaint against *ratio*, then, is that it subserves the egocentricity of the natural man. It ministers to his persistent tendency to look at everything, including God, from his own point of view, as it affects himself and his own interests. From a theocentric point of view, however, this must be regarded as a prostitution of reason, for it results in the perversion of man's natural knowledge of God and leads, not to true religion, but to idolatry. How more precisely this comes about it is not difficult to understand.

In the first place, knowing something of the sovereign power of God, men tend to see in it a possibility of securing the fulfilment of their own desires. They seek to make His divinity, as it were, a means to their own ends.

In this, therefore, they erred [says Luther, referring to the heathen of old] that they did not leave the divinity bare and worship it, but they changed and adapted it to their own wishes and desires. And everyone wanted divinity to be in that whereby he might please himself, and so they changed the truth of God into a lie.[67]

For no people were ever so reckless as not to set up or cultivate some form of worship; but every man sets up as his god that from which he hopes to obtain good, help, and comfort. So the heathens, whose sole aim was power and dominion, made Jupiter their highest god, while the others selected Hercules, Mercury, or Venus, according as they desired wealth, fortune, or pleasure and delight . . . and so on; each one taking for his god what his heart desired. . . . But they erred herein, that their faith was false and wrong, for it was not centred in the only God beside whom verily there is no god in heaven or earth. Wherefore the heathens make an idol of their own invented dream and fancy of a god.[68]

But the heathen are not alone in their error. It is Luther's constant complaint against catholic piety that it is rooted in human selfishness.

How many there are even now also [he laments] who do not worship Him as God, but as they imagine Him to themselves! . . . For is not this to change the glory of God into the likeness of an imagination and a dream, if thou neglectest the work that thou owest and worshippest Him with a work thyself hast chosen, and . . . believest God to be such an one as should have respect unto thee and thine?[69]

Such worshippers sin against the First Commandment,

because they do not seek the things of God, but their own, even in God Himself and His saints; and they are their own ultimate end (as it is called) and idol of this work of theirs, using God, enjoying themselves.[70]

In the second place, it must be said that men naturally do not imagine they can obtain what they desire from God, or from their gods, simply for the asking. They retain at least some consciousness of His righteousness, some awareness 'that He is just and that He punisheth the wicked'. But this, Luther holds, only gives occasion for another and more subtle form of idolatry. Because God is the God of the law, men assume that He must deal with them on a legal basis of merit and reward, and they seek to establish their own relationship with Him accordingly. They seek to gain His approval by performing what they elect to regard as 'good works'.

For this [says Luther] is the imagination of them all: If I do this work, God will have mercy upon me: if I do it not, He will be angry. And therefore every man that revolteth from the knowledge of Christ, must needs fall into idolatry, and conceive such an imagination of God as is not agreeable to His nature: as the Charterhouse monk for the observing of his rule, the Turk for the keeping of his Alcoran, hath this assurance, that he pleaseth God, and shall receive a reward from Him for his labour.[71]

Luther regards this as 'the worst form of idolatry'.

It concerns the conscience alone [he says] which seeks help, comfort, and salvation in its own works: . . . it would gain heaven by force . . . as though it would accept nothing from Him gratuitously, but would itself earn reward and do service over and above what is required; as if He must be our servant and debtor, and we His masters. What else is this but to turn God into an idol or wooden image, and to set up ourselves as a god?[72]
    For to trust in a work . . . is to give glory to oneself and take it from God . . . but this is complete perversity, for it is to please and enjoy oneself in one's own works and to adore oneself as an idol.[73]

All the children of Adam, Luther affirms, are idolaters, for they try by one means or another 'to take God captive',[74] as he puts it, or 'to bewitch God',[75] as if He should conform to their ideas or be subservient to their interests. Their wishful thinking prevents them from taking seriously all that is implied in the knowledge that God is Creator of heaven and earth.[76] They should know that 'one cannot put God in one's pocket';[77] that 'God does not exist for man's sake, but man for God's';[78] and that 'we must adapt ourselves to Him, for He will not adapt Himself to us'.[79] 'By the right of creation' He can and does require of us whole-hearted obedience to His commandments, and He would owe us nothing even if we rendered it.[80] Yet men offer to God their self-chosen works, as if they could put Him into their debt and obtain a reward from Him; and so doing, they make reward their god, 'for that for which a man does anything, that is his god'.[81] The fact is, however, that we owe to the Creator all that we have and are, and can therefore never become His creditors. From this point of view, Luther can say that 'there is no other worship of God than thanksgiving'.[82] The offering of thanks gives God His divine honour, it allows Him to be and remain God, the

Creator and Giver of all things; but the offering of works robs Him of His honour and does not allow Him to remain God, but makes Him into an idol.[83]

It is catholic piety, with its eudemonism and moralism, that Luther clearly regards as the most subtle and perilous form of idolatry. For its professors cannot believe that they are idolaters, and they are indignant at the very suggestion of it. They do not bow down to graven images; they give their utmost endeavours to serve the true God; they worship Him in the name of Christ. Luther gives them full credit for their good intentions; he knows they are sincere. But they are sincerely wrong.[84]

It is not enough [he points out] to say or think: 'I am doing it to God's glory; I mean it for the true God; I will serve the only God.' All idolaters say and intend that. Intentions and thoughts do not count, or those who martyred the apostles and the Christians would also have been God's servants, for they, too, thought that they were doing God's service, as Christ says in John 16; and Paul in Romans 10 testifies for the Jews that they are zealous for God, and says in Acts 26 that by serving God night and day they hope to come to the promised salvation.[85]

The fact is, that although such people may appear to be seeking and serving God, and may quite sincerely believe that they are doing so, yet they do not seek Him as He wills to be sought.[86] They worship Him, not as He is, but as they imagine Him to be; they seek Him for their own ends, and serve Him in ways of their own choosing. If they use the name of Christ, they misuse it, for theirs is a corruption, an egocentric perversion, of true Christianity; it is at its best only a refinement of the religion of the natural man. 'And herein', Luther asserts, 'the Papists, under the name of Christ, have showed themselves to be seven-fold more wicked idolaters, than ever were the Gentiles.'[87]

The anthropocentric religion of the natural man, based on his natural knowledge of God, is false religion, with a false conception of God and a false relationship to Him. The religion of the 'Papists' is in no essential way different from this, for although it calls itself Christian, it has no proper understanding of Christ. It fits Him into the scheme of natural religion, instead of allowing Him to 'do His proper work' and revolutionize the whole religious relationship. This does not mean that Luther denies the existence of any true Christians 'under the Papacy', as we saw in an earlier chapter;[88] nor does he for a moment claim that a profession of Evangelical faith is a sufficient guarantee that the one who makes it, truly lives by it. On the contrary, he believes it is possible for a man to have at least some measure of true faith in God without being explicitly aware of it, as it is also possible for a man not to have it and yet not to know that he lacks it.[89] In our present context, however, he is not primarily concerned with the religious status of individual men, but with doctrines and practices that express and encourage the egocentricity of the natural man, wheresoever it may be found. Such doctrines and practices detract from the glory that belongs to God alone 'as the one who does, gives, and has all things'; for the natural man is a faithful reproduction of his prototype, Adam, who 'stole the glory and took it for himself', and no vice is so deeply rooted in him as the desire to be of importance. Over against him, Luther sets Christ, who, in the proper understanding of Him,

has restored God's glory to Him by teaching us that everything of ours is nothing but mere wrath and disfavour before God, so that we may in no way boast nor please ourselves therein, but . . . that our glory and self-pleasing may be cast down to the ground.[90]

12. THE PARTICULAR OR PROPER KNOWLEDGE OF GOD IN CHRIST

We must now consider in more detail the nature and function of Luther's 'particular' or 'proper' knowledge of God; and here it is first of all important to be quite clear about the meaning of his frequent and vigorous assertion that apart from Christ there is no real knowledge of God at all.

In view of his conception of the general knowledge, he plainly does not hold that Christ furnishes the sole ground for any belief in God whatsoever, nor that those who are without knowledge of Christ are unable to say or think anything that is in any sense true about God. Neither does he maintain that God is not to be encountered anywhere in the world outside the specific sphere of the Christian revelation. On the contrary, God is at work everywhere throughout the whole of His creation, actively manifesting Himself as a God of power and law in nature and in the consciences of men. But, although all men are in some measure aware of Him, they do not properly understand Him.

They may confess, rightly, that He exists, is powerful and just, and is to be worshipped, yet they place the wrong construction on these facts and adopt a quite false attitude toward Him, so that it can be said with truth that they do not really know Him at all. They are ignorant of His essential character, His inmost purpose and will, which alone determines the meaning of the things they do know about Him. This ignorance Luther finds dispelled in Christ and in Christ alone.

Men should, no doubt, have recognized the true nature of God, even from their general knowledge, at least sufficiently to avoid idolatry—otherwise they could hardly be said to be 'without excuse'.[91] Indeed, Luther can actually assert that the very heathen would have been saved, if only they had rested content with their bare general knowledge and had not 'changed and adapted it to their own wishes and desires'.[92] They would, however, owe their salvation ultimately to Christ, for their knowledge would be by no means full and complete until it was perfected by 'the Christ who was to come'.[93] Such was the case with those heathen in the Old Testament, who came to believe, albeit in a very dim and inchoate way, in the God of Israel and were thereby justified 'before Christ was revealed, when that faith yet reigned, which believed in Christ to come'.[94] Abraham and the saints of the Old Covenant, of course, were justified by faith in the Christ who was to be revealed, as Christians are justified by faith in the Christ who has been revealed.[95] It is interesting that Luther can suggest a possibility of salvation for men who have never actually heard of Christ; and we may notice that he also ventures to hope that Cicero 'and men like him' may be saved.[96] But on such matters he does not dogmatize; they are for God, not Luther, to decide. What is more important is that he cannot conceive of any *saving* knowledge of God, that is, representing a right relationship to God, except a knowledge which, explicitly or implicitly, may be said to contain Christ. It is in this sense that we must understand his assertion that 'without Christ there is nothing else but mere idolatry, an idol and a false imagination of God'.[97]

The particular knowledge of God, we may therefore say, is not opposed to the general knowledge in itself, but to what men have falsely made of it; and it furnishes the necessary principle for its correct interpretation.[98]

Because men have abused their knowledge of God from His works [Luther says] God has willed to be known anew from His sufferings . . . so that it suffices and profits no one now to know God in His glory and majesty, unless he also knows Him in the humility and ignominy of the Cross.[99]

True Christian divinity [he therefore asserts] setteth not God forth unto us in His majesty, as Moses and other doctrines do. It commandeth us not to search out the nature of God; but to know His will set out to us in Christ, whom He would have to take our flesh upon Him, to be born and to die for our sins.[100]

At the same time, it is very important to notice that it is precisely the God of majesty who is revealed to us in Christ. If Luther urges us to abstain 'from all cogitations and searching of the majesty of God, and look only upon this man Jesus Christ, who setteth Himself forth unto us to be a mediator', he does so because 'thus doing, thou shalt perceive the love, goodness, and sweetness of God: thou shalt see His wisdom, power, and majesty tempered to thy capacity.'[101]

In this revelation of God in Christ, Luther finds 'a most manifest distinction' between Christianity and all other religions in the world[102]—including the misinterpretation of Christianity itself in medieval Catholicism, which is the chief concern of his reforming work. For Catholicism forfeits its title to the Christian name, inasmuch as it fails to give to Christ His due place as the one mediator between God and man.

There are three characteristic aspects of medieval religion, which Luther condemns as human attempts to have dealings with 'God in His majesty', or with 'the naked God', to the virtual exclusion of the revelation of God in Christ. Dr. Nygren has described his attack upon them as a 'Campaign against the "Heavenly Ladders"'.

The Medieval interpretation of Christianity [he says] is marked throughout by the *upward tendency*. This tendency asserts itself no less in the moralistic piety of popular Catholicism than in the rational theology of Scholasticism and the ecstatic religiosity of Mysticism. . . . They all know a Way by which man can work his way up to God, whether it is the Way of merit known to practical piety, the ἀναγωγή of mysticism, or the Way of speculative thought according to the 'analogy of being' (*analogia entis*). Man must mount up to God by means of one of the three heavenly ladders. Against this upward tendency or ascent Luther makes his protest. He will have nothing to do with this 'climbing up into the majesty of God'. In place of this 'theologia gloriae' he demands a 'theologia crucis'.[103]

Against scholastic rationalism, Luther never tires of warning us that 'we must abstain from the curious searching (*speculatio*) of God's majesty'.[104] We must not imagine that by that means 'anything concerning God can be known to our salvation'.[105]

It is perilous [he declares] to wish to investigate and apprehend the naked divinity by human reason without Christ the mediator, as the sophists and monks have done and taught others to do. . . . There has been given to us the Word incarnate, that is placed in the manger and hung on the wood of the Cross. This Word is the Wisdom and Son of the Father, and He has declared unto us what is the will of the Father toward us. He that leaves this Son, to follow his own thoughts and speculations, is overwhelmed by the majesty of God.[106]

With rationalism, Luther closely connects mysticism. 'It was Dionysius with his Mystical Theology, and others who followed him,' he says, 'that gave occasion for these speculations concerning the naked majesty of God'; and he exhorts us to 'detest as a veritable plague that Mystical Theology of Dionysius and similar books'.[107] The mystical ascent is a false way to God, for God

will not have thee thus ascend, but He comes to thee and has made a ladder, a way and a bridge to thee. . . . He comes first to us and we do not first mount up to heaven to Him, but He sends His Son down into the flesh . . . He speaks: This way, brother, 'The Father is in Me, and I in the Father'; keep thine eyes fixed on Me, through My humanity is the way to the Father.[108]

Only the eyes that are fixed on Christ can attain the beatific Vision of God which the mystic otherwise vainly seeks,

for to see His face, as the Scripture says, means rightly to perceive Him as a gracious, good Father, to whom we may look for all good things. But this only comes through faith in Christ.[109]

Even more emphatically, Luther condemns legalism and the doctrine of salvation by merit.

All hypocrites and idolaters [he asserts] go about to do those works which properly pertain to divinity and belong to Christ solely and alone. They do not indeed say with their mouth: I am God, I am

Christ, yet in fact they arrogate to themselves the divinity and office of Christ. And so in effect they say: I am Christ, I am saviour, not only of myself, but also of others. And so the monks have taught and persuaded the whole world of this, that they can, by that hypocritical holiness of theirs, justify not only themselves, but also others to whom they communicate it.[110]

For he who says: I shall be saved through my works, says nothing other than: I am Christ, since the works of Christ alone save as many as ever are saved.[111]

It was because the religion of the Papacy, in such ways as we have just mentioned, and especially by its doctrine of merit, effectively if not deliberately dispensed with the mediation of Christ, that Luther came to denounce the Pope as Antichrist.[112] His own evangelical Christianity, on the other hand, is entirely Christocentric. There is no other way by which man can attain true knowledge of God and fellowship with Him, than the way through Christ, who is Himself the Way and the Truth. In this, however, we must recognize once again Luther's assertion of his theocentric point of view against all anthropocentricity in religion.[113] For the rationalism, mysticism, and moralism he attacks are all means by which man is presumed to make his own way to God, whereas Christ, although in a certain sense He may be described as man's way to God, is primarily and essentially God's way to man. To remove Christ from the central place, therefore, is to remove God Himself from the centre of things and, by consequence, to make true knowledge of Him and a right relation to Him impossible. How this is so, we shall see more particularly, when we consider in the next chapter Luther's conception of the Person and Work of Christ.

NOTES

1. E.g. *Gal.* E.T. 274(iv.8f.): 'God will or can be known no otherwise than by Christ, according to that saying of John 1. "The only begotten Son, which is in the bosom of the Father, he hath declared Him." '

2. ibid. 277: 'All men naturally have this general knowledge, that there is a God, according to that saying, Romans 1. "Forasmuch as that which may be known of God was manifest in them." For God was manifest unto them, in that the invisible things of Him did appear by the creation of the world.'

3. ibid. 277f.   4. ibid. 278.   5. ibid. 277.

6. ibid.: ' . . . here some think one thing, and some another. The Jews imagine this to be the will of God, if they worship Him according to the rule of Moses' law; the Turk, if he observe his Alcoran; the monk, if he keep his order and perform his vows.'

7. ibid.

8. *S.W.* I.187. The passage continues: 'So, there are before our eyes the creation of the world and the power of God; but the chief thing of all is to know, the end for which, and the design with which, God made them.' cf. *W.A.* XXXIX.1; 177.24f.: 'Nay, to know God is indeed something other than to know that He is the Creator of all things.'

9. *Gal.* E.T. 274.

10. W. Temple, *Malvern 1941*, 12f.

11. Something of the effects of the Fall on 'reason', as Luther conceives them, may be seen in a later section of this chapter.

12. cf. Aulén, *Gudsbilden*, 191: 'The significance of the Nominalist theology, in one aspect of it, lies in the fact that it has dissolved this rational knowledge of God. Men have no longer any confidence in their ability to decipher by rational means the character of the Divine will from the course of the world.'

13. *Our Knowledge of God*, 194.

14. Luther understands the biblical use of 'know', of which he says: 'The verb *Iada* has a wider sense than *cognoscere* with us. For it not only signifies speculative knowledge, but feeling and experience, so to speak'—*W.A.* XLII.179.15ff.

15. cf. Törnvall, *Andl. o. världsl.* 28f.: 'Whereas the scholastic knowledge of God culminated in an abstract idea, Luther's conception of God is marked by a peculiar concreteness with a footing in the created world. Instead of man's moving, as it were, in scholastic fashion, toward the Deity as a metaphysical object in order to attain knowledge of Him, it is characteristic of Luther's thought that God descends into the created world and, as it were, takes shape in its ordinances, even making man himself a medium and instrument of His revelation.'

16. Baillie, op. cit. 147.

17. cf. ibid. 193: 'When Luther condemns the *theologia gloriae*, he is condemning precisely the kind of natural theology practised by St. Thomas—the attempt to reach God from "the things that are made". So far, then, Luther's criticism of the *theologia gloriae* corresponds exactly to our own criticism of Thomism.'

18. Exodus 3320; cf. Proverbs 1715, 2527—quoted by Luther, e.g., *Gal.* E.T. 11f.(i.3).

19. *W.A.* XLII.296.22ff. cf. *Gal.* E.T. 11ff.

20. *W.A.* XL.1; 174.3: *Ideo universa creatura est eius larva. Gal.* E.T. 60(ii.6): 'Now this veil of God is every creature.'

21. *Gal.* E.T. 60(ii.6): 'God here in this life dealeth not with us face to face, but covered and shadowed from us: that is, as Paul saith in another place, "We see now as it were through a glass darkly: but then we shall see face to face" (1 Corinthians 13¹²). Therefore we cannot be without veils in this life.'

22. *W.A.* XL.1; 463.9.

23. cf. the lines from *Ein' feste Burg*:
> Er heisst Jesus Christ,
> Der.Herr Zebaoth,
> Und ist kein andrer—Gott;
> Das Feld muss er behalten.

24. *Gal.* E.T. 61(ii.6).   25. *W.B.* 37.   26. *W.A.* XIX.226f.

27. cf. Wingren, *Kallelsen,* 129: '[For Luther] God meets man, not in the thoughts and feelings that arise in him when he isolates himself from the world, but in that which *happens to him,* the outward and palpable things that occur in his vicinity.'

28. *Our Knowledge of God,* 178ff., 196.

29. *Gal.* E.T. 60(ii.6): 'This the natural man cannot see: but the spiritual man only discerneth . . . the veil of God from God Himself. . . . But here wisdom is required, which can discern the veil from God Himself: and this wisdom the world hath not. The covetous man, hearing "that man liveth not by bread alone . . ." eateth the bread, but he seeth not God in the bread . . . so he doth with gold and other creatures, trusting to them so long as he hath them: but when they leave him, he despaireth. And thus he honoureth not the Creator, but the creatures, not God, but his own belly.'

30. *W.A.* XLII.631.36ff.   31. *Römerbr.* 19.1ff.

32. *Gal.* E.T. 277(iv.8f.).   33. *W.M.L.* II.355.

34. *Römerbr.* 18.27ff.   35. *Gal.* E.T. 277(iv.8f.).

36. *The Nature and Destiny of Man,* I.141. Niebuhr includes a third element in his 'general revelation', describing it as 'the longing for forgiveness' or 'the longing for reconciliation'. But this is an effect of the revelation rather than a part of it, and with it we are not here concerned. It was, of course, far from unfamiliar to Luther, who sees in all non-Christian religions, and even in some types of Christianity, false attempts to secure reconciliation or, as he would term it, 'justification'.

37. cf. Aulén, *Gudsbilden,* 190: 'It is thus chiefly the motifs of power and of judgement that stand out here. The God of the "general knowledge" is for Luther, we might say, primarily the God of Nature and of Law.'

38. *B.o.W.* 43.   39. ibid. 244.   40. *W.A.* XLII.374.11ff.

41. *Römerbr.* 37.15ff.   42. *Gal.* E.T. 357(v.14).

43. *Römerbr.* 37.25ff. Luther, like Augustine and the Schoolmen after him, speaks of Matthew 7¹² as the 'natural law'. cf. *E.A.*²8.69: 'For there is no one but must feel and confess that that is right and true which the natural law saith, Matthew 7¹² . . . So they carry a living book with them in the bottom of their hearts'; cf. *W.A.* I.480.1ff.; II.120.22ff.

44. *W.A.* XXXIX.1; 454.4ff.: 'It was not Moses that was the author of the Decalogue, but from the foundation of the world the Decalogue has been inscribed on the minds of all men. . . . For there has never been any nation under the sun so brutal or barbarous and inhuman as not to be aware (*quin senserit*) that God is to be worshipped and loved . . . even if it has gone astray in the manner and methods of worshipping God. Similarly with regard to honour and obedience toward parents and superiors; likewise they detested vices, as is to be seen in the first chapter to the Romans. . . . So Moses was only as it were the interpreter and illustrator of laws written on the minds of all men wherever they are in the world under the sun.'

45. *W.A.* XXXIX.1; 361.19ff.: 'All men indeed have naturally a certain knowledge of the law, but it is very weak and obscured. Hence it was and always is necessary to hand down to men that knowledge of the law that they may know the greatness of their sin, of the wrath of God, etc.' op. cit. 454.61ff.: 'But afterwards, since men had come at length to such a pitch that they cared neither for God nor for men, God was compelled to renew those laws through Moses, and to set them before our eyes written with His finger on tables, in order that we might be admonished what we were before the fall of Adam, and what some day we are to be in Christ.'

46. *W.A.* XVI.447.10ff.

47. As a glance at his *Institutes*, I.iii–v, will quickly show.

48. Brunner, *Das Gebot und die Ordnungen*, 579.

49. *Gal.* E.T. 12(i.3).

50. *Tischr.* 372f.nr.627.

51. *Gal.* E.T. 199.

52. cf. *W.A.* XVI.447.26ff.: 'If the natural law were not written and given in the heart by God, one would have to preach long before the conscience were smitten. One would have to preach to an ass, horse, ox, or cow for a hundred thousand years before they accepted the law, although they have ears, eyes and heart as a man. They too can hear it, but it does not enter their heart. Why? What is wrong? Their soul is not so formed and fashioned that such a thing might enter it. But a man, when the law is set before him, soon says: Yes, it is so, he cannot deny it. He could not be so quickly convinced, were it not written in his heart before.'

53. *Gal.* E.T. 278(iv.8f.).

54. ibid. 275: 'Every man that revolteth from the knowledge of Christ, must needs fall into idolatry.' ibid. 378(v.19): 'All the highest religions, the holiness and most fervent devotions of those which do reject Christ the Mediator . . . are nothing else but plain idolatry.' ibid. 379: 'All the worshippings and services of God and all religions without Christ are idolatry and idol-service.'

55. *Römerbr.* 47.24: '. . . an idol, i.e. false and mendacious doctrine.'

56. *W.A.* I.399.11ff.: 'All the sons of Adam are idolaters and offenders against this First Commandment. But we must know that there are two kinds of idolatry, one exterior, the other interior. The exterior is that by which a man worships wood, stone, beasts, stars. . . . But this proceeds from the interior. The interior is that by which a man, either from fear of punishment or from love of gain, outwardly indeed omits the worship of the creature, but inwardly there remains love and trust toward the creature. For what sort of religion is it, not to bow the knees to riches and honours, etc., and yet to give one's heart and mind, the noblest part of oneself, to them? This is to worship God in the body and the flesh, but inwardly to worship the creature in the spirit.'

57. *W.A.* XLII.112.23ff.: 'A monk is an idolater. For he imagines that if he has lived according to the rule of Francis or Dominic, that is the way to the kingdom of God. But this is to invent a new god and become an idolater, because the true God declares the way to the kingdom of heaven to be, if thou believest in Christ. When, therefore, faith is lost, there follows unbelief and idolatry, which transfers the glory of God to works. Thus Anabaptists, Sacramentarians, Papists, are all idolaters; not because they worship stocks or stones, but because they worship their own cogitations, having relinquished the Word.'

58. The only difference between them is the material of which they are made. So long as we are dealing merely with our own conceptions and ideas of God, we are dealing with something produced by ourselves, and something that is in our power to alter and modify at will. We are not dealing with the living God, who so far from being created by us is our Creator, and who so far from being at our disposal has us at His. This fact is too often overlooked in much that passes for religious and theological discussion.

59. *Works*, I.315 (*Journal* for 15th June 1741).

60. *W.A.* X.1; 207.5f.

61. ibid. 203.4f.

62. *W.A.* XXXIX.1; 175.9ff.

63. For the substance of this paragraph, see *W.A.* X.1.203-7.

64. It should perhaps be specially emphasized that Luther regards reason as in need of redemption only in matters of religion. In relation to what he calls 'the things beneath us', i.e. the affairs of this world, which it is within man's province to order and govern, reason is an excellent instrument when properly used, no matter who uses it. But in relation to 'the things above us', i.e. matters pertaining to God, the reason of the natural man is vitiated by the anthropocentric assumptions which he uncritically makes and regards as entirely rational. Enlightened by the Gospel, however, it becomes a most excellent instrument even in matters of religion. cf. Hazlitt, *Table Talk*, 34, LXXVI.

65. *Pace* Dr. R. S. Franks, who attributes the difficulty of interpreting Luther to 'the fundamental irrationalism which characterizes his doctrine even in its clearest statements, and which becomes almost its hall-mark and distinguishing stamp.' (*Work of Christ*, I.353). The words 'rational' and 'irrational' are much too uncritically used in the discussion, not only of Luther, but of many other subjects. Far too often, the speaker or writer dismisses as 'irrational' anything that he does not understand, or that disagrees with his own views.

66. *B.o.W.* 268.

67. *Römerbr.* 19.3ff.

68. *W.B.* 36.

69. *Römerbr.* 20.3ff.

70. *W.A.* I.425.2ff.

71. *Gal.* E.T. 275(iv.8).

72. *W.B.* 37.

73. *W.A.* I.358.4ff.

74. ibid. XI.33.10f.

75. *Gal.* E.T. 380(v.19).

76. *W.A.* X.1.1; 241.20f.: 'If they truly believed in a God who has created heaven and earth, they would know also that the same God was also a creator above their conceit and might make, break, direct the same as He would.'

77. ibid. XXX.1; 134.21f.

78. ibid. VIII.655.12.

79. ibid. X.1.1; 70.16.

80. *Sermons*, 130: 'If we were able to fulfil all the commandments of God, and in all things to satisfy His justice, notwithstanding we had not as yet deserved grace and salvation . . . for that He may by the right of creation require as due service, all those things of us His creatures, created to live unto Him; wherefore it should yet come of grace and mercy, whatsoever should come from Him unto us: this Christ declared very well, Luke 177-10.' cf. the exposition of the first article of the Creed in the *Short Catechism*, which begins: 'I believe that God has created me and all that exists; that He has given and still preserves to me body and soul . . .', and concludes: ' for all which I am in duty bound to thank, praise, serve and obey Him.' cf. also *W.A.* X.1; 122.13f.

81. *W.A.* VII.800.25ff.

82. ibid. XVII.1; 401.20f.

83. ibid. XXX.2; 602.30f.: 'For he who does not give thanks, but wishes to merit, has no God and makes inwardly in his heart and outwardly in his works another god out of the true God.'

84. *W.M.L.* VI.398-403.

85. ibid. 402.

86. cf. *Römerbr.* 75.23ff.

87. *Gal.* E.T., 191(iii.13).

88. See above, pp. 23,32(nn.60,63).

89. *W.M.L.* I.317: 'For without true faith it is impossible to please Him, as Saint Paul says in Hebrews 11. Now there are many who, hidden in their hearts, have such true faith, and themselves know not of it; many there are who do not have it, and of this, too, they are unaware.'

90. *W.A.* X.1; 88.14-89.6.

91. cf. p. 85 *supra.*

92. *Römerbr.* 19.14ff.

93. ibid. 38.19ff.

94. *Gal.* E.T. 139f.(iii.2), *et al.*

95. *W.A.* XLII.567.25ff., *et al.*

96. *Tischr.* 372.nr.626.

97. *Gal.* E.T. 278(iv.8f.).

98. cf. Niebuhr, *The Nature and Destiny of Man,* I.139f., where there is an exactly similar relation between what Niebuhr calls 'general' and 'special' revelation.

99. *W.A.* I.362.5ff.

100. *Gal.* E.T. 11(i.3).

101. ibid. 12.

102. *S.W.* I.179.

103. *Agape and Eros,* II.ii.482.

104. *Gal.* E.T. 11.

105. ibid. 23.(i.4). Where the religious relationship is not in question, however, it is another matter; cf. ibid. 12, quoted on p. 83 *supra.*

106. *W.A.* XXXIX. 1; 389.10ff. cf. *Gal.* E.T. 12: 'If thou wouldest be in safety and out of peril of conscience and salvation, bridle this climbing and presumptuous spirit, and so seek God as Paul teacheth thee (1 Corinthians 123f.) . . . Therefore begin thou where He began, namely, in the womb of the Virgin, in the manger, and at His mother's breasts, etc. For to this end He came down, was born, was conversant among men, suffered, was crucified and died, that by all means He might set forth Himself plainly before our eyes, and fasten the eyes of our hearts upon Himself, that He thereby might keep us from climbing up into heaven, and from the curious searching of the Divine majesty.'

107. *W.A.* XXXIX.1; 389f. It is curious that Wesley should have thought Luther to be 'deeply tinctured with Mysticism throughout' (*Works,* I.315). If Mysticism is not Methodist (*Works,* IX.49), neither is it Lutheran; and Luther would thoroughly approve of Wesley's many criticisms of it. The chief of these are that it is unscriptural; that the mystics teach that we are justified by 'our own righteousness'—not, indeed, the righteousness of virtuous actions, but of virtuous habits or tempers—and so 'lay another foundation'; and finally, that Mysticism leads to the forsaking of Christian fellowship, of the ordinances of God, and of good works. (See, for instance, *Works,* XIV.232ff.).

108. *W.A.* XVI.144.16ff.; cf. *Römerbr.* 132.24ff.

109. ibid. XXXII.325ff.

110. ibid. XL.1; 406.17ff.; *Gal.* E.T. 172(iii.10).

111. ibid. VIII.619.14ff.

112. *Gal.* E.T. 172: 'The Pope . . . by publishing and spreading his divinity through-out the whole world hath denied and utterly buried the office and divinity of Christ. . . . He that knoweth all these things rightly, may certainly judge that the Pope is Antichrist.'

113. cf. Obendiek, *Der Teufel,* 30: 'Only Christocentric theology is theocentric, because it takes seriously the revelation of God in Christ, and renounces the theoretical (*gedankliche*) construction of a conception of God.'

H

CHAPTER FOUR

THE THEOLOGY OF THE CROSS

13. THE INCARNATE DEITY

LUTHER's entire theology can be said to stand or fall with the divinity of Christ. Nothing is more important to him than the Nicene *homoousios*.[1] In Christ, he maintains, we are confronted by God Himself, for Christ is 'very God'.[2] If his theology is Christocentric, in the sense we have described, it is not less true to say that his Christology is theocentric.

There may be truth in the view, largely deriving from Ritschl, that Luther focused attention in a new way on the historical Jesus. No one can speak more vividly or with deeper feeling than he about the human Figure of the Gospels, His words and works and, above all, His sufferings and Cross. Yet Luther is most strongly convinced

that it is not enough nor is it Christian, to preach the works, life and words of Christ as historical facts, as if the knowledge of these would suffice for the conduct of life, although this is the fashion of those who must today be regarded as our best preachers.[3]

It would clearly be quite wrong to attribute to him anything like the modern interest in 'the Jesus of History'.[4] If he tells us that 'the Scriptures begin very gently, and lead us on to Christ as to a man', we must observe that he continues, 'then afterwards to a Lord over all creatures, and after that to a God'.[5] The Scriptures do not lead to a merely human witness to God, a teacher about God, or even to one who 'has the value of God'. On the contrary, Christ is for Luther quite literally 'God incarnate and clothed with man's nature'.[6] When he says that 'true Christian religion . . . beginneth not at the highest, as other religions do, but at the lowest',[7] he is thinking of the Incarnation, by which the God of supreme majesty, in infinite compassion, has condescended to sinful man. 'For the humanity', he says, 'would be no use, if the divinity were not in it; yet on the other hand, God will not and cannot be found except through and in this humanity.'[8] That is why he bids the anxious seeker after salvation 'know that there is no other God besides this man, Christ Jesus'.[9]

We have already seen how Luther speaks of the Incarnation as, on the one hand, a 'veil' in which the God of majesty confronts us, and on the other, as a 'glass' or 'mirror' in which He is to be beheld. The double metaphor is illuminating. If glass suggests manifestation, veil suggests concealment. Both of these are characteristic of Luther's idea of Divine revelation, as we saw in his conception of the creatures as *larvae Dei*. He can therefore speak of the divinity of Christ as 'hidden' (*abscondita*) in the humanity.[10] The theologian of the Cross, he says, is one who speaks of God crucified and hidden;[11] and he even contrasts 'God hidden in His sufferings' with 'God manifest from His works'.[12] This is important, since Luther's idea of the 'hidden God' is often wrongly taken to refer only to God as He is apart from the revelation in Christ, as if in Christ He were held to be plainly visible and were nowhere else to be seen. But Luther is not so naïve.

Luther recognizes that it is by no means obvious, either to physical sight or to 'rational' insight, that Jesus, the crucified Man of Nazareth, is the incarnate Son of God, the Second Person of the Blessed Trinity. That is something which can only be apprehended by faith, not demonstrated by 'reason'.[13] Moreover, even when it is so apprehended, there remains deep mystery in it; for faith is still faith and not sight. The 'glass' that mirrors God does not disclose all that might conceivably be learnt about Him; and even what it does disclose is something that passeth understanding.[14] In fact, it can be said that God is more deeply hidden in Christ crucified than He is in His creation; for the natural man, at any rate, more easily connects divinity with power and justice than with the humiliation and suffering of the Cross. It is such points as these that Luther has in mind, when he speaks of the divinity as hidden in the humanity of Christ.

The similarity between Luther's conception of the way in which God is revealed in Christ and in creation, is remarkable and important. In neither case is it a question of the communication of 'truths' or 'doctrines' about God, still less of man's arriving at theoretical conclusions about Him. Both in the *larvae* of the creatures and in the *involucrum* of the Incarnation, the Divine majesty Himself is actively confronting men, presenting Himself to them with a 'mediated immediacy'.[15] In both cases He is at once hidden and revealed.[16] The essential difference between them is that in Christ the Divine nature is revealed to a far greater depth. The character and will and inmost heart of God are disclosed—to the eye of faith—here as nowhere else. That is why 'we ought to learn to recognize God in Christ'.[17]

If we now ask what it is in Christ that Luther regards as the essential revelation of the Divine, we must first of all observe that, according to him, Christ is represented in two different ways: as a Gift or Sacrament, and as an Example.[18] He has a twofold office, for He is both a Lawgiver, or rather—since the Law is already given, as we have seen—the Interpreter of the Law, and also a Mediator and Saviour.[19] As both He ought to be understood and preached; yet His two offices must be most clearly distinguished. Christians ought certainly to follow the example of Christ and do such good works as He teaches, but they must not imagine that they are thereby justified.[20] Where the establishment of the religious relationship is in question, they must look to Christ in a different way, as a gift, not as an example.[21] To impenitent sinners, however, Christ must be presented as one who, both in His teaching and His life, stands over against them as the embodiment of the utmost demands of God's Law. Only as they are brought to consciousness of their sin by this means, so that they become humble seekers after salvation, can He be rightly presented to them as a gift and a Saviour. Moreover, it is only when they receive Him as Saviour, that men begin to be truly able to follow His example.

Of these two offices of Christ, that of Mediator and Saviour constitutes what Luther calls His 'proper' office, 'for the which He came principally into the world'. By contrast with this, His teaching and example, and even His miracles, are to be regarded as an 'accidental or by-office'. Others than He, both apostles and prophets, have taught and performed miracles; and in these things He is not substantially different from them.[22] Others, moreover, such as 'Abraham, Isaiah, John Baptist, Paul, and other saints', may furnish examples of holy life; 'but', says Luther, 'they cannot forgive my sins, they cannot deliver me from the power of the devil and from death, they cannot save me and give me everlasting life'.[23] Christ certainly interprets the Law, and He makes it exacting, as we shall see, to the point of impossibility;

but this like the work of His Forerunner, John the Baptist, is simply preparatory to His specific mission.[24] His proper office is, 'after the Law hath pronounced a man to be guilty, to raise Him up again, and to loose him from his sins, if he believe the Gospel'.[25] Therefore 'Christ, according to His true and proper definition, is no Moses, no lawgiver, no tyrant, but a mediator for sins, a free giver of grace, righteousness, and life'.[26] And He gives these things, we must note, not simply as the apostles in a sense gave them by preaching the Gospel, but as their author and creator.[27]

It need hardly now be said that it is in the proper office of Christ that Luther finds His essential divinity and His revelation of God. For, he says,

to give grace, peace, everlasting life, to forgive sins, to make righteous, to quicken, to deliver from death and the devil, are not the works of any creature, but of the Divine majesty alone.

[Christ] hath the divine works not of a creature, but of the Creator, because He giveth grace and peace: and to give them, is to condemn sin, to vanquish death, and to tread the devil underfoot.

Since, then, He does what no creature can do, Luther holds, 'it must needs follow that He is very God by nature'.[28]

14. CHRIST AS INTERPRETER OF THE LAW

(a) The Condemnation and Curse of the Law

Although Christ's interpretation of the Law is described by Luther as merely His 'accidental or by-office', it is of very considerable importance, not only for the understanding of His proper office as Luther conceives it, but also for the explanation of the apparently contradictory attitudes which, as is well known, Luther himself adopts toward the Law. We must therefore devote some attention to this matter before we go on to consider the work of Christ as Saviour.

The Law of God, as Luther understands it, is revealed in three main stages. The first is the Natural law, or the awareness which, as we have seen, all men naturally have, that they ought to worship God, and that they ought to do to others as they would have others do to them. The second is the Mosaic law, the Decalogue, of which the first table states more explicitly man's duty to God, and the second his duty to his neighbour—Moses being not so much the lawgiver as an interpreter of the Law already given by nature but obscured by sin. The third stage is that of the Gospel commandment of love toward God and our neighbour, by which our Lord reveals the true inwardness of the Law, and which He illustrates both by His teaching and His example. These three stages in no sense represent different ethical principles, but are all alike expressions of the one Law of God, which alone is binding on the whole world.[29] They differ only in the degree, so to speak, in which they reveal the essential meaning and content of the Law. This content is nothing more nor less than love.[30] Love is the requirement of the law of Nature[31] and of the law of Moses[32] no less than of the commandment of Christ, in whose light alone their true significance is seen.

If we are rightly to understand the Law, Luther holds, we must first of all distinguish between the 'moral' and the 'spiritual' observance of it,[33] or between 'doing the works of the Law' and 'fulfilling the Law'.[34] The works are done, when our behaviour conforms to the letter of the Law, even though in our hearts we would rather do otherwise, were it not for the constraint of the commandment. The Law is fulfilled, however, only when our behaviour is governed by love in our hearts, and love of such a kind that we would 'do the works' even if they were not commanded. This fulfilment is what the Law essentially and inexorably requires. Unlike the laws of men, God's Law cannot be satisfied merely with works, for God judges according to what is at the bottom of the heart, and His Law makes its demands upon the inmost heart and will.[35] It requires perfect love, free from every selfish consideration. It can therefore be fulfilled only by a pure heart and a cheerful will, such as are entirely unmoved by any thought of penalty or reward.[36] If men judge the doer by his deeds, God judges the deeds by the doer,[37] and no work can please Him unless it is done out of willing love.[38]

The love that the Law requires is of precisely the same character as that which Luther finds revealed in Christ.[39] It is the love that 'seeketh not its own', that 'betakes itself not where it finds a good to enjoy, but where it may confer good upon the evil and the needy'. It is the antithesis of self-love. Luther differs, 'with all due respect', from the view of Saint Augustine and others, that Christ's commandment of love bids us love God first, then ourselves, and then our neighbour. We have no need to be told to love ourselves, he contends, for we do so without any telling; and that is how we ought to love our neighbours, according to Christ's commandment. If we did so, we should cease from self-love altogether.[40]

If our love were what it ought to be, Luther says, it would flow forth out of a pure heart toward all men, both friends and enemies, like that of our heavenly Father, who lets His sun rise on the evil and the good, and sends His rain on the thankful and the unthankful. We should not reserve our love for those who are well-disposed to us, or from whom we derive some profit or pleasure; for to do so is typical of the self-love that does nothing freely, but seeks its own advantage and not its neighbour's.[41] Nor should we let our love be governed by the deserts or worthiness of others, loving them for the good things we see in them, as a young man may love a maid for her beauty; for such love also is a form of the self-love that seeks its own enjoyment, and it lasts only as long as the desirable qualities endure that evoke it. It is undeniable, Luther admits, that a good man is more worthy to be loved than a bad one, and that we are naturally more drawn to him;[42] but true love is independent of such external considerations, and it seeks out primarily not those who are most attractive, but those who are most in need.

True love [he says] ought to be such as floweth out of a continual fountain, and proceedeth from the bottom of the heart, as a fresh and continual water always springeth forth, which cannot be stopped and is never dried up.[43]

This is called true, divine, entire, and perfect love;[44] [and] thus should they preach, which will rightly teach love required of the law.[45]

Now here it must be noticed that, for Luther, 'law' always signifies a demand made upon us and supported by sanctions temporal or eternal. In the case of the Law of God, eternal life is bound up with obedience to it, death with disobedience. Christ's interpretation of the Law, however, makes it impossible to fulfil and brings all men under its condemnation. Its effect is to reveal and, indeed, to increase sin, for which, in the nature of the case, it provides no remedy.[46] It is not, of course, the 'effective cause' of sin, but it shows man to be a sinner, and by forbidding sin it stimulates sinful activity.[47] To be under the Law, therefore, is to be under a curse, under Divine condemnation and wrath.

The Law demands nothing less than perfection, Luther maintains, and all who fall short of this are under its condemnation.[48] But to demand perfection is to demand 'impossible things'[49] —not because perfect love is in itself an impossibility, but because it is entirely beyond the capacity of fallen man.[50] To be 'fallen' means to have a will at variance with the Divine will expressed in the Law, and for that very reason to be under the Law. The Law, as the apostle says, is not made for the righteous man; and if we were righteous, if our will were in full harmony with God's, then His will would not stand over against us as Law at all.[51] Only those are not under Law who 'of their own accord' and 'of their own voluntary will' do good and abstain from evil, delighting to do so and having no trace of desire to live otherwise than the Law requires.[52] This, however, is just what fallen man does not and cannot do; and the Law, so far from enabling him to do it, positively disables him. It can control his behaviour, inasmuch as he is impelled by fear of punishment or hope of reward to observe its letter; but it is powerless to change his heart and implant in him a good will and a right spirit.[53] The Law demands spontaneity, yet operates by compulsion; it demands unselfishness yet appeals to self-interest; it demands love, but of a kind that cannot possibly be produced to order. As long, therefore, as man is under the Law, it is impossible that he should ever fulfil the Law.

It is important here to observe Luther's insistence on the absoluteness of the Law's demand, which he will not allow to be in any way modified or accommodated to human weakness.[54] His Gospel of the unlimited Divine forgiveness of sins is bound up with the unqualified rigour of his interpretation of the Divine Law, and it is in the light of this alone that his conception of sin can be rightly understood.[55] 'Sin is known by the Law', he says, 'forasmuch as we learn thereby, how our affection is not set upon that which is good.'[56] Since the Law requires that we abstain not merely from evil deeds, but also from evil desires, we sin by having such desires.[57] Even though we do the works of the Law in spite of our contrary impulses, we sin in the doing of them, inasmuch as we fall short of fulfilling the Law. This does not mean that the works thus done are in themselves evil, Luther assures us, for they are not; it is we who do them, that are evil.[58] The Law requires us to love with our whole heart and our whole strength, and we sin if we do less.[59] It demands free and willing fulfilment, and therefore 'there is as much sin as there is unwillingness, difficulty, necessity, resistance'.[60] Resistance to the Law, moreover, means resistance to the Divine will of which it is an expression; it means hostility to God Himself, which ranges us on the side of His chief adversary. Inasmuch, therefore, as we do not willingly and cheerfully perform all that the Law requires, Luther bids us take warning that we are 'damned and under the dominion of Satan'.[61]

If the Law thus exposes the nature of sin, it does nothing to cure, but rather aggravates the disease. If it restrains men outwardly from sinful behaviour, as it is meant to do, it only intensifies the sinfulness of their hearts.[62] It shuts men up as it were in a prison, Luther says, and that in two ways.[63] It prevents them from behaving as they would really like and giving free rein to their own desires, and it prevents them from doing what they ought and performing freely of their own accord all that it commands. Sinful men, it is true, naturally imagine that so long as they perform the works of the Law, they are righteous; and indeed, they do possess a certain righteousness, but it is not such as to justify them before God.[64] To presume that it is, is to commit the sin of sins; it is to be filled with ungodly self-confidence and pride, to despise the mercy and grace of God, to be possessed by the devil.[65] On the other hand, when the true inwardness of the Law is brought home to such men, so that they realize that they do not and cannot fulfil it, they are not thereby set free from the bondage of self-will. They become all the more resentful against both the Law and the Lawgiver for making such impossible demands upon them, until they are driven by the devil to despair, not only of themselves, but of the very mercy of God;[66] and this is 'the supreme sin and irremissible', Luther declares—though he hastens to add: 'unless grace recall them at an acceptable time'.[67]

In a vivid simile, borrowed from Saint Augustine, Luther likens the effect of the Law on fallen human nature to that of water on lime.[68] There is in lime, he says, a certain ardent and fiery nature, which is kindled when water is poured over it. This is not the fault of the water, but of the lime, whose latent qualities are thus stimulated to activity. In a similar way, the Law stimulates our sinful human will. Standing over against us with its commandments and prohibitions, which run counter to our desires, it only succeeds in inflaming these. 'For', as Luther observes, 'we are all by nature such that we desire the more those things that are forbidden to us.' This is not, of course, the fault of the good, righteous, and holy Law, but of our sinful nature, which does not will what the Law wills, and would rather, if it were possible, that there were no Law. But to wish that there were no Law (which is an expression of the will of God) is virtually to wish that there were no Lawgiver, and that God Himself were not.

The Law, therefore, as Luther sees it, provokes and exposes sin, but cannot cure it. It is not in fact intended to do so, as we shall see, but its purpose is rather to bring home to man his desperate condition and make him ready to have it cured. The cure is found in the Gospel, which, when it is applied to the sin-sick soul, has an effect precisely opposite to that of the Law. It acts, according to Luther, not like water, but like oil poured upon lime; for by oil the fiery qualities of the lime are not kindled, but extinguished. The content of the Gospel, however, is nothing else but Christ in His proper office, to the consideration of which we shall turn in due course.

(b) The Law of Nature and of Christ

Luther's view of the Law, as we have just stated it, differs quite considerably from the well-known account of it given by Ernst Troeltsch.[69] According to Troeltsch, Luther

found the objective revelation of the moral law . . . not in the Sermon on the Mount, but in the Decalogue, [which thus] developed its characteristic absolute meaning within Protestantism, as the complete expression of the *Lex Naturae* and of the Protestant ethic with which it was identified.[70]

Now Troeltsch may or may not be right in what he says about Protestantism, but he must certainly be said to misrepresent Luther.

In the first place, Luther invariably interprets the Ten Commandments, which he delights to expound, in terms of the Sermon on the Mount and not vice versa.[71] He explicitly declares, moreover, that the whole Decalogue requires nothing but love toward God and our neighbour, and forbids nothing but self-love.[72] Troeltsch, it is true, admits this of the earlier Luther, but maintains that his attitude had changed by 1532. The document on which he relies to prove his case, however, as Karl

Holl has pointed out, is certainly not authentic, at any rate in its present form.[73] Furthermore, there is evidence from genuine sources of a later date, that Luther did not regard the strict letter of the Decalogue as binding for Christians. When we have Christ, he says, we can make new Decalogues, as Paul does in all his Epistles and as Christ Himself does in the Gospel; and these new Decalogues are better than that of Moses.[74] Nothing that Moses has commanded is binding for us, unless it is also contained in the Natural law;[75] and since what the Natural law requires is love, any law that is contrary to love, Luther asserts, is no law at all.[76] Love is the 'queen and mistress' of all laws, and has authority to set them aside, whenever their literal observance would do more harm than good.[77] Love is the fulfilling of the Law, Luther maintains with Saint Paul, and therefore, where there is love, there is no need of law, and where love is not, no law is ever sufficient[78]—though it is not necessarily useless, as we shall see.

In the second place, Troeltsch gives an account of Natural law[79] that has no parallel in Luther. To begin with, there is an ambiguity in his conception of it, from which Luther is quite free. He appears to identify it, on the one hand, with certain 'conditions' that are the 'product of nature' or of 'reason', and on the other, with a moral imperative that is, presumably, dictated by these conditions. He then distinguishes between an absolute and a relative law of Nature. The former is equated with the teaching of the Sermon on the Mount and is said to represent a purely religious ideal, an inward morality for the individual; whilst the latter represents a modification of the former, consequent upon the Fall, and decrees an external 'official' morality, a 'secular ethic of professional life'. Between these two, according to Troeltsch, there is a sharp opposition, resulting in a dualism in Lutheran ethics, which is modified only by the gradual supersession of the inward by the external morality.

Now it must be said that Troeltsch's entire conception is quite foreign to Luther. Luther nowhere equates the Natural law with any 'conditions' produced either by nature or by reason. It is always for him a moral, or better, a Divine imperative. This, it need hardly be said, the Fall has in no way modified—unless we are to suppose that it can have changed God's will of love. What man's disobedience has done is to dim and distort man's apprehension of God's will. But man's misapprehension does not relativize the Natural law, nor constitute an independent ethical principle; and Troeltsch's 'secular ethic of professional life', which is inconsistent with the Sermon on the Mount, would be regarded by Luther as highly unethical. For Luther, there is only one ethical principle—the Divine will of love. If this is called the Natural law, it is natural, ultimately, in the same sense as we shall see that the God of love is for Luther the 'natural God'.[80]

In the third place, Troeltsch's idea of a professional and official ethic reveals a serious misconception of what Luther understands by 'office' and 'station' (*Amt, Stand*) as Divine ordinances. Troeltsch appears to regard these as belonging to those natural 'conditions' which, by making ethical demands of their own, give rise to an independent, secular ethical principle, the relative Natural law. That, however, is far from Luther's view, if we consider what he actually says of the 'offices'.

As Luther describes them, the offices represent various relationships in which a man can stand to his fellowmen, his neighbours. We have already seen one list of these which he gives, and we may recall it here. It includes: 'the prince, the magistrate, the preacher, the schoolmaster, the scholar, the father, the mother, the children, the master, the servant'. We have also seen that Luther describes these as *larvae Dei*, media of Divine revelation and instruments by which God governs the world. This does not mean, of course, that the actions of any given person in his various offices necessarily give expression to the will of God. Indeed, it is Luther's constant complaint that they are all too often the expression of rebellious human self-will. The offices are in themselves the good creatures and ordinances of God; but as Luther sees it, the devil ceaselessly strives to gain control of them, or to prevent the proper use of them by perverting the will of those who occupy them. Nevertheless, the offices themselves are and remain *larvae Dei*, in and through which God Himself confronts men in the midst of their concrete environment.

Now it is precisely in virtue of the Divine confrontation of man, as we have seen, that man possesses such natural knowledge of God as he has; and this knowledge includes a consciousness of the 'natural law', which is nothing else but God's unalterable will of love. The Natural law is not conceived by Luther as a part, so to speak, of the inward, psychological furniture of human nature,[81] but as something given in and with the 'theological conscience', that is, the awareness of being confronted, with a mediated immediacy, by the living God Himself.

The stations and offices, or neighbourly relationships, might well be said to be concrete embodiments of the Natural law and its demand for neighbourly love. They are creatures or ordinances of God, [82] through which He calls men to the service of their neighbours; and they can therefore also be described as 'commands' and 'vocations' (*Befehl, Beruf*). There is no one who is not thus called by God, Luther insists, since everyone is in a station of one kind or another—as a married man or woman, for instance, or as a son or daughter, or a prince, or a lord spiritual or temporal. He laments, moreover, that people neglect these commands and vocations in favour of pilgrimages and other supposedly holy works, so that no one takes his station seriously. [83] When, therefore, he wishes to show the meaning of neighbourly love, it is quite natural for Luther to speak in terms of vocation, of station and office.

We are to live, speak, act, hear, suffer, and die [he says] each one in love and service for others and even for enemies, the husband for his wife and children, the wife for her husband, the children for their parents, the servants for their masters, the masters for their servants, the rulers for their subjects and the subjects for their rulers, so that the hand, mouth, eye, foot, yea heart and mind of the one is also the other's —that means truly Christian and naturally good works. [84]

Luther then contrasts these works with 'the works of the Papists', such as pilgrimages, fastings, and various rites and ceremonies, which have no reference to their neighbours, but which they offer to God with a view to securing their own salvation. So doing, they neglect their vocation, fail to take their station seriously, and are therefore disobedient to the will and commandment of God. [85]

Men ought, Luther holds, to remain in their vocations, whether they do so willingly and out of genuine love, or simply in submission to the Divine will and commandment expressed in them. He does not mean, of course, that a man may not change his occupation. If some of the stations, such as those of parent and child, brother and sister, are unalterable, others are not; and there are occasions when men not only may, but should, seek fresh employment. [86] No man, however, can do God's will except in a divinely ordained office and vocation, and none is divinely ordained that does not involve real service of one kind or another to one's neighbours, for that is what God wills. From this it should be clear that Luther is innocent of Troeltsch's distinction between an absolute and a relative Natural law. It is still more clear when we notice that the stations and offices that embody the law belong to that temporal order which Luther calls *politia*, and which is usually, but very inadequately, translated as 'the State'.[87] *Politia*, so far from being a consequence of the Fall, as Troeltsch's interpretation would suggest, was created before it;[88] and although certain particular arrangements may have been necessitated within it, in order to meet the situation created by the Fall, this in no way means the institution of a relative Natural law. It is not the law and ordinances of God that have fallen, but men, who either misuse their offices for selfish ends, or abandon the vocations they have from God in order to perform self-chosen works by which they hope to secure their salvation.

Since the Fall, it is true, the needs of a sinful world call for measures that would never have been necessary apart from sin. Princes and magistrates, for example, must enact and enforce special laws in order to keep in check the more dangerous expressions of human self-will, which might otherwise ruin that whole system of neighbourly relationships which is *politia*. But this means no modification of God's natural law of love. Neighbourly love itself, in fact, requires that such measures should be taken, in accordance with the needs of time and place and circumstance. It also furnishes the indispensable criterion by which all measures actually taken must be judged, for none of them can be legitimate, according to Luther, unless it serves the purposes of love.[89] Furthermore, even if the office of prince or magistrate itself, and not simply the ways in which it must be exercised, should be regarded as a consequence of the Fall, there is still no justification for the idea that it could mean the substitution of a relative Natural law, or an official morality, for the original absolute ethic of love. It would mean, what is in fact the case, that Luther does not conceive of *politia* as consisting of an unalterably fixed number of stations and offices, but as capable of new developments to meet new needs.[90]

We may sum up and illustrate Luther's position on this issue as follows. Love, which is immutable in character, is mutable in action, in order that it may render true service to its neighbours according to their several necessities. The same neighbourly love, excluding all self-love, is required by all stations and vocations; but the neighbourly services to be rendered must obviously differ in the different relationships in which a man stands. The office of a school-master is not the same as that of a magistrate, nor that of an employer as of a parent, nor of a brother as of a husband. Yet neither the differences between the offices, nor the conception of the offices in general, can be said to contain any suggestion that Luther envisages any other ethical principle than that of love. There is no place here for the 'dualism' Troeltsch alleges in Luther's ethic. Luther's teaching shows no trace of an opposition between a purely religious ideal and a secular, official morality,[91] which would be little else but a revised version of the familiar double standard of Catholicism that he so vigorously attacked. As Luther sees it, it is irreligious to neglect the office and vocation ordained by God; it is to yield to the temptation of the devil, who delights in the selfish abuse and contempt of the ordinances of God.

Finally, it should be pointed out that Troeltsch's whole interpretation of Luther's ethic is vitiated by his misinterpretation of Luther's religion.[92] This he removes 'out of the material substantial sphere . . . into the intellectual, psychological sphere', making it wholly a matter of the inner life of the individual believer.[93] The accompanying ethic is then said to be purely spiritual,[94] and to consist in aloofness from the world and concentration on the question of personal salvation.[95] It is not surprising, therefore, that Troeltsch finds 'the deduction of ethical behaviour from the religious element . . . not very certain'.[96] The uncertainty, however, arises from Troeltsch's own presuppositions, which are not Luther's.

For Luther, as we have seen, God is one who comes down, veiled in the *larvae* of His creatures, and meets man precisely in the 'material substantial sphere' of the external world. In the stations, offices, and vocations He ordains, His divine will of love confronts men. It confronts them, of course, primarily as Law; but for those who have eyes to see, the Gospel is there as well. God gives and does so much good to us by means of His creatures, which remain good despite our sinful abuse of them, Luther maintains, that we should be able to recognize that He is a gracious God. Just as the *larvae Dei* can be said, as it were, to contain Christ, so it can be said that 'God has placed forgiveness of sins in all His creatures'.[97] How, then, can Troeltsch assert that, for Luther, 'there is no real inner connexion between God and Nature';[98] or how can he interpret Luther's 'faith' as something purely inward and psychological? For Luther, faith means a certain relationship of the whole man to the God who meets him in the outward circumstances of his daily life.[99] In this relationship, moreover, the believer, so far from concentrating on his personal salvation, is governed by the love of God, both as Law and as Gospel, which delivers him from preoccupation with himself and enables him to serve his neighbour as God wills.[100] His relationship to God naturally and inevitably determines his dealings with his neighbours, so that 'ethical behaviour' and the 'religious element' are inseparable in Luther's thought. Faith, however, is the work of the Gospel, not of the Law, and to the Gospel we may now turn our attention. Its meaning and content are to be found, not in Christ's 'by-office' as interpreter of the Law, but in His 'proper office' as the Saviour of sinful men who are under the condemnation and curse of the Law.

15. CHRIST AS MEDIATOR AND SAVIOUR

(a) *The Work of Redemption and Atonement*

What Luther wishes us above all to see in Christ is the Divine Victor and Deliverer, who has broken the power of what he calls the 'Tyrants' that hold sway over human life.[101] He uses very varied metaphors to describe the Work of Christ, but most characteristic is that of a conflict on a cosmic scale between the Redeemer and forces hostile to the will and purpose of God. Of these he gives various lists, but five are constantly named, which may be said to include all that is essential to the conception. They are as follows: sin, death, the devil, the Law, and the Wrath of God. It will be noticed that we have had occasion to mention all of these in our preceding discussion, especially in connexion with the nature and significance of the Law. If it seems strangely contradictory that the Divine Law and the Wrath of God should be counted among the forces hostile to the Divine will, of which they are actually expressions, we may recall that we have seen how they nevertheless prevent the full and perfect realization of that will in and through man, because they render him impotent to fulfil it. That is why they are numbered amongst the Tyrants against which Christ in His proper office contends.

Now by His Incarnation, Cross, and Resurrection, Luther holds, Christ has won the decisive battle against all the tyrannical powers; and although the warfare is not ended, but must continue until the Last Day, yet the final issue is assured. In his victory, moreover, Christ gives all believers to share, and it is thus that He fulfils His proper office and proves Himself the Saviour of men.[102]

Luther's conception of the Work of Christ has fundamentally the same significance as his doctrine of justification. He speaks of the two in the same breath and in identical terms.[103] Both are opposed to anthropocentricity in religion, and especially to its expression in religious legalism. Luther maintains that men are justified and saved by Christ's work and not by their own. To deny the divinity of Christ, therefore, is to deny the article of justification, and to reject the article of justification is to reject the divinity of Christ. This is what the popish schoolmen have done with their doctrine of salvation by merit. They may say in the words of the Creed, that Christ came down from heaven for us men and our salvation, but they will not let Him fulfil His divine, saving office. Nothing remains for Him, therefore, but His other office of lawgiver and judge; and it is Luther's constant complaint that the Papists have made of Christ a tyrant and a taskmaster harsher than Moses.[104]

Against this legalism, Luther sets his doctrine of justification; and to be justified means to be made participant in Christ's victorious strife against the Tyrants. The imagery he uses to depict this strife is sometimes quite grotesque, like that of the Greek Fathers, but there is profound insight behind it. Legalism, as we have seen, means a false conception of God and a false relationship to Him, which will not permit Him to be truly *God*. It thwarts the Divine will and purpose and sets up hostility between God and man, which has powerful and disastrous consequences for human life. This situation cannot be altered by any willing or doing of man, since all that he wills and does is determined precisely by his false attitude to God. Hence it is

I

no mere phantasy when Luther, like the New Testament, describes man as in bondage to evil forces from which he cannot liberate himself, but whose power has been broken through Christ. He is, of course, well aware that he is using metaphors and images, which must not be taken with crude literalism; but he believes that the thought of conflict and victory best expresses the significance of the Work of Christ.[105]

The view taken here of Luther's conception of the Work of Christ is that maintained by Bishop Aulén, who describes it as the Classic Theory and emphasizes its close resemblance to Patristic conceptions.[106] The same view is taken by Professor Ragnar Bring, who has shown, at greater length and with much ampler evidence, how what may be called the 'dramatic-dualistic' motif runs through the whole of Luther's thought.[107] Dr. Sidney Cave, however, while recognizing the value of Aulén's thesis, ventures to criticize it as one-sided. Luther, he contends, taught not only the Patristic view, but also the Penal Theory of the Atonement, or at least gave interpretations of Christ's Work of which the Penal Theory is a rationalization.[108] An older interpreter of Luther, Theodosius Harnack, might seem to lend support to this view, when he maintains that Luther's chief emphasis falls not primarily on Christ's conflict with the powers of evil, but on His relation to the Law, not on Redemption, but on Atonement.[109]

Now it is true that Luther quite frequently uses very different imagery from that of conflict and victory to express the significance of the Work of Christ. He speaks of Christ's satisfaction of the Law, His merit, His sacrifice, His pacification of the Wrath of God. At first sight, these conceptions appear to have little in common with the view we have outlined above; and for those who are determined to believe in Luther's incapacity for consistent thought, appearances will no doubt settle the matter. But the question may legitimately be raised, whether there may not be a consistent purpose underlying all Luther's statements about the Work of Christ, however diverse they may be superficially. The importance of this question is easily shown with reference to Harnack's contention. What he says would be true only if Christ's victory over the Tyrants, as Luther represents it, had no essential connexion with the Law. In fact, however, the Law itself is not only numbered among the Tyrants, but can practically be said to be the chief among them, since apart from their connexion with it, the rest would lose their significance. The truth of this assertion will be seen if we recall Luther's view of the situation of man under the Law.

The Law is an expression of the will of God, we have heard Luther argue, yet it makes sinful men not better, but worse. It exposes and intensifies the deep and subtle hostility between human self-will and the Divine. It can therefore be called a revelation of sin; for if we were not sinners, if our will were in perfect harmony with the will of God, His will would not stand over against us as Law at all. The revelation of our sin, moreover, is at the same time a revelation of Divine wrath;[110] for inasmuch as our will is opposed to God's, His will is opposed to ours—actively opposed, since He is the living God. God cannot adapt His will to ours without ceasing to be holy and righteous and good, that is, to be God. But neither can we, so long as we are under the Law, adapt ourselves to Him; for the Law itself, as we have seen, renders us impotent to do so. It is when we are in this situation that Luther asserts us to be damned and under the dominion of Satan.[111] To be under the Law, therefore, is to be under a curse and subject to death, for the Law condemns the sin it exposes, and dooms to perdition whatsoever is opposed to the holy and righteous and good will of God. From this it should be clear that to separate, as Harnack suggests, the thought of Christ's conflict with the Tyrants from that of His concern with the Law, is to set up an unnecessary and, indeed, a false antithesis.

This does not, however, quite dispose of Dr. Cave's allegation that Luther teaches what is virtually a Penal Theory of the Atonement. If the charge could be substantiated, it would reveal a profound and irreconcilable contradiction in Luther's thought. For the Penal Theory, as Dr. Cave points out, implies the primacy of Divine justice, which requires that the claim of God's Law and Wrath should be satisfied before His Love can do its work. In other words, the Penal Theory implies a fundamentally legalistic conception of God's character and of His dealings with men.

But is it possible that Luther, who is otherwise so implacable an opponent of legalism, could have failed to perceive this fact? Even when he uses language suggestive of the Penal Theory, may it not be that his meaning is quite the opposite? Saint Paul, as is well known, has sometimes been accused by his shallower

critics of doing serious harm to Christianity by interpreting it in
terms of the law-court. But if only a little attention is paid to his
arguments, it is perfectly clear that, while he uses the language of
Jewish legalism in order to meet his contemporary opponents on
their own ground, yet he employs it in such a way as to shatter
beyond repair every legalistic conception of religion. In a similar
way, Luther makes use of current terms such as satisfaction, merit,
and sacrifice, in order to convey a meaning precisely contrary to
that commonly accepted among his opponents. He employs them
in connexion with the Work of Christ, in deliberate opposition to
the Roman doctrine that men must acquire merit in order to
secure their salvation, must make satisfaction for the sins they
commit, and must ensure the favour of God by offering the
sacrifice of the Mass.

Luther leaves us in no doubt that he does not like the term
satisfaction. If it is to be used in theology at all, he says, we must
be quite clear that it cannot have the same meaning there as it
has in other connexions.[112] He has retained it, he explains, to
please the Papists—but only on the understanding that it signifies
something done, not by us, but by Christ. If the Papists are
not content with this, he will send the word home to the judges,
lawyers, and hangmen, from whom the Pope has stolen it.[113] It
could hardly have been more plainly stated, that the idea of
satisfaction is quite unessential to Luther's own thought, and that
he knows it can be very misleading unless we see why he uses it.
His purpose is to exclude the anthropocentric doctrine of his
opponents and to assert his own theocentric point of view. Hence
he insists that, if we are to speak of satisfaction for sin at all, it
must have reference, not to the work of sinful men, but of Christ,
who is divine.[114] It is certainly not to Christ as man (*qua homo*),
representing men, that Luther points us here. From his point of
view, it would be quite impossible for Christ as man to make satisfaction to God for sin, because as man Christ was laden with the
sins of the whole world, which He freely took upon Himself, as
we shall see. Furthermore, Luther makes it quite plain that he
understands Christ's satisfaction, no less than His victory, to be a
Divine work and a revelation of the infinite and boundless
mercy of the Father.[115]

This same point of view is just as clearly represented in Luther's
references to the merits of Christ, which he consistently opposes to

all human merit.[116] He makes Christ's merit, moreover, synonymous with 'free mercy'[117] and with 'spirit and life, grace and truth';[118] and since he also represents it as the object of faith and the sole ground of justification, its meaning for him cannot be other than *sola gratia*.[119] It is not something offered to God, to satisfy His justice and enable Him to forgive,[120] but it is given to believers, who just by the receiving of it are made effectively participant in Christ's victory.

Thanks be to God [cries Luther, echoing Saint Paul]—Thanks be to God, which giveth us the victory through our Lord Jesus Christ. That is to say, the Law makes us sinners, and sin makes us guilty of death. Who hath conquered these twain? Was it our righteousness, or our life? Nay, it was Jesus Christ, rising from the dead, condemning sin and death, *bestowing on us His merits*, and holding His hand over us. And now it is well with us, we keep the Law, and vanquish sin and death.[121]

The merit of Christ is thus virtually equivalent to that justifying righteousness of God (*iustitia qua iustificat nos*), which is Christ Himself, and which is given to us.[122] Christ Himself, apprehended by faith and dwelling in the believing heart, Luther says, is the merit of Christians and the only means of their justification, that is, of their deliverance not only from the guilt, but also from the power of sin.[123]

Now just as Christ's merit signifies for Luther that free mercy of God which is the sole ground of justification, so also the sacrifice of Christ is a work of free mercy and equally opposed to all legalistic conceptions.[124] Speaking of the Old Testament sacrifices, Luther says that they were commanded by God, but that they were never intended as a means whereby men might secure for themselves Divine favour.[125] Men misinterpreted and misused them with this end in view, however, and that was the reason why the prophets condemned the whole sacrificial cultus, ordained of God though it was.[126] The sacrifices could only have pleased God as pointing to the sacrifice of Christ in which they were to find their fulfilment.[127] For men to offer sacrifices in the hope of placating and propitiating God, is in Luther's eyes a mark of false religion and idolatry; and he therefore sets the sacrifice of Christ in absolute opposition to all sacrifices offered by men. He opposes it most sharply of all to the sacrifice of the Mass,

which cannot but seem doubly blasphemous to him, inasmuch as
it is offered by men in order to obtain favour from the God who has
shown Himself freely and eternally favourable in Christ.[128] In
the Mass, Luther ceaselessly insists, we do not offer a sacrifice to
God, but we receive gifts from Him; we do not repeat Christ's
sacrifice, but we remember it and share its benefits, for it is
eternally sufficient and complete. Christ's sacrifice, moreover,
like His satisfaction, is entirely a Divine work; it is God's sacrifice
of Himself, to which He was moved by nothing else but His
inestimable love for men.[129] When Luther speaks of Christ's work
in sacrificial terms, therefore, it is clear that he does so in order to
assert yet again his theocentric point of view. Christ's sacrifice,
like his merit, means *sola gratia*.[130]

But let us at this point hear Luther's own words on the subject
of Christ's atoning work.

Christ alone [he says] was able, and satisfied for us, who of the infinite
mercy of the Father was sent for the same cause, and that to us. . . .
Without all doubt it was no merit, but only boundless mercy, that
Christ came to us and merited and obtained for us remission of sins
unto eternal salvation. Now he calls Him 'the day-spring from on high',
which signifieth unto us His divinity . . . for He proceedeth from the
Father, as the beams do from the sun.[131]

Moreover, this He did of inestimable love: for Paul saith, 'which
loved me'. . . . For He delivered neither sheep, ox, gold, nor silver,
but even God Himself entirely and wholly, 'for me', even for 'me', I
say, a miserable and wretched sinner. . . . These words (which are
the pure preaching of grace and Christian righteousness indeed) Paul
setteth against the righteousness of the Law. As if he said: be it so that
the Law is an heavenly doctrine, and hath also his glory: yet notwithstanding it loved not me, nor gave itself for me: yea, it accuseth me,
terrifieth me, and driveth me to desperation. But I have now another
which hath delivered me from the terrors of the Law, sin, and death,
and hath brought me into liberty, the righteousness of God, and
eternal life.[132]

The way in which Christ's atonement becomes effective for the
Christian, Luther describes as follows:

Faith taketh hold of Christ [he says] and hath Him present, and
holdeth Him inclosed, as the ring doth the precious stone. And
whosoever shall be found having this confidence in Christ apprehended
in his heart, him will God account for righteous. This is the mean, and

this is the merit, whereby we attain the remission of sins and righteousness. 'Because thou believest in me, saith the Lord, and thy faith layeth hold upon Christ, whom I have freely given unto thee that He might be thy mediator and high-priest, therefore be thou justified and righteous.' Wherefore God doth accept and account us as righteous, only for our faith in Christ. And this acceptation, or imputation, is very necessary . . . because we are not yet perfectly righteous, 'but while we remain in this life, sin dwelleth in our flesh'; and this remnant of sin God purgeth in us. . . .[133]

Such passages as these make it abundantly clear that Christ's atoning work is, for Luther, God's own work, and that so far from being directed toward God in order to change His attitude to men, it is directed toward men in order to bring them into a new relationship to God, if only they receive Christ into their hearts by faith.

Nevertheless, it may be asked, does not Luther connect Christ's work of satisfaction and sacrifice with the idea of the fulfilment of the Law and the pacification of God's wrath? And does not this suggest the primacy of Divine justice, whose claims had to be met before free mercy and justifying grace could be shown to sinful men? Although Luther has effectively excluded legalism from his conception of the Christian's relationship to God, has he not, perhaps unwittingly, retained it in his thought of the Divine nature itself?

In answer to these questions, it must first of all be said, that Luther uses the idea of satisfaction to show, not only that the Law has been fulfilled and therefore satisfied, but that it has been actually abolished by Christ. It has been abolished, moreover, not in order that mercy and grace might become available for men, but precisely because they have been made available. What this means, it is not difficult to see, if we consider what is implied by Christ's fulfilment of the Law. It means that He has shown toward men just such a love as the Law vainly commands men to show toward others, a love which by its very nature excludes all legalistic considerations, as we have already seen. That is why the Law is abolished as a basis for the religious relationship. But we must also recall that the love required by the Law is such that it cannot be produced to order and in response to the dictates of the Law. Only one who is free from the Law and, as it were, above the Law, is able to fulfil it. This fact has much to do with

Luther's repeated insistence on the divinity of Christ, which we have already pointed out, and on the voluntariness of Christ's work, which we shall have further occasion to notice. Christ's work is the work of God Himself; and it is done, not at the behest of the Law, but out of free and spontaneous love. God is not subject to the Law, for the Law is an expression of His will, not its master. The idea of the fulfilment and satisfaction of the Law, therefore, in no way indicates the primacy of Divine justice, although it may be said to have a certain positive value inasmuch as it stands for the consistency and righteousness of the Divine will.

There is nothing essentially inconsistent with what has just been said, when Luther speaks of Christ's atoning work as having appeased the Wrath of God. To begin with, he is aware that such language is not quite appropriate to his own outlook. In a passage attacking the satisfactions and sacrifices of men, and insisting that there is one sacrifice alone, namely Christ's, whereby God is 'placated', Luther adds: *ut ita dicam*—'so to speak'.[134] He is clearly conscious of an approach to his opponents' standpoint here, and he does not wish to be misunderstood. Secondly, the Work of Christ, as Luther represents it, in no way creates, but presupposes a gracious God. The very Wrath that is pacified by it is, for him, the 'strange work' (*opus alienum*) of a God whose 'proper work' (*opus proprium*) is forgiveness and grace, and it is at the service, not in control, of that proper work.[135] It stands for the purity and holiness of a love that will forgive at the cost of utter self-sacrifice, but will never for a moment condone or compromise with sin. Since this love is the antithesis of all legalism, it is only when Wrath is viewed in isolation from love, that any suggestion of legalism can arise; and it is when this happens, that Wrath becomes a Tyrant, the worst of all the Tyrants from which Christ came to deliver us.

Finally, it is most important to notice that the Law and the Wrath of God have not ceased to be, as a result of Christ's work. They are realities that have continually to be overcome, if sinful men who are under them are to be saved. They are overcome, however, not in order that love may be free to do its proper work, but just to the extent that it actually accomplishes it. Christ's atonement is effective for sinners only in so far as by faith they receive the benefits of His sacrifice, have His merits imputed to them, or become partakers of His victory, which means the same thing. What it means is an intimate and vital union of believers with Christ Himself, who delivers them from Wrath inasmuch as He deals with both the guilt and the power of sin in their lives.[136] To this subject we shall return; but here it is chiefly important to insist that neither Wrath nor even the Law itself signifies for Luther anything in the nature of legal justice whatsoever.

If any further evidence were required to support our thesis here, we might point out that Luther very often speaks of Christ's satisfaction, merit, sacrifice, and pacification of God's Wrath, in the same context and virtually in the same breath as he speaks of the conflict and victory over the Tyrants.[137] From this it is plain that Luther himself can have had no sense of incongruity or inconsistency in the ideas he intended to express. The fact is that he is simply giving utterance to one and the same fundamental idea in a variety of ways. He uses all the means at his disposal to bring it home to his hearers or readers, and he is not afraid to adopt their terms of reference, if in that way he may help them to see. One thing he is not trying to do, it should perhaps he said, and that is to elaborate a dogmatic theory of the Atonement.

There can be no doubt, however, that Luther's own characteristic point of view finds its clearest and most consistent expression in the thought of Christ's conflict and victory. He actually defines the proper office of Christ in these terms.

The true and proper office of Christ [he says] is to wrestle with the Law, with the sin and the death of the whole world, and so to wrestle that He must suffer and abide all these things; and by suffering them in Himself, conquer and abolish them, and by this mean deliver the faithful from the Law and all evils.[138]

This conception Luther describes as *capitalia nostrae theologiae* and as

the principal article of all Christian doctrine, which the popish schoolmen have altogether darkened.

For [he explains] it belongeth only to the divine power to destroy sin and to abolish death, to create righteousness and to give life. They have attributed this divine power to our own works, saying, If thou do this work or that, thou shalt overcome sin, death, and the wrath of God; and by this means they set us in God's place, making us in very deed naturally, if I may so say, God Himself.[139]

(b) The Redeemer, Human and Divine

Luther's emphasis on the divinity of Christ is such that he might easily be thought to give little weight to the humanity. Yet that is by no means the case. He firmly maintains the Chalcedonian doctrine of the Two Natures and insists upon both the necessity and the full reality of the human nature.[140]

For the humanity would be no use [he says] if the divinity were not in it; yet on the other hand, God will not and cannot be found except through and in this humanity.[141]

Luther is, of course, well aware of the problems raised by the assertion that Christ is God and Man in one Person. How can God have been crucified and died? How can Christ, who is Man, have created the world? In connexion with these, he has recourse to the old doctrine of the *communicatio idiomatum*, the communication of the attributes, according to which, whatever is predicated of the divinity must be predicated also of the humanity, and vice versa.[142] As a metaphysical explanation of the union of the two Natures, this is singularly unconvincing; but in view of Luther's reiterated objection to 'speculation' about matters concerning God, we can take it as certain that he never intended it as such. In fact, he as good as tells us so himself.

As for the man [he says] who . . . wants to be subtle and to reckon up how it can sound correct that God and man are one Person—let him go on and be subtle and reckon up, and see what he gains by it. How many a man has become a fool by all this![143]

According to Karl Holl, when Luther seeks to express his view of Christ in terms of the traditional dogmatic formulae, he borders on the heresy of monophysitism. For this, Holl blames the old dogma, on the grounds that, being formulated in terms of Hellenistic metaphysics, it is ill-adapted to Luther's thought.[144] It is possible, however, to argue that Luther in fact has perceived that the dogma, despite its terminology, is not metaphysical speculation at all. For the primary purpose of its formulation was not to explain *how* Christ could be both human and divine, but to assert *that* He indeed was truly both. In other words, the dogma is not theoretical explanation, but religious affirmation, the utterance of faith. At any rate, it is certain that Luther's treatment of it must be regarded in that light.

The doctrine of the communication of the attributes is an expression of Luther's religious conviction about the relation of God to mankind and the nature of His dealings with men.[145] His account of it is exactly similar to his description of the relationship between Christ and the Christian believer, or between Christ and the Church, under the figure of a marriage.[146] Just as the bride and bridegroom are joined in a personal union so intimate that they become 'one flesh' and everything that belongs to either comes to belong also to the other, so God in Christ has imparted to humanity His divine gifts and has taken upon Himself human weakness and evil, thereby delivering from these all who are united with Him by faith. It is in this light that we must understand Luther's exhortations, which we have noticed, to cleave to the humanity of Christ and to know no other God but this God incarnate and clothed with man's nature.

In Luther's thought, divinity and humanity are not as such mutually exclusive; they are not, so to speak, metaphysically incompatible. Although there is an unalterable distinction between the Creator and the creature, yet the most intimate personal fellowship and communion between them is not only possible, but divinely intended. This is hindered, not because human nature is inherently evil, but because it is in the grip of alien and hostile forces from which no man can set himself free. The thought of sin, death, and the rest as objective powers and 'Tyrants' is no doubt foreign to the modern mind. But it is drawn from the New Testament, and it has importance as showing among other things that Luther regards these forces, including sin, as fundamentally alien to human nature as a good creature of God. Now, as Luther sees it, it was precisely in order to break the power of these Tyrants and deliver man from them, that God became Man in Christ. The humanity of Christ is essential to the fulfilment of His proper office. Since the conflict between God and the Tyrants takes place in human life, where God and His adversaries contend, as it were, for the mastery of Mansoul, it is in human life that the victory must be won, at any rate if it is to effect man's salvation, and if God is to be truly God *for man*.

Here it is important to observe how Luther more precisely conceives the victory to have been won.

In the first place, God in Christ entered into such a vital and intimate union with humanity, that He became subject to the same conditions, the same Tyranny, under which men suffer. Indeed, He can be said to have become more truly Man than any other, because He suffered more deeply than any.

For [says Luther in a sermon on Ephesians 48-10] He descended into the deepest of all depths, under the Law, under the devil, death, sin, and hell; and that, I think, is verily the last and lowest depth. Therefore this text claims that the Person who has descended and ascended, is not only true God, but also true man.[147]

No man ever descended so deep as Christ, and no mere man ever could, but God alone was able to take upon Himself the whole weight of the world's sin and bear the whole tyranny of death, the devil, and the curse. At the same time, it was only by assuming true human nature, or as Luther puts it, by taking upon Him our person, that God in Christ was able to enter into the domain where the Tyrants hold sway.

Christ, therefore, became 'like us, a man and our brother',[148] and the decisive battle against the Tyrants was fought in His Person; He won it *in se ipso*, in Himself. He won it, Luther says,

without war or weapons, in His own body, and in Himself, as Paul delighteth to speak: 'Spoiling', said he, 'all principalities and powers, and triumphing over them in Himself' (Colossians 215), so that they cannot any more hurt those that do believe. And this circumstance, 'in Himself', maketh that combat much more wonderful and glorious. For it sheweth that it was necessary, that these things should be accomplished in that one only Person ... and that so the whole creature through this one Person should be renewed.[149]

Here we can see the significance of Luther's idea that there are found in Christ 'two things so contrary and so repugnant' as, on the one hand, the sin, death, and curse of the whole world, and on the other, righteousness, life, and blessing that are invincible because divine.[150] The Tyrants launched their attacks on Christ in His human nature as they could not have done otherwise, since He would have been beyond their reach. But they were powerless to overcome the divinity that was 'hidden' in His humanity, and their tyranny was therefore broken. The victory is God's, but it has been won where alone it could be won, in true and complete human nature.[151]

In the second place, all that Christ has done, He has done freely and voluntarily. He did not come under the power of the Tyrants because of any obligation or necessity as do sinful men. He joined Himself to sinners 'of His own accord';[152] He bore their sins 'of His own good will';[153] He submitted to the punishment of the sins He bore, and 'was willingly made a curse for us'.[154] Furthermore, lest anyone should suppose that there was a division in the Godhead, as if this burden were laid upon a merciful Son by the Father's vengeful justice, Luther assures us that what Christ willingly did was done also 'by the will of His Father',[155] and 'through the love of the Divine Majesty'.[156] Even passages in which Luther quite explicitly speaks of Christ as bearing the punishment of our sins, do not signify anything like a Penal Theory of the Atonement. They do, however, show a very proper recognition of the fact that by making Himself a friend of publicans and sinners, God in Christ exposed Himself to all the pains and penalties of their sinful situation, which indeed He actually suffered. But His suffering, we must notice, was not passively, but actively borne. It was not a penalty imposed upon Him for His own sin, for in Himself He is innocent of sin, but it was vicariously endured for our sake. 'All the weight of the matter', says Luther, 'standeth in this word "For us" ';[157] and his repeated emphasis on the pronouns—for *us*, for *me*, for *thee*—shows what great importance he attaches to this fact. It was only because Christ did everything freely and voluntarily, for our sake, not His own, that He both fulfilled and abolished the Law, and thereby vanquished all the Tyrants, whose power, as we have seen, is inseparably bound up with the Law.

In the third place, by virtue of His spontaneous and selfless love, which is highest righteousness, Christ achieved His victory *stricto iure*—that is, neither by force nor by fraud, but by unquestionable right.[158] Even when Luther attributes the defeat of the devil to his deception by the Incarnation, there is no suggestion of fraud. The devil, he says, failed to perceive the divinity that was hidden in the humanity of Christ, and thought he could swallow Him up, like all other men, in death. But death could not prevail over immortal life, nor the devil over God, and both were cheated of what had seemed their choicest victim, just when they appeared to have Him most securely in their grasp.[159] By this Luther does not mean that God has employed an unworthy artifice to deceive and vanquish His foe. On the contrary, the idea of the deception is entirely in keeping with Luther's view that God is always hidden just where He is revealed; or to put it another way, that God reveals Himself in a manner precisely opposite to that which the natural man, at any rate, would normally and naturally expect.[160] The devil, therefore, who might be said to be the archetype of all natural men, was prevented by his very nature from recognizing God in the despised Man Christ. How could the one who is the quintessence of egocentricity—of self-seeking, self-assertion, and pride—understand that the way of humiliation, of suffering, of self-sacrificing love, was the way in which the Almighty God would fight and would prevail? The devil was deceived exactly as unbelieving men are deceived, because it never occurs to them that God might act otherwise than they themselves would act if they were in His place. The Incarnation was no Divine fraud, but was entirely in character with the sovereign righteousness of God.

It was, then, because the Tyrants had no right over Christ, that they had no ultimate power; and in seeking to vanquish Him, they were themselves vanquished.[161] When sin, the universal Tyrant of the world, assailed Him, it did so in vain, for He was 'a person of invincible and everlasting righteousness'. Nevertheless, the tyrant Law accused and condemned Him to death, as if He must Himself be a sinner and under its jurisdiction, because He was found in the company of sinners. In a very real sense, it is true, Christ *was* under the Law, since He had entered into a sinful world where it held universal sway; but in another sense He was by no means under it, since He had come and submitted to it freely and without any of its constraint.[162] In condemning Him, therefore, the Law acted unjustly and condemned itself. For if it is within its rights in tyrannizing over sinful men, it exceeded them in attacking Christ, who was not only innocent, but 'right-eousness itself'. It was a wonderful combat (*mirabile duellum*), Luther therefore says, when the Law, which is a creature, assaulted its Creator, who might easily have abolished it by an act of sheer power from on high, but who chose instead the way of humiliation and suffering because of His inestimable love for men. In a similar way, the curse, 'which is the wrath of God upon the whole world', sought to overcome the blessing, that is, 'the grace and eternal mercy of God in Christ'. But the blessing is divine and everlasting, and therefore the curse must needs give place. For if the blessing in Christ could be overcome, then should God Himself be overcome.

Such statements as those just quoted, and especially the subordination of the Law as a creature and the virtual identification of the eternal blessing with God Himself, are sufficient by themselves to dispose of any suggestion of the primacy of justice in Luther's thought of God. They are, in fact, unequivocal assertions of the primacy of grace. Their meaning is clearly this, that God, so far from being governed by legalistic considerations, is such that not even His own uncompromising antagonism to sin can deter Him from taking the part of sinful men and seeking their salvation, regardless of the cost to Himself. That is precisely what Luther wishes us to see Him doing in Christ. For Christ, he says,

making a happy change with us . . . took upon Him our sinful person, and gave unto us His innocent and victorious person. . . . Now He, thus bearing the sin of the whole world in our person, was taken, suffered, was crucified, and put to death, and became a curse for us. But because He was a person divine and everlasting, it was impossible that death should hold Him. Wherefore He rose again the third day from death, and now liveth for ever: and there is neither sin nor death found in Him any more, but mere righteousness, life, and everlasting blessedness.[163]

Finally, we must notice that the climax of Christ's work, where the defeat of the Tyrants is irrevocably sealed, is reached in the Cross and Resurrection. These two are for Luther inseparably one. Whenever he speaks of either, the thought of the other is certainly implied. He can attribute Christ's victory to the Cross, where Christ, he says, 'performed His mightiest work and vanquished sin, death, world, hell, devil, and all evil'.[164] He can also attribute it to the Resurrection, saying that Christ 'rose again to make us righteous and in so doing, He hath overcome the Law, sin, death, hell, and all evils'.[165] Here the decisive battle in the cosmic conflict between God and the forces of evil has been won. The final issue of the war is certain, though the end is not yet. Christ will triumph, because He has triumphed; and in His victory He gives all believers to share. It is therefore to Christ

crucified and risen, that Luther will have us look if we would find
the true and saving knowledge of God. 'This image and mirror',
he says, 'we must have continually before us, and behold the same
with a steadfast eye of faith.'[166] This is the heart of his *theologia
crucis*, where Incarnation and Atonement, Redemption and
Revelation are all one, and all are God's own work.

16. THE MAJESTY OF UNCREATED LOVE

For Luther, the acting subject in all Christ's work is God Himself.
The Christocentricity of his thought, therefore, in no way con-
flicts with its fundamental theocentric motif. It is important,
however, to notice here that he never precisely equates God with
Christ. There is a marked element of what may be termed subor-
dinationism in his Christology. Christ is God's gift to men, and 'in
His words and works we should not so much look upon Him as
upon the Father'.[167] As Conqueror of the Tyrants, He is the agent
of God the Father, who 'hath delivered us out of the kingdom of
the devil . . . by His own Son'.[168] Although He now reigns
as Victor, He will one day have 'delivered up the kingdom to God
His Father', as Saint Paul says, 'and God shall be all in all'.[169]
Contrary to what at first might appear, this means no modification
of Luther's essential theocentricity, but a strengthening of it.
It means that Luther does not make of Christ a substitute for
God. He does not regard Him as filling the whole Divine horizon,
or as furnishing an exhaustive revelation of God. God cannot be
defined simply and solely as the Incarnate. But in and through the
Incarnate, He has revealed His essential character, in the light
of which all His works and ways are to be interpreted, and He
Himself is to be trusted where He cannot be traced.

Christ, says Luther, is described as the Word of God; and a
word is the best means of signifying what is in the speaker's
heart.[170] God's revelation of Himself in Christ, therefore, enables
us to know 'what is going on in the Supreme Majesty' (*wie es in
suprema maiestate zughet*). This is a far greater thing than if God
had revealed how He created heaven and earth, for here He
discloses His inmost self, His very essence or substance (*suam
substantiam*).[171]

If we ask what precisely the 'substance' of God is, Luther can
answer very simply. 'What', he says, 'will you find in Christ that

does not breathe mere love?'[172] It was out of mere love that
Christ undertook His whole redeeming work:[173] and the love that
is in Him is none other than God's own. He could not have
shown love to us, 'except the will of God by His eternal love had
so appointed'.[174]

The Incarnation and Passion of Christ [therefore] are set forth for our
contemplation, in order above all that we may behold and know the
love of God toward us. So John 3 says: God so loved the world, etc.[175]
[Here God] pours out not sun and moon, nor heaven and earth, but
His own heart and His dearest Son, and even suffers Him to shed His
blood and die the most shameful of all deaths for us shameful, wicked,
ungrateful people. How can we here say anything else but that God is
nothing but an abyss of eternal love?[176]

We have received from God naught but love and favour, for Christ
has pledged and given us His righteousness and everything that He has,
has poured out upon us all His treasures, which no man can measure
and no angel can understand or fathom, for God is a glowing furnace
of love, reaching even from the earth to the heavens.[177]

The chief marks of Divine love are as follows. First of all, it is
spontaneous. God 'so loveth us, that of His own accord He joineth
Himself unto us, seeketh to have to do with us, voluntarily showeth
and offereth His grace unto us'.[178] It can be described as a
quellende Liebe, a love that wells up and flows forth out of the loving
heart, quite independently of all external considerations.[179]
It is entirely free from all eudemonistic or legalistic calculation,
and is neither kindled by any worth nor quenched by any unworthiness in its object.

It knows nothing but to do good; it lives . . . unto the benefit of others,
having no view to private advantage; it does all things freely and without any regard to the merit of others; it anticipates all things with its
benefits. [180]

Such love seeks not its own, but its neighbour's good;[181] and it
can actually be defined as 'nothing but benefiting and doing good
unto all men, both friends and enemies'.[182] Although it takes
especial care not to show kindness to one at the expense of another,[183] yet its nature finds clearest and fullest expression in
kindness shown to the unthankful and the evil.[184] It can therefore
be described as a *verlorene Liebe*, a lost love; for although it by no

K

means always meets with a favourable response, yet even when love's labour is lost, Divine love still goes on loving.[185] It cannot be checked by ingratitude or even hostility, but is the same toward all, friends and enemies alike.[186]

Above all, Divine love is *amor crucis*, the love of the Cross.[187] In the Cross there is displayed, in all its unfathomable mystery, the breadth and length and depth and height of God's redeeming love. Here, in utter selflessness, God sacrifices Himself on behalf of sinful men, creatures yet enemies of His own, whom He does not love because they are lovable, but who are lovable only because He loves them.[188] In thus freely loving sinners, however, Divine love never for a moment condones their sin, nor compromises with evil, but seeks actively to overcome it. For the Cross, we recall, is the scene of the decisive encounter between Christ and the hostile Tyrants, that is, between Incarnate love and the forces of lovelessness and selfishness—for in the last analysis it is with these that the Tyrants stand or fall. Had love failed here, had God ceased from loving, He would have abdicated His Godhead and left His creatures to perish for ever. But in fact Divine love proved invincible, and God is still God even in a world that denies and crucifies Him.

But how does the conception of God as love, in the sense we have described, accord with our natural knowledge of Him as a Lawgiver and righteous Judge, and as an omnipotent Creator? At first sight, the two seem entirely opposed to one another.

For this is to know God aright [says Luther] when He is understood of us, not under the name of power or wisdom (which is a terror unto us), but under the name of goodness and love;[189] [and] in Christ we see that God is not a cruel exactor or a judge, but a most loving and merciful Father, who, to the end that He might bless us . . . 'spared not His own Son, but gave Him for us all', etc. (Romans 832). This is a true knowledge of God, and a divine persuasion, which deceiveth us not, but painteth out God unto us lively.[190]

Nevertheless, this true knowledge of God, upon which Luther's entire theology is based, by no means excludes either Divine power or Divine law. What Luther means here is simply that, if we construe the will of God in terms either of legal justice or of arbitrary power rather than of giving and forgiving love, then we misconstrue it and stand in a wrong relationship to God.

As many as know not the article of justification [Luther says] take away Christ the mercy-seat (*propitiatorem*) and will needs comprehend God in His majesty by the judgement of reason, and pacify Him with their own works.[191]

Man's attempts to establish the religious relationship by means of rational speculation and the works of the law, are opposed to the way to the Father that is given through Christ. 'I speak from experience', Luther assures us;[192] and we at once recall the young and devoted monk, desperately trying to meet the requirements of the Divine law in order to find a gracious God, and tormented by the deep mysteries of Divine predestination. It is in vain, he now insists, that we endeavour to climb up into heaven by rational inquiry into God's power and wisdom, 'how He created the world and how He governeth it'; and equally vain are all efforts to come to terms with God by 'making thy works a means between Him and thyself'.[193]

It is characteristic of Luther to link together these two ways, of 'reason' and 'law', by which men think to find God. They may almost be said to be one and the same; for natural human reasoning is inveterately legalistic, and it assumes without question that God's will and ways must be understood in terms of distributive justice, if they are 'rationally' intelligible at all.[194] But this way of understanding God can only lead in the end either to presumption or to despair—to presumption, when a man actually imagines that he is meriting the favour of God,[195] and to despair, when he feels sure he is not.[196] But 'it is as great a sin to despair on account of our own unworthiness as to presume on account of our own righteousness'.[197] Nor does it help to take what seems the middle way, so often recommended, of doubt and uncertain suspension between the two.[198] Doubt, despair, and presumption alike are symptoms of an anthropocentric attitude to God, which will not let Him be Himself, that is, gratuitously good. We must therefore keep to what alone, in Luther's view, can truly be called 'the middle way', the way of faith in the Divine love and grace revealed in Christ.

The way to God through faith in Christ thus supplants the way of 'reason' and 'law'; but this does not mean that the love and grace of Christ exclude either the righteousness or the sovereignty of God. On the contrary, these latter are not less, but even more strongly asserted in Luther's evangelical theology than in the scholastic doctrine he learnt as a monk. They are, however, differently understood in the light of the love of God in Christ. Although it is not a simple matter to reconcile such love with law and power, Luther wrestles hard to solve the problem; and we have already had some indication of the way in which he deals with it, in our discussion of his understanding of the Law. The general character of the solution at which he aims, can be quite simply stated. Instead of the subordination of love to justice, on the one hand, or to arbitrary might on the other, which he found in Scholasticism, he seeks to represent both law and power as at the service of love. Indeed, it can be said that he finds precisely *in* the love, both the essential righteousness and the unassailable sovereignty of God. God's righteousness is no longer conceived in terms of distributive justice, but is identified with the grace by which He justifies the ungodly;[199] and precisely this grace is the surest sign of His omnipotence, since He is a greater God, more really *God*, who can forgive and save sinners, than one who only knows how to punish and destroy.[200]

Such love as we have described, then, is the nature, or essence, or substance of God. These latter terms have lost in Luther's thought all trace of the physical or quasi-physical associations they originally had; and love is no longer one among other 'divine attributes' attached to an otherwise unqualified 'divine nature'. God's substance is His essential character, which is determinative of everything He is and does. Here we see the deepest import both of the Nicene *homoousios*, the 'substantial oneness' of the Son with the Father, and also of the subordinationist element in Luther's Christology. In Christ, God is manifested as personal will actuated simply and solely by love; but this will is not confined to its manifestation in Christ. God is ceaselessly active throughout the whole creation, and wheresoever and howsoever He acts, His activity springs from no other source than the love that is revealed in Christ.

For those who have eyes to see, the same Divine will of love is manifested in Creation as in the Incarnation,[201] and 'all creatures', Luther claims, 'give evidence of our theology'.[202] As he looks upon them, the creatures of God are, so to speak, mirrors of the Divine love that seeketh not its own.

For [as he points out] no tree produces fruit for itself, but it gives its fruits to others; indeed, no creature lives for itself or serves itself, except man and the devil. The sun does not shine for itself, water does not flow for itself, etc. So every creature observes the law of love, and its whole being is in the law of the Lord; for even the members of the human body do not serve themselves; only the disposition of the mind is ungodly . . . seeking in all things, even in God Himself, the things that are its own.[203]

Furthermore, just as Divine love is the same toward all, good and bad alike, so a fig-tree bears figs, and a vine grapes, whether it is planted among thorns or among roses;[204] and just as Divine love never faileth, even toward its enemies, so the silver did not turn to ashes, even when Judas the traitor got it.[205] In such ways as these, therefore, it can be said that everything in creation— except man and the devil—bears open testimony to the constancy and selfless generosity of the Creator's love.

It is the sovereign freedom with which God loves and gives and forgives, that is His glory,[206] and that constitutes, if we may so express it, His Godhead.[207] It makes Him truly 'a God above all creatures'. The creatures at their best are but channels and instruments of His love; while at their worst, like the devil and wicked men, they oppose themselves to it in vain. These will not truly acknowledge Him as God and let Him be God for them; but He is God none the less. In Christ, suffering and triumphant, He has decisively asserted His Godhead in the midst of a hostile world; and in the Incarnate and Crucified Saviour we behold the supreme majesty of that 'uncreated love, which is God Himself'.[208]

NOTES

1. Though he does not greatly like the *word* (*vocem*), he says in *W.A.* VIII.117.33, yet he maintains what it is meant to signify (*rem*); see Loofs, *D.G.* 749, A. Harnack, *H.D.* VII.225.

2. *Gal.* E.T. 13f.(i.3). cf. *Römerbr.* 91.34: 'For Christ also is God'; *W.A.* I.400.2: 'But Jesus is the true, the one, the only God'; *W.A.* X.1; 57.1: '. . . that Christ is also true God.'

3. *W.M.L.* II.326—in the *Treatise on Christian Liberty* (1520).

4. cf. Nygren, *Agape and Eros*, II.ii.486; Aulén, *Gudsbilden*, 179f.; Bring, *Dualismen*, 137f.

5. *E.A.* xii.412. The process envisaged is perhaps indicated in Luther's advice to 'run straight to the manger, and embrace this infant, and the Virgin's little babe in thine arms, and behold Him as He was born, sucking, growing up, conversant among men, teaching, dying, rising again, ascending up above all the heavens, and having power above all things.'—*Gal.* E.T. 13.

6. *Gal.* E.T. 12; *W.A.* XL.1; 78f.: *deus incarnatus et humanus deus.*

7. *Gal.* E.T. 13.

8. *W.A.* X.1; 208.22ff.

9. *Gal.* E.T. 12.

10. *Römerbr.* 10.15ff.

11. *W.A.* I.613.23.

12. ibid. 362.8.

13. 'Reason', which 'delights in splendid things' (*W.A.* XLII.317.36), finds it 'a ridiculous thing, that the One God, the high Majesty, should become a man' (Nygren, *Agape and Eros*, II.ii.485).

14. Even for the believer, it is never an obvious thing, or something to be taken for granted, that God should have 'so loved the world . . .' ((John 316). cf. *M.H.B.* 371:

> Amazing love! how can it be
> That Thou, my God, shouldst die for me!

> 'Tis mystery all! The Immortal dies;
> Who can explore His strange design?

M.H.B. 66:

> Love moved Him to die,
> And on this we rely;
> He hath loved, He hath loved us: we cannot tell why.

15. Here again Luther anticipates modern thought. cf. W. Temple, *Nature, Man and God*, 317: 'There is no such thing as revealed truth. There are truths of revelation, that is to say, propositions which express the results of correct thinking concerning revelation; but they are not themselves directly-revealed.' ibid. 322: 'What is offered to man's apprehension in any specific Revelation is not truth concerning God but the living God Himself.'

16. It is interesting that in his comment on Galatians 13, when speaking of Christ as a 'mirror', he quotes Colossians 23: 'In whom are all the treasures of wisdom and knowledge *hidden*' (*Gal.* E.T. 12f.), while in his comment on Galatians 26, where he is explaining that 'we cannot be without veils in this life', he quotes 1 Corinthians 1312: 'For now we see in a *glass* darkly . . .' (op. cit. 60).

17. *E.A.* xlix.426.

18. *Gal.* E.T. 343(v.8); *W.A.* XXXIX.1; 462ff.; *W.A.* X.1; 11f.; etc.

19. *Gal.* E.T. 257(iv.4); *W.A.* XXXIX.1; 535f.; etc.

20. *Gal.* E.T. 98(ii.18): 'The example of Christ is to be followed. . . . What then followeth? Thou shalt then be saved and obtain everlasting life. Nay, not so. I grant indeed, that I ought to do good works, patiently to suffer troubles and afflictions, and to shed my blood also, if need be, for Christ's cause; but yet I am not justified, neither do I obtain salvation thereby.' cf. ibid. 163(iii.9).

21. *Gal.* E.T. 163: 'In this matter we must set nothing before our eyes, but Jesus Christ dying for our sins, and rising again for our righteousness; and Him must we apprehend by faith as a gift, not as an example.'

22. ibid. 257(iv.4).

23. ibid. 343(v.8).

24. cf. *W.A.* XXXIX.1; 533.4ff.

25. *Gal.* E.T. 92(ii.17).

26. ibid. 19(i.4).

27. ibid. 14(i.3).

28. loc. cit.; cf. *W.A.* XX.337f.

29. 'Nor is less care necessary in understanding that very common distinction of the Law of Nature, the written Law, and the Law of the Gospel. For since the Apostle here says, that they all agree in one sum and substance, Love is certainly the end of every Law, as he tells Timothy, I. 15. But Christ also (Matthew 7.12) expressly declares that what they call the Law of Nature—*All things which ye would that men should do to you, do ye also to them*—is the same with the Law and the Prophets. Now as He Himself teaches the Gospel, it is clear that these three Laws do not differ so much in their real purpose, as in the misunderstandings of their interpreters. Moreover this written Law, *Thou shalt love thy neighbour as thyself*, says exactly the same thing with the Law of Nature: *What ye wish that men should do to you*—for this is to love oneself—*even so do to them*:—this is plainly to love others, as oneself. But what else does the whole Gospel teach? Therefore there is one Law, which has spread to all ages, known to all men, written on the hearts of all: nor does it leave anyone excusable from the beginning to the end; although among the Jews ceremonies were added to it, and in other nations their own special laws, which did not bind the whole world—an obligation peculiar to this, which the Spirit writes on the hearts of all, without intermission.' (Quoted by J. C. Hare, *Vindication*, 60f., as from *Luther's Latin Works*, ed. Jen. p. 418.)

30. cf. *Gal.* E.T. 181(iii.12): 'the law commandeth nothing else but charity, as we may see by the text itself: "Thou shalt love the Lord thy God with all thy soul," etc.' cf. ibid. 169.

31. *W.A.* XI.279: 'Nature teaches, as love does, that I am to do what I would have done to me. . . . But where thou neglectest love and the natural law (*natur recht*), thou wilt never succeed in pleasing God, even though thou hadst swallowed all the law-books and lawyers . . . it is love and the natural law (*naturlich recht*) that gives such a free judgement.' cf. ibid. 272.11 and XXX.2; 562.10.

32. *Sermons*, 348: 'If we consider the commandments of Moses, they have respect altogether unto love.' *W.A.* XVIII.80f.: 'Thus it is not merely Moses' law . . . but also the natural law . . . as Paul teaches in Romans 2. Also Christ in Matthew 7, Himself sums up all the prophets and the law in this natural law: "What ye would that men should do to you, that do ye also to them." . . . So also does Paul in Romans 13 where he sums up all the commandments of Moses in love, as the natural law also naturally teaches: "Love thy neighbour as thyself" . . . Inasmuch as Moses' law and natural law are one thing, the law remains and is not abolished outwardly, but only through faith spiritually, which is nothing else but the fulfilling of the law.'

33. *Gal.* E.T. 178(iii.10).

34. *W.M.L.* VI.449; cf. *W.A.* XI.120.23ff.

35. *W.M.L.* VI.447f.; cf. *Römerbr.* 45.5ff.; 91.12ff.; 322.14ff.; *W.A.* XXXIX.1; 387.8ff.

36. *W.A.* I.461.28ff.: '[The Law] is called spiritual because it is fulfilled with the spirit alone and requires the spirit; that is, unless it is fulfilled with the heart and a cheerful will, it is not fulfilled. . . . Wherefore, whenever any law is heard, commanding this or that, we should always think and understand, that it commands us to do such things with a will, that is, freely without fear of penalty and with cheerfulness. . . .' *W.A.* XXXIX.1; 460.17ff.: 'As if the Law said: I am spiritual, that is, I require a pure and spiritual heart, I am not satisfied except with a cheerful heart and a spirit renewed by the Holy Spirit; thou indeed doest fine-seeming works, great and useful, but because thou doest them with an impure heart and spirit, or with love of thyself and fear of penalties, thou art not he that hath satisfied me.'

37. *Sermons*, 254.

38. *W.M.L.* II.125.

39. For a detailed analysis, see Nygren, *Agape and Eros*, II.ii.508-15.

40. *Römerbr.* 336f.; cf. 304f.

41. *Sermons*, 166f.; cf. 233f.

42. ibid. 168.

43. ibid. 169.

44. ibid. 166.

45. ibid. 169.

46. *W.M.L.* VI.448, 456, 458; *Gal.* E.T. 208ff.(iii.19), 222f.(iii.20), 230ff.(iii.25), *et passim.*

47. *W.A.* XXXIX.1; 555.20f.

48. *Gal.* E.T. 95(ii.17); 276(iv.8); 360f.(v.16).

49. ibid. 95; 137(iii.2). cf. *W.A.* I.105.14ff.: 'But this understanding of the Law spiritually is much more deadly, because it makes the Law impossible to fulfil . . . for no one is without anger, no one without *concupiscentia*; such we are from birth. But what will a man do, whither will he go, burdened with such an impossible Law?'

50. *W.A.* XXXIX.1; 515.16: 'God does not command impossible things. But man himself through sin has fallen into impossible things.' *W.A.* VI.24.12ff.: 'The Divine law shuts up all men under sin. It does not therefore follow that God has commanded impossible things. For what was impossible through the law of works, has been made possible by the law of faith.'

51. cf. *Gal.* E.T. 209(iii.19): ' . . . yea, this restraint sheweth plainly that the world is wicked and outrageous . . . for otherwise, it need not be bridled by laws that it should not sin.' If our will were in perfect harmony with God's, He might still give us commandments, of course, bidding us do this or that; but since we should have no other desire than to do as He willed us to do, such commandments would have a far different significance for us from that which the Law now has.

52. *Sermons*, 268.

53. *Gal.* E.T. 242(iii.27): 'The law then maketh us not children of God. . . . It cannot beget us into a new nature, or a new birth. . . .' cf. *W.A.* XXXIX.1; 372.7ff.; 202.2ff.: 'The works of the law are those that are done apart from faith by the human will. Which will the law either compels with threats and penalties, or allures with promises and rewards. Yet this will is never true and right, but always seeking the things that are its own.'

54. cf. *W.A.* I.368.21ff.:'But they say: God does not require this perfect commandment from us. I ask: From whom then does He require it? From stocks and stones? From beasts? . . . Therefore it is commanded for us, from us it is required. Through that most false understanding of this statement, "God does not require perfection", it has come to be said that anything done with less than perfect love is not sin; whereas the reason why He does not require it, is because He forgives, not because it is lawful and not sin.'

55. In the *Sermo de triplici iustitia, W.A.* II.43ff., Luther distinguishes three aspects of sin. The first is open defiance of the Law in one's conduct. The second is the inner desire of the will that is contrary to the Divine. The third covers all the 'works', including the 'good' ones, performed by that unregenerate will.

56. *Sermons*, 255.

57. *W.A.* I.227.16ff.

58. ibid. XXXIX.1; 253.26ff.

59. ibid. I.368.10ff.

60. ibid. 367.22ff. cf. *W.M.L.* III.376: 'For he who does unwillingly what he must, or thinks he must, sins in his heart.'

61. *Sermons*, 357.

62. *Gal.* E.T. 208(iii.19); *W.A.* XXXIX.1; 557.18ff.

63. *Gal.* E.T. 230f.(iii.23).

64. It is a fundamental principle of Luther's thought, that righteousness in relation to men is not necessarily righteousness in relation to God. cf. *W.A.* XXXIX.1; 247.18f.: 'There is a double forum, theological and political. The righteousness that justifies before Pilate, does not forthwith justify before God.' At the same time, it should be noticed that Luther is far from denying *all* value to 'political' righteousness, as he calls it; for he firmly maintains that it is willed by God. What he denies is that it can have any *justifying* value. It cannot furnish the ground of our acceptance with God.

65. *Gal.* E.T. 207, 209(iii.19).

66. *W.B.* 126.

67. *W.A.* XXXIX.1; 50.28f.

68. *W.A.* V.257; XXXIX.1; 555; *Tischr.* 178.nr.285. The simile is found in Augustine, *De civitate Dei*, 21.4.3.

69. *Social Teaching*, II.465-561.

70. ibid. 504.

71. cf. the two *Catechisms*; the *Treatise on Good Works* (*W.M.L.* I.184-285); the *Short Explanation* (*W.M.L.* II.354-67); etc.

72. *W.M.L.* II.364, 367.

73. *Ges. Aufs. I.*249. The document is the *Auslegung der Bergpredigt*, of which the Weimar editors say that its origin is unknown.

74. *Disput. p.* 12, *Drews Th.* 52-4 (1535)—quoted by Holl, op. cit. 249.

75. *W.A.* XVIII.81.7ff.; XVI.386.3ff., 390.1ff.—quoted by Holl, op. cit. 249f.

76. *W.A.* XLII.505.11ff.; cf. *W.M.L.* VI.371f.

77. *W.A.* XLII.503. 37ff., 505.11ff. (*Commentary on Genesis*, 1535-45).

78. *W.A.* I.436.14f.

79. op. cit., esp. 503ff.

80. See p. 75 *supra* for Luther's use of this expression.

81. cf. Bring, *Tro och g.*, 201f.

82. Luther equates *creatura* and *Ordnung*; cf. Törnvall, *Andl. o. världsl.* 173.

83. *W.A.* X.1.1; 308f. It should perhaps be noticed here that Luther speaks of two 'vocations'. Besides the one described above, there is also the call of the Gospel, in response to which a man becomes a Christian.

84. *W.A.* X.1.2; 41.5ff.—quoted from Wingren, *Kallelsen*, 132.

85. This is, of course, the root of Luther's objection to monasticism, and his justification for renouncing the monastic vows.

86. cf. *W.M.L.* III.241: 'Therefore, should you see that there is a lack of hangmen, beadles, judges, lords, or princes, and find that you are qualified, you should offer your services and seek the place, that necessary government may by no means be despised and become inefficient or perish.'

87. Our modern conception of the State is much narrower and more rigid than Luther's *politia*. *Politia* is one of the two essential means by which God governs the world; the other being *religio*, or *ecclesia*, the 'Church'. But neither *ecclesia* nor *politia*, it should be noted, is conceived essentially in terms of political or ecclesiastical institutions. They are rather concrete expressions of the Law and the Gospel respectively, which are the twin forms, as we shall see, of the eternally creative Word of God.

88. *W.A.* XL.3; 20: *Politia creata in paradiso*, '*Politia* was created in Paradise'. The argument of R. E. Davies, *The Problem of Authority*, 51, that the State in Luther's view is infralapsarian, appears to depend upon the identification of *ubirkeytt* ('government'— perhaps better rendered as 'the powers that be') with *politia*, and the equation of both with the State. It would be quite possible for Luther to hold without contradiction that *ubirkeytt* is necessitated by the Fall, whereas *politia* was created before it.

89. cf. *W.M.L.* III.249: 'If the State and its sword are a divine service, as was proved above, that which the State needs in order to wield the sword must also be a divine service. . . . Therefore, when such duties are performed, not with the intention of seeking one's own ends . . . there is no peril in them. . . . For, as was said, love of neighbour seeks not its own, considers not how great or small, but how profitable and how needful for neighbour or community the works are.' cf. p. 180 *infra*, n. 55. See also my *The State as a Servant of God*, 34ff., 41ff.

90. For instance, whether *ubirkeytt* (see n. 88 *supra*) itself was or was not a feature of the *politia* that was created in Paradise, its legislative and coercive functions can certainly be said to be developments necessitated by the Fall. Such new developments, as Luther sees them, are manifestations of the creative activity of God; for creation in his view is not simply something that happened once long ago at the beginning of time, but something upon which God is ceaselessly engaged.

91. cf. Bring, *Tro och g.* 185; Törnvall, *Andl. o. världsl.* 82.

92. Holl suggests, rightly, that Troeltsch has been misled by his determination to make Luther's Christianity conform to what he chooses to regard as the 'Church-type' as opposed to the 'sect-type'. It can also be said that Troeltsch has read into Luther far too much of Melanchthon and later Lutheranism; cf. Bring, *Tro och g.* 209.

93. Troeltsch, op. cit. 469f.

94. ibid. 471.

95. ibid. 495.

96. ibid. 496.

97. *Tischr.* 316.nr.534; cf. Wingren, *Kallelsen*, 20.

98. Troeltsch, op. cit. 473. A detailed investigation of Luther's conception of creation is much to be desired. Troeltsch is quite right in saying that Luther has 'a new conception of Nature'; but the account he gives of it is very unsatisfactory.

99. cf. Bring, *Tro och g.* 33.

100. As Luther sees it, the Gospel governs the believer's 'conscience', the Law his 'flesh'; or to put it another way: in so far as a man has true faith, he is free from the Law—free to fulfil it!—but inasmuch as sinful impulses remain in him, even though they are forgiven, he is under obligation not to give way to them, and in that sense is subject to the Law.

101. See, e.g., his exposition of Galatians 3:13 (E.T. 185-95), and 4:4 (E.T. 255ff.), and of the Second Article of the Creed in his *Catechisms* and elsewhere; cf. also the same theme in his hymns (e.g. *M.H.B.* 210 and 494).

102. *Gal.* E.T. 6(1.1): 'Christ's victory is the overcoming of the law, of sin, our flesh, the world, the devil, death, hell, and all evils; and this His victory He hath given unto us.' ibid. 190: 'Therefore all they which believe not, do lack this inestimable benefit and glorious victory.' cf. ibid. 102ff.(ii.19).

103. ibid. 190: 'To abolish sin, to destroy death, to take away the curse in Himself: and again to give righteousness, to bring life to light, and to give the blessing, are the works of the divine power only and alone . . . wherefore they that deny the divinity of Christ, do lose all Christianity, and become altogether Gentiles and Turks. We must learn therefore diligently the article of justification (as I often admonish you). For all the other articles of our faith are comprehended in it: and if that remain sound, then are all the rest sound. Wherefore, when we teach that men are justified by Christ, that Christ is the conqueror of sin and death, and the everlasting curse: we witness therewithal that He is naturally and substantially God.'

104. ibid. 45f.(i.16): 'The madness and blindness of the Papists hath been so great, that of the Gospel they have made a law of charity, and of Christ a lawmaker, giving more strait and heavy commandments than Moses himself.' ibid. 254(iv.4): 'We . . . which have been so nusled up in this pernicious doctrine of the Papists . . . although we confessed with our mouth that Christ redeemed us from the tyranny of the law, yet in very deed in our hearts we thought Him to be a lawgiver, a tyrant, and a judge, more terrible than Moses himself.'

105. *W.A.* XXXVI.159ff.; XXXVII.63ff.; XLVI.305ff.; XLIX.310ff.

106. *Christus Victor*, cap. vi.

107. *Dualismen, passim.*

108. *Work of Christ*, 157f.

109. *Luthers Theologie*, I.365f.

110. *W.A.* XXXIX.1; 348.29: 'The Law and the exposure of sin, or the revelation of wrath, are convertible terms.'

111. Satan, as Luther conceives him, has a semi-independent existence, but is ultimately an instrument of the Wrath of God.

112. *W.A.* XLIV.468 (*Commentary on Genesis*, 1535-45): 'Nor must we dispute here about satisfaction, as the Papists are wont to do, as if God required satisfaction for sins, for there certainly is none. Even Joseph does not exact it from his brethren, although he could with entire justice put them to death on account of the injustice done to him. But he does not do so, because he knows that there is no satisfaction in the human race for sins, except civil satisfaction, which the magistrate requires. But that has nothing to do with theology, in which Christ our Lord is the only victim, by which the wrath of God has been satisfied.'

113. *W.A.* XXIV.1; 301ff.; cf. *E.A.* xi.306 (quoted in Herrman, *Communion*, 138).

114. *S.W.* I.137: '. . . when thou hearest of satisfactions, do thou determine to speak of no other satisfaction than that which is the true satisfaction, and which is called, and is, the satisfaction of faith—that Jesus Christ bore thy sins.'. . . But what does the Monk? What does the Turk? What does the Jew? They perform many works, they devise many ways whereby they endeavour to serve God, but with this view and confidence:—that they shall cleanse themselves from their sins and appease God. And what else is this but to deny Christ, who was for this end appointed of God, that He might make satisfaction for us . . .?'

115. *Sermons*, 57—quoted in text, p. 122.

116. cf. *Gal.* E.T. 99(ii.18): 'In their confessions they make no mention of faith or the merit of Christ, but they teach and set forth the satisfactions and merits of men.'

117. *S.W.* I.93: 'For there is only one ground of justification:—the merit of Christ, or free mercy. . . .'

118. *W.A.* II.427: 'The merits of Christ are spirit and life, are grace and truth, as John 1 says, Grace and truth came by Jesus Christ.'

119. Bring, *Dualismen*, 179: '*Meritum* here means the same as *sola gratia*.'

120. There are passages, it is true, which speak of Christ's work as a satisfaction made to God; and Luther may well have used this idea at times for pastoral purposes. He would then be adopting deliberately the standpoint of those to whom he was speaking, knowing that they thought in such terms. His intention would be to emphasize the objectivity of Christ's work, so as to release troubled consciences from preoccupation with themselves by pointing them to Christ and saying, in effect: 'Your acceptance with God does not depend on *your* merits, but on Christ's.' At the same time, Bring, *Dualismen*, 180ff., gives considerable evidence that many of the passages in Luther that represent Christ's work from such a legalistic standpoint are found in texts that have suffered from the work of editors.

121. *W.M.L.* I.169. (*italics* mine).

122. *W.A.* I.309: 'The merit of Christ can be of advantage to us in three ways. First, by being the sum of our confidence and the head of righteousness, according to that saying of Paul: Who hath been made unto us righteousness from God, that is, who has made His righteousness ours, just as He made our sins His.'

123. *Gal.* E.T. 84f.—quoted in text, p. 122f.

124. ibid. 117(ii.20): 'Let us learn therefore to give a true definition of Christ, not as the school-divines do, and such as seek righteousness by their own works, which make Him a new lawgiver, who abolishing the old law hath established a new. . . . But let us define Him as Paul here doth: namely, that He is the Son of God, who not for our desert or any righteousness of ours, but of His own free mercy offered up Himself a sacrifice for us sinners, that He might sanctify us for ever.'

125. *W.A.* XVII.2; 228ff.

126. ibid. XL.2; 465f.

127. ibid. XVII.2; 206, 21ff.

128. *W.A.* XLII.539f.; XLV.398. *W.A.* VIII.442: 'What is remission of sins but grace, salvation, inheritance, life, peace, eternal glory in God Himself? And thou, mad and ungodly Papist, by thy sacrifice makest for thyself another god in the Eucharist! Dost thou not see that all sacrificers are idolaters, and that they commit idolatry as often as they sacrifice?'

129. *Gal.* E.T. 116(ii.20)—quoted in text below.

130. If there are passages in Luther which seem to represent Christ's sacrifice as a propitiatory offering to God, the following points should be borne in mind. (1) Luther's typical practice is to set Christ's sacrifice as the work of God over against the works of men, in order to exclude legalism; and therefore Christ's sacrifice clearly means *sola gratia*. (2) Most of the passages that suggest a legalistic view, according to Bring, *Dualismen*, 194f., are found in texts edited and published by others than Luther himself. (3) In speaking of sacrifice, as of merit and satisfaction, Luther deliberately adopts current terminology, but not with the meaning currently attached to it; and therefore, even when he expresses himself in legalistic language without expressly repudiating legalism, we are not entitled to assume that a legalistic view is implied, but should consider both what he says and why he says it, in the light of the organic unity of his thought.

131. *Sermons*, 57.

132. *Gal.* E.T. 116(ii.20).

133. ibid. 84.f.(ii.16).

134. *W.A.* VIII.442: 'Finally, that He may take from thee the sacrilegious thought of placating Him . . . He Himself marks and shows to thee that whereby He is to be, and is, placated, by saying: "Which is given for you, Which is shed for you." . . . There is one onliest and uniquest sacrifice whereby He is placated (so to speak).'

135. For further discussion of this subject, see pp. 155–60 *infra*.

136. The failure to recognize this fact—although Luther repeatedly insists that God in Christ not merely pardons, but also conquers sin—is responsible for a good deal of misinterpretation and mistaken criticism of his doctrine of justification by faith.

137. See *Gal.* E.T. *passim.*

138. ibid. 257(iv.4).

139. ibid. 190f.(iii.13).

140. *W.M.L.* V.223: 'The immortal God becomes something that must die, suffer, and have all the human *idiomata*. What would that man be, with whom God is personally united, if He were not to have true human *idiomata*?'

141. *W.A.* X.1; 208.22ff.

142. cf. *W.M.L.* v.222ff.; *Gal.* E.T. 177(iii.10).

143. *E.A.* xix.15.

144. *Ges. Aufs. I.* 72.

145. Luther uses the idea of *communicatio idiomatum* in other than specifically Christological connexions; e.g., in describing how the Christian can be 'at once both flesh and spirit, righteous and a sinner, good and evil'—*Römerbr.* 172.22ff. He also uses it in illustration of the relation between faith and works—*Gal.* E.T. 177.

146. *W.M.L.* II.320ff.; *Gal.* E.T. 110(ii.20); *W.M.L.* III.193.

147. *W.A.* XXIII.702ff.—quoted from Bring, *Dualismen,* 147f.

148. *W.M.L.* V.223.

149. *Gal.* E.T. 189(iii.13).

150. ibid. 188f.

151. cf. *W.M.L.* V.223: 'We Christians must know that if God is not in the scale to give it weight, our side of the scale sinks to the ground. That is to say, if it cannot be said that God, not a mere man, died for us, we are lost. . . . He could not be in the scale, however, unless he had become a man like us. . . . For in His own nature, God cannot die; but when God and man are united in one Person, then, if the man dies with whom God is one thing, or one Person, then it can truly be called God's death.'

152. *Gal.* E.T. 186(iii.13).

153. ibid. 191.

154. loc. cit.

155. ibid. 186.

156. ibid. 187.

157. ibid. 186.

158. *W.A.* XLIV.697: 'For He not only redeemed us, but also claimed us as His own by right, so that the Devil and hell were compelled to let Him go by strict right, because they had slain the innocent Son of God. . . . Why didst thou, O Devil, death, hell, slay the unoffending? We have a law, they said, and according to the law He ought to die, because He made Himself the Son of God. Look upon Him then, rising from the dead and triumphing over you: I am the Son of God, I am an un-conquered Person. What now, Satan, law, death, hell? Death is swallowed up in victory, etc. I have lost, cry they all together; they acknowledge themselves vanquished with supreme and full right and most justly.' cf. ibid. XXXII.39ff.; XL.1; 565 (*Gal.* E.T. 255).

159. For Luther, death is 'the devil's henchman'. cf. *W.A.* XLV.367; where he says that the devil has raised a banner on which is written: 'I am a god and prince of the world; and that it may be true, I have a fellow with me, death, who devours the whole world.' The devil and his henchman were deceived by the humanity of Christ, which Luther describes in Patristic fashion as the bait that concealed the fish-hook of His divinity; cf. *W.A.* XX.334f., XXXII.41f., XL.1; 417, etc. The devil had swallowed up in death all men, great and small; and he thought he had

an excellent tit-bit in Christ. But this tit-bit disagreed with him as grass with a dog, and he was forced to yield up Christ as the great fish yielded up Jonah. Christ is true God and could not be holden of death (*W.A.* XX.334f.).

Grotesque as Luther's imagery is, we should not allow its crudity to obscure its significance. Underlying it there is a religious conception according to which humanity as a whole has fallen victim to the power of sin and evil and is under a curse that it is beyond human power to remove. For those who repudiate such a conception, of course, Luther's imagery will appear not only in very bad taste, but probably quite meaningless as well.

160. It should perhaps be emphasized here that, for Luther, the hiddenness of God does not refer to God as He is apart from the revelation of Himself in Christ, as if in Christ He were not at all 'hidden'. Even where God is revealed, the revelation is apprehended by faith, not by sight. It is not beyond dispute that the suffering Son of Man is God incarnate.

161. For the rest of this paragraph, see Luther's expositions of Galatians 313 and 44; cf. *Sermons*, 394ff.

162. It is simple fact (1) that our Lord became incarnate by His own free choice, not at the behest of any law; (2) that by becoming incarnate, He entered into a legalistic situation, for Judaism was the religion of law *par excellence*; (3) that He observed the provisions of the Jewish Law—was circumcised, kept the Sabbath, paid the Temple-tax (Matthew 1724ff.); (4) that He was nevertheless attacked and put to death in the name of the Law, and that the ultimate cause of this was His friendship for publicans and sinners. It is therefore not a very far-fetched idea when Luther represents the Law itself as assaulting Christ, especially when he makes it clear that he is using a figure of speech; cf. *Gal.* E.T. 255f.: 'And to make the matter more . . . apparent, he [Paul] is wont to set forth the law by a figure called *prosopopoeia*, as a certain mighty person, which had condemned and killed Christ.' Historically, it was Jewish legalism that crucified Christ; but for Luther legalism is typical of the natural man, whatever his religion, and Christ's conflict with the Law is something that concerns the whole world. In this, too, Luther is not far wrong.

163. *Gal.* E.T. 191.

164. *W.M.L.* III.178.

165. *Gal.* E.T. 6(i.1).

166. ibid. 191.

167. *Gal.* E.T. 20(i.4); cf. *W.A.* XLII.296.19f.: '. . . . the Son of God, who paints for us the mind and will of His Father, that He wills not to be angry with sinners, but to have mercy on them through the Son.'

168. ibid.22.

169. ibid. 360(v.16).

170. *W.A.* XI.225.35ff.

171. ibid. 5ff.; cf. 226.5f.: 'So Scripture preaches the divine nature and substance. By this Word He portrays Himself.'

172. *Römerbr.* 338.28ff.

173. *S.W.* I.173.

174. *Sermons*, 58; *W.A.* II.140.36f.

175. *W.A.* I.341.36ff.

176. *W.A.* XXXVI.426.34ff.

177. *W.M.L.* II.420; cf. *W.A.* XXXVI.424.16ff.: 'If anyone would paint and aptly portray God, then he must draw a picture of pure love, as if the Divine nature were nothing but a furnace and fire of such love, which fills heaven and earth. And again, if it were possible to paint and picture love, we should have to make such a picture as would be not of works nor human, yea not of angels nor heavenly, but God Himself.'

178. *Sermons*, 113.

179. For *quellende Liebe* cf. *W.A.* XXXVI.360.8ff. The simile of a perennial spring is a favourite of Luther's for describing the freedom and spontaneity of Divine love and goodness. cf. *W.B.* 117: '[God] is like an everlasting and inexhaustible spring, which, the more it flows and runs over, the more it gives forth'; ibid. 37: 'He is an eternal source which overflows with pure goodness.'

180. *S.W.* I.474.

181. *W.A.* I.365; cf. *W.A.* XI.115.12ff.: 'Here you have the nature and habit of true divine love. It does not have good done to it, but does good itself, etc. . . . If it is divine . . . it loves, not for its own advantage, but its neighbour's, for it loves the poor, the weak, etc.'

182. *S.W.* I.474.

183. ibid. 474.

184. ibid. 476: '[Christ] gives a still more convincing proof of the nature of charity; seeing that, He exercises it toward those, on whom what benefit soever you bestow, is lost; and from whom, if you do them a kindness, you meet with nothing but evil in return.' cf. *W.A.* XXXVII.148.7ff.

185. For *verlorene Liebe* cf. *W.A.* XXXVI.435.30ff. cf. *W.A.* XXXVII.148.1ff.: 'So Christ did . . . and so the Father still does, for His sun still shines on the good and the evil. But what if He should say: . . . they are ungrateful; I will let it shine no longer and will let them die?' cf. *W.A.* XXXVI.460.6ff.: 'He gives . . . all things to all men, and what has He? That they curse Him and crucify His Son. That is a thanks written with black ink. Christ sweats a bloody sweat, etc., and then is rewarded, alas, as He has not deserved; for they say that we are saved by our works and not by Christ.' cf. *W.A.* XLII.103.12ff.: '. . . Let us be God's children and do good even to our enemies, as God has done and still does to us, His enemies and evildoers.'

186. *S.W.* I.470: '[Christ] treated Judas as a friend, but Judas did not treat Him as a friend: for Judas accounted Him an enemy and hated Him. . . . Love must always be round, and be kind toward all men alike.'

187. For *amor crucis* cf. *W.A.* I.365—quoted p. 69(n.50) *supra*.

188. ibid.

189. *Sermons*, 58.

190. *Gal.* E.T. 274(iv.8f.).

191. *Gal.* E.T. 11(i.3).

192. *Expertus loquor*; cf. *Gal.* E.T. 12, 19(i.4); *W.A.* VI.562.11f.

193. *Gal.* E.T. 11f.

194. ibid. 274f.(iv.8f.): 'This is the highest wisdom, righteousness, and religion, that reason can judge of; which is common to all nations, to the Papists, Jews, Turks, Heretics, etc. They can go no higher than the Pharisee did (Luke 18.11f.). . . . For the Turk thinketh the self-same thing that the Charterhouse monk doth: namely, If I do this or that work, God will be merciful unto me; if I do not, He will be angry.' ibid. 16(i.4): 'Man's reason would fain bring and present unto God a feigned and counterfeit sinner. . . . It would bring him that is whole, and not him that hath need of a physician.' *S.W.* I.188: 'For reason and human sense argues thus:—I feel that I have sinned . . . therefore I have an angry God; therefore all grace is taken away from me.' It is interesting to notice that Wesley makes precisely the same criticism of 'reason' as Luther does, in *Works*, I.96 (*Journal*, May 1738).

195. *Gal.* E.T. 178(iii.10): 'For he walketh in the presumption of his own righteousness against God, whilst he will be justified by man's free-will and reason . . . they work many things, but in the presumption of their own righteousness . . . as the Pharisee did (Luke 18) and as Paul did before his conversion.'

196. *Gal.* E.T. 269(iv.6): 'For men do not lean to the promises of God, but to their own works and merits. Therefore they cannot be assured of the goodwill of God toward them, but must needs doubt thereof, and so at length despair.'

197. *S.W.* I.192.

198. *Gal.* E.T. 266(iv.6): '. . . that devilish opinion of the whole kingdom of the Pope, which taught that a man ought to be uncertain and to stand in doubt of the favour of God toward him. If this opinion be received, then Christ profiteth nothing. For he that doubted of God's favour toward him, must needs doubt also of the promises of God, and so consequently of the will of God, and of the benefits of Christ, namely that He was born, suffered, died, and rose again for us, etc. But there can be no greater blasphemy against God, than to deny His promises, to deny God Himself, to deny Christ, etc.' Notice that the assurance Luther wishes us to have in place of this doubt is an assurance about God, not about ourselves.

199. *W.A.* X.1; 106.3f.: 'Divine righteousness, that is, the divine grace, which justifies us through faith.' *S.W.* I.173: '. . . this term "righteousness" cost me much labour. For they used generally to explain it thus:—that righteousness signifieth that truth, whereby God condemns according to desert, or judges the undeserving. And they set righteousness in opposition to that mercy, whereby those who believe are saved. This exposition is most perilous. . . . Wherefore, remember ye, that the righteousness of God is that, by which we are justified, or receive remission of sins.'

200. *Sermons*, 327: 'Whosoever take not away sins, they are no gods, but idols; . . . for other gods will find and not bring godliness, but the Almighty God doth not find it, but bring it.' *S.W.* I.98: 'For what would God be, if He knew nothing else but to frighten and destroy? This is the work of Satan, of sin, and of a man's own conscience. But to be God, is to be able to do, and to do, something above all this—to comfort, to lift up, to give life in the midst of all these perils, and to declare that He knows how to do, and can do, more than Satan, the law, and I, know and can do.'

201. *W.A.* XXXIX.289.6ff.: 'God does all things and wills all things to be done in redemption according to His revealed will, which He has revealed abundantly enough in that He has created heaven and earth, though supremely in that He has given us His Son.'

202. ibid. XL.1; 462: *omnes creaturae dant testimonium nostrae theologiae.*

203. ibid. V.38.11ff.

204. ibid. III.77.3ff.

205. ibid. X.1, 2; 180.8ff.

206. *S.W.* I.447: 'For the glory of God is, that He bestows blessings with a certain bounty and overflowing abundance.' *Römerbr.* 339.17: 'the wondrous glory of God, that is glorified when sinners are received.' *Gal.* E.T. 18(i.4): 'thou preachest unto me the glory of God; for thou puttest me in mind of God's fatherly goodness toward me, wretched and damned sinner.'

207. *W.A.* IV.269.25: 'But this it is to be God: not to receive good things, but to give them, and so to requite good for evil.' *W.A.* XLII.585.4: '. . . just as God is God, that is, beneficent and good. . . .' *W.A.* X.1; 100.19: 'Divine nature is nothing else but pure beneficence.' *S.W.* I.191: 'God, in His proper form, is such a God who loves the afflicted, who pities the broken, who pardons the fallen, and comforts the languid.' *Sermons*, 134: 'Herein God showeth His majesty and grace in this life, that He taketh away and pardoneth men's sins.'

208. *W.A.* XXXIX.1; 319.15.

CHAPTER FIVE

THE DOCTRINE OF THE WORD

17. CHRIST THE WORD

LUTHER often asserts that there can be no right understanding and no genuine worship of God without His Word.[1] This means nothing essentially different from his contention, already discussed, that there is no true knowledge of God apart from Christ. Christ and the Word are virtually interchangeable terms for Luther.[2] At times, however, he appears to identify the Word with the written word of Scripture or even with the spoken word of the Christian preacher. This is at first sight confusing; but it constitutes no real difficulty, if we consider what he understands by Scripture and by Christian preaching.

'In the whole Scripture', Luther holds, 'there is nothing else but Christ, either in plain words or involved words,'[3] Although there are passages that are obscure and difficult of exegesis, yet the content of Scripture as a whole is perfectly plain, and it is nothing else but the revelation of God in Christ.[4] This is true no less of the Old Testament than of the New, though in a rather different way. The former must be interpreted in the light of the latter before we can see how 'the entire Old Testament refers to Christ and agrees with Him';[5] and this is what ought to be done, for the law and the prophets are not rightly preached and understood, unless we find Christ wrapped in them.[6] They are the 'swaddling clothes and manger in which He was wrapped and laid'; they 'truly contain Him', 'speak only of Him and give testimony of Him and are His certain sign as He Himself says, John 539'.[7] On the other hand, 'the New Testament is nothing else but an opening and revelation of the Old Testament', and 'we see in the Apostles how all their preaching was nothing else but the exposition of the Scripture and building themselves on it'.[8] They refer us back to the writings of Moses and the prophets, 'that we may read and see how Christ is wrapped in the swaddling clothes and laid in the manger, that is, how He is contained in the Scripture of the prophets'.[9] Quite strictly speaking, Luther can say, only the Old Testament is 'Scripture', for the content of the New is

L

essentially something to be preached rather than written down.[10]
Few of the apostles wrote, and those who did wrote little. Their
reason for writing was simply to give a true account of Christian
teaching, which would exclude false versions of it.[11] 'Christ',
Luther therefore says, 'has two witnesses of His birth and government. One is the Scripture, or word comprised in letters; the
other is the voice, or word spoken out through the mouth.'[12]

But how, more precisely, does Luther conceive of Old Testament
Scripture and New Testament preaching as witnessing to Christ?
In his *Preface* to the two Testaments[13] he makes it quite clear what
he considers to be their essential message. The New Testament
primarily sets forth the Gospel, which is nothing else but 'good
tidings' of how Christ has conquered the 'Tyrants' and broken
their power over those they held captive. That is a reason why it
is more appropriately proclaimed by word of mouth than simply
committed to writing. It is joyful news of a victory won. It is also
called a 'Testament', because Christ before His death bequeathed
this 'evangelical and divine news' to be preached to all the world,
so giving to all who believe it a share in His victory.[14] This is not,
however, the whole content of the New Testament books, for
Christ and His apostles also 'give many commandments and
doctrines and expound the law'; but these are not the main thing.[15]
When we turn to the Old Testament, we find that it is primarily a
book of laws and commandments, 'which teaches what men are
to do and not to do, and gives besides examples of how these laws
are kept or broken'.[16] It is called a 'Testament' because 'in it God
promises and bequeathes to the people of Israel the land of
Canaan, if they keep it'; but it is a legal covenant, resting upon
men's works, not upon God's grace.[17] Yet there is grace in the
Old Testament, for it not only contains many direct promises of
the Gospel, of which Luther gives examples,[18] but there are also
parts of it that are to be understood allegorically, in the manner
illustrated by New Testament writers, as referring specifically to
Christ.[19] Furthermore, even the Law in the Old Testament can
be said in a sense to have a Christological reference. For, as we
have already heard Luther say, salvation under the Old Covenant
was by faith in 'Christ to come'; and he now explains that the
ultimate purpose of the Law was to make men aware of their sin
and helplessness and their need of the promised Saviour.[20]

It is not difficult to understand the relation between the two

Testaments as Luther conceives it. The Old is related to the New, first, as foreshadowing it by its promises of the coming Saviour, and secondly, as preparing the way for it by revealing through the commandments man's need of salvation. This two-fold relationship can be summed up as that between the Law and Gospel,[21] provided we do not forget the promises in the Old Testament, on the one hand, and the commandments and interpretation of the Law in the New, on the other. But in fact, as we shall see in a later section, the Law and the Gospel are ultimately inseparable; for the latter always presupposes the former, and the former, rightly understood, actually implies the latter. It is important to remember this especially when New Testament preaching is defined simply as the proclamation of the Gospel. The Gospel teaches nothing but Christ,[22] Luther asserts again and again; but Christ has two 'offices', we may recall, as Saviour and as interpreter of the Law. Of these, the former alone constitutes the Gospel in the strict sense,[23] but it is not to be preached alone. 'God has instituted', as Luther does not allow us to forget, 'two ministries of preaching'[24]—the Law and the Gospel—and both of these are words of God.[25] When Luther speaks of the Word of God, therefore, he means, on the one hand, the Law as interpreted by Christ, and on the other, the Gospel as constituted by Christ, who is Himself the Word. This Word is the essential content of both Old Testament Scripture and New Testament preaching, through which He is set forth and presented to men.

Now this setting forth of Christ, it is important to notice, is never a mere narration of historical happenings, and still less is it the exposition of abstract doctrine.

To me [Luther says] it is not simply an old song of an event that happened fifteen hundred years ago; it is something more than an event that happened once—for it is a gift and a bestowing that endures for ever.[26]

In order to see what this means, we must first remind ourselves that Christ as the Word of God is the concrete expression of the Divine will of love. This love, which is in God's heart from all eternity, has found its fullest and deepest and most decisive utterance in the Word incarnate. But it has also spoken—'by divers portions and in divers manners'—in the creative Word,[27] in the word of commandment given to Adam in Paradise,[28] in the Commandments and Promises of the Old Testament; and it speaks still to us in the apostolic preaching of the Redeemer, whether as written in the New Testament books or as spoken by the mouth of a contemporary of our own. This means that, for Luther, wherever there is a manifestation or utterance of the Divine will of love, there is the living Word of God. But where in our contemporary world is this Word of love more clearly and decisively spoken to us than in and through the words of the 'two witnesses', Scripture and Christian preaching, which bring to our eyes and ears the message of Christ, incarnate, crucified, risen, and reigning 'for us'?[29]

In the light of what has now been said, it is understandable that Luther can speak at times as if he simply equated the written words of the Bible, or the spoken words that convey the biblical message, with the Word of God itself. Yet that is never quite his meaning. For him, the Word is always fundamentally Christ, even when he does not explicitly say so; and although his exegesis may not be modern, and he can find Christ in what seem to us unlikely places, yet he is no 'fundamentalist'.[30] The creaturely words, whether written or spoken, are for him rather the vehicle or media of the Divine, creative Word, by which God addresses Himself directly and personally to us.[31] Apostles and preachers are *larvae Dei*, and we are to have regard, Luther says, not so much to them as to 'Christ speaking in them, and the word which they bring and preach unto us'.[32] They are 'the mouth of our Lord Jesus Christ, and the instrument whereby He openly preacheth the Word';[33] and since, as we have seen, Christ the Word is the utterance of God's own heart, 'when thou hearest the Word,' Luther says, 'then thou hearest God'.[34]

18. THE WORD AS LAW AND GOSPEL

The Word of God, we have heard Luther say, comes to us in two forms, as Law and as Gospel. Both of these are to be preached, but they must never be confused, and it is the mark of a true theologian to be able rightly to distinguish between them. They differ from one another as a demand made upon us differs from a gift offered to us. They are inseparable, but everything in our theology depends upon which of them we take as our starting-point. It is of vital importance that the Law should be understood in the light of the Gospel, and not the Gospel in the light of the Law.

Now Luther frequently represents the Law and the Gospel as entirely hostile to one another. He numbers the Law among the 'Tyrants' that have been vanquished by Christ, and speaks of it in terms which, as is well known, John Wesley denounced as blasphemous.[35] If Wesley had read his copy of the *Commentary on Galatians* with a little more care, however, he would have noticed that Luther also repeatedly asserts with Saint Paul that the Law is 'holy and righteous and good'. Knowing that he seems to speak blasphemously of the Law, he explains that he does not mean it to be despised, for 'it ought to be had in great estimation'.[36] He describes it as 'the perfect rule of the will of God';[37] says that it is given 'to be a light and a help to man, and to show him what he ought to do, and what to leave undone';[38] and declares that, next to faith, it is 'the best, the greatest and most excellent of all corporal blessings of the world'.[39] Rightly understood, the Law belongs together with the Gospel and serves the purposes of the Gospel; but it can be misapplied, so that it becomes positively hostile to these and then 'it is no more the holy Law of God, but a false and devilish doctrine . . . and therefore must be rejected'.[40]

For Luther, the Law is both good and evil, divine and devilish; but it is so, as he is careful to say, 'in divers respects'.[41] In itself, as an expression of the will of God, it is divine; but when it is allowed to prescribe the terms and conditions of justification, then it is devilish. When it governs a man's 'conscience' and becomes determinative of his relationship to God, it is a Tyrant. Good as the Law is, and good as the works of the Law in themselves are, they cannot justify us.[42] Regarded as the way to salvation, they are in fact a hindrance to it, and therefore where the religious relationship is in question (*in loco iustificationis*), they have no place.

But out of the matter of justification [Luther says] we ought with Paul to think reverential of the Law, to commend it highly, to call it holy, righteous, good, spiritual, and divine (Romans 7 14). Out of the case of conscience we should make a God of it, but in the case of conscience it is a very devil.[43]

That is why, as he points out, Saint Paul himself applies 'such odious and, as it appeareth to reason, blasphemous terms to the

Law, which is a divine doctrine revealed from heaven'.[44] When
Luther speaks 'blasphemously' of the Law, therefore, he is simply
repudiating religious legalism and the 'pernicious opinion of the
Law, that it justifieth and maketh men righteous before God'.[45]
The reason for this we have already seen. It is not merely that
fallen man, as Luther maintains, is incapable of fulfilling the real
requirements of the Law. It is rather that God's dealings with
men are not governed by legal considerations, so that even if a
man could and did fulfil the Law, he would not be justified
thereby.[46] The attempt, therefore, to secure salvation by 'good
works', or 'the righteousness of the Law', means in effect a refusal
to let God deal with us in His own way, a refusal to let Him be God.

When Luther sets the Law and the Gospel in sharp opposition
to one another, there are two points in particular that we must
bear in mind if we are not to misinterpret him. In the first place,
it cannot be too strongly emphasized that he is not opposing ethics
to religion. That is something which Luther never does. What he
is doing is to contrast the Law as one kind of *religious and ethical*
principle with the Gospel as a *religious and ethical* principle of a
quite different kind. Or to put it in other terms, he is contrasting
two ways of salvation, the legal and the evangelical, the false and
the true. In the second place, it is most important to notice that,
strongly as Luther maintains that the Law cannot justify, he no
less strongly insists that it is not therefore useless.[47] *As a way of
salvation* it has been abolished by Christ. We are saved by grace,
not by the works of the Law. But the Law itself is not abrogated.
The will of God is still the will of God. Antinomianism is therefore
as great an evil as legalism. Indeed, it is a greater, for if those
who seek salvation by the works of the Law 'are rightly called the
Devil's martyrs',[48] those who flout the Law because they have
learnt they are not saved by it 'are become bondslaves of the
Devil, and are seven times worse . . . than they were before'.[49]

For both sorts [Luther asserts] do offend against the Law; the one on
the right hand, which will be justified by the Law, and the other on
the left hand, which will be clean delivered from the Law. We must
therefore keep the highway, so that we neither reject the Law, nor
attribute more unto it than we ought to do.[50]

When the Law is not regarded as a way of salvation, it 'stands
with the promises, and serves the promises and grace'.[51] Yet

it must still be clearly distinguished from the Gospel, as a demand from a gift. There is a time for each, Luther says, and each must be allowed to fulfil its own proper function. The Law has a double 'use' and the Gospel a two-fold 'office', which must be maintained in their due order and proportion.

Of the two uses of the Law, Luther describes one as 'civil', or 'political', the other as 'spiritual'.[52] With regard to the former, it cannot be too much emphasized that he is not thinking in terms of a fixed, statutory code of laws. Even in its 'political' use, the Law means for him essentially the will of God as it is expressed in that whole series of 'offices' and 'stations', which we have already had occasion to consider.[53] All the neighbourly relationships in which we human beings are placed—as parents, children, teachers, scholars, masters, servants, rulers, subjects, and so forth—make manifold and ever-varying demands upon us, which Luther sees as concrete expressions of the Law of God.[54] Written, enacted laws are necessary in this sinful world, because the 'offices' are liable to abuse; but such laws also vary with time and place and circumstance, and they possess no claim to validity except as they are in harmony with the Law that is at once natural and Divine.[55] For Luther, the Law is always something much wider and more fundamental than mere State legislation, although this may be included in it. It is something so inextricably woven into the very fabric of human life—nay, into the texture of the universe itself—that no one can be quite ignorant of it, nor can it be ignored with impunity. Although, as we have seen, the Law cannot make men good, so that they freely and willingly do all that it requires, yet it can control their behaviour and prevent them from giving free rein to their contrary impulses. This it is intended to do, for in its 'civil' or 'political' use its function is, as Luther puts it, 'to bridle the flesh', 'to punish transgressions' and 'to restrain sin'. Inasmuch as it does so, the Law is a very great blessing to mankind, and it can be described as 'the best gift of God that the world has'.[56]

The second use of the Law Luther describes as 'divine and spiritual' and says it is 'to increase transgressions'.[57] We have already seen how the Law does this when it is applied, not simply to our conduct, but to our heart and conscience.[58] We must now observe that, in Luther's view, it is precisely intended to do this. It is meant thereby to reveal to man the depth of his sinfulness,

the inward hostility of his heart toward God, even while it
restrains him from giving outward expression to the impulses of
his self-will. It is meant to convince him of his utter impotence
to fulfil its real requirements and deliver himself from its condemnation and from the Wrath of God.[59] The Law, Luther says,
'is a glass that sheweth unto a man himself, that he is a sinner,
guilty of death, and worthy of God's everlasting wrath and
damnation'.[60] It is the 'hammer of God' that breaks and shatters
all man's self-righteousness and self-confidence before God. That
'pernicious and pestilent opinion of man's own righteousness . . .
suffereth not God to come to His own natural and proper work',
and therefore it must be brought to naught.[61] To bring it to
naught is 'the proper and spiritual use of the Law';[62] and in this
way the Law serves as 'a minister that prepareth the way unto
grace',[63] and as 'our schoolmaster to bring us unto Christ'.[64]
By revealing to us that we suffer from a disease for which there is
no cure in ourselves, it prepares us for the remedy of the Gospel,
for salvation by God Himself, who can now come to His 'proper'
work. For it is 'His nature', Luther says,

to exalt the humble . . . to comfort the miserable . . . to justify sinners,
to quicken the dead, and to save the very desperate and damned.
For He is an almighty creator, making all things of nothing.[65]

In its spiritual, no less than in its political use, therefore, 'the Law
is an excellent thing'[66] and the servant, not the enemy, of the
Gospel.[67]

When we turn to the Gospel, we must first of all note that Luther
often speaks as if it alone were the Word of God. But then it is
necessary to bear in mind that the Gospel has been said to have
two 'offices'. The first of these is to interpret the Law and to effect
that 'spiritual use' of it, which we have just described.[68] Luther
terms this the 'strange work' (*opus alienum*) of the Gospel, and
identifies it with that 'strange work of God', which is the Divine
wrath.[69] The expression is borrowed, as he tells us, from Isaiah
28 21; and he explains that God's 'strange work' must necessarily
be performed before He can come to His 'proper work'.[70] Sinful
men must be made aware of their disease before they will seek its
cure, they must acknowledge their sin before they can receive
forgiveness, they must despair of themselves before they can truly
believe and hope in God. The Gospel, therefore, bids us not only

to believe, but first to repent; it proclaims us sinners before it offers us grace. It comes to us as *Cacangelium*, bad and unwelcome news, before it is heard as *Evangelium*, or good news.[71] Luther always most strongly insists that the good news of the Gospel is by no means to be preached to men who do not acknowledge their sin. Such persons must be hammered by the Law until their pride and stubbornness of heart is crushed; only then can it be right to preach to them forgiveness and grace.[72]

The 'second and proper and true' office of the Gospel is nothing else but the preaching of Christ in *His* 'proper office', or the proclamation of the 'proper work' of God.

To this office [Luther says] belong those words: Come unto me all ye that labour and are heavy laden, and I will refresh you (Matthew 11₂₈), or again: Son, be of good cheer, thy sins are forgiven thee (Matthew 9₂).[73]

The Gospel in the strict sense of the term, therefore, has precisely the opposite effect to the Law. Where the Law demands, the Gospel gives; where the Law reveals sin, wrath, condemnation, death, the Gospel reveals forgiveness, grace, righteousness, life.[74] The Gospel is that Word whereby God discloses His inmost heart, manifesting Himself a gracious God, who wills to deal with us, not as an angry Judge, but as a merciful Father. Inasmuch as we believe this Word, accepting it not merely as an abstract doctrine, but as addressed by God Himself quite personally to us, we enter into a quite new relationship to God. We exchange the condition of servants and slaves for the life and liberty of sons. We are delivered from the tyranny and curse of the Law, and we are 'justified' by our faith. With our new relationship to God, more-over, all things else begin to be made new. The justified sinner can be said to be 'righteous' inasmuch as he is in a right relation-ship to God, although in himself, since the deep infection of original sin is not eradicated in a moment, he is still a sinner.[75] Yet he is 'on the way to righteousness',[76] Luther insists, for 'justi-fication is a kind of regeneration',[77] and 'faith is accompanied by the beginning of a new creature'.[78] The Gospel furnishes the remedy not only for the guilt but also for the power of sin, which is both forgiven and conquered by Christ.[79] What the Law demands, therefore, but renders man impotent to accomplish, the Gospel increasingly enables the believer to perform.[80]

To be a believer, is to be no longer under the Law, but under grace; it is to stand in a filial, not a legal, relationship to God. In this sense the Law is abolished by the Gospel—and only in this sense. Believers are free from the Law, inasmuch as it no longer tyrannizes over their conscience, driving them to despair on account of their sin. It cannot do so, because their sin is forgiven by the Author of the Law. But they are not therefore free to do what the Law forbids, or to omit what it commands. The 'civil' or 'political' use of the Law, which we discussed above, must still be maintained,[81] and even its schoolmasterly function does not entirely cease, so long as there remains any sin in believers.[82] Indeed, it can be said that God deals even with the justified in wrath as well as in grace. Luther finds both the *opus alienum* and the *opus proprium* of God revealed in Christ—the former in His Cross, the latter in His Resurrection—and it is a characteristic thought of his, that Christians must be 'conformed' to their Saviour. Now 'this conformity to the image of the Son of God', he says, 'includes both those works';[83] and he explains the *opus alienum* as 'the crucifixion of the old man and the mortification of Adam', while the *opus proprium* is 'justification in the Spirit and the vivification of the new man, as Romans 425 says'.[84] The Gospel, Luther constantly asserts, brings the Cross with it; and he thinks of this Cross quite concretely in terms of the disciplines of duty and of suffering to which Christians must submit in this life, as the means appointed by God for what he terms the 'crucifixion of the old man', or, as we might put it, to break their self-will and pride that would hinder His 'proper work'. The 'strange work' of God thus stands in the service of the Gospel and grace.

God's 'proper work', as its name is meant to indicate, always retains the primacy in Luther's thought, and all else must be understood in the light of it. When this is done, the Law and the Wrath of God clearly do not imply any legal character in God's dealings with men. It is man's misconception of them, when he either views them quite apart from the Gospel, or gives them the primacy over the Gospel, that gives rise to legalism. Legalism means that man not only has a false conception of God, but also is in a false relationship to Him, so that he worships in fact, not the true God, but an idol, as we have seen. But such idolatry brings a man under the wrath of the true God. For the God whose nature is revealed in the Gospel as pure love and grace is no mild sentimentalist, and Luther can actually speak of His 'wrathful love', His *zornige Liebe*.[85] Love's wrath, however, is neither the evil passion of offended self-esteem, nor the cold severity of violated justice, but the intensely personal reaction of the Father's all-holy will against sin. Wrath represents the purity of that Divine love which, while it freely and fully forgives sin, never pretends that it is not sin and does not matter.[86] The grace and favour shown toward sinners, therefore, always shine out, and shine the more brightly, against the dark background of Wrath. The same situation can be expressed in terms of Divine righteousness. Since the essential righteousness of God, as Luther sees it, is that whereby He justifies sinners, rather than whereby He punishes them, it clearly cannot be conceived in terms of distributive justice.[87] Yet since the justifying righteousness, which is identical with grace,[88] does not exclude punishment, it is also clear that this latter cannot be equated with distributive justice either—unless there is to be sheer contradiction in the Divine nature itself. Instead, we must say of it what we have already said of Wrath, which is in fact only another name for it, that it is an assertion of the purity of that forgiving love, which wills not only to pardon sin, but utterly to purge it away.[89] To the unbelieving, no doubt, the idea of Wrath is the opposite and the very negation of grace; and even for the believer the tension between them may be acute. Yet faith holds fast to the Word of Divine grace, which is Christ,[90] and maintains, despite all appearances to the contrary, that even Wrath itself is the work, the 'strange work', of a gracious God.[91]

For Luther, both the righteousness that punishes and the righteousness that justifies, both wrath and grace, both Law and Gospel, are works of one and the same God, whose inmost nature is pure love. If any further evidence of this is needed, we may notice that, just as we have seen the Law to be included in the Gospel, so Luther also finds the Gospel implicit in the Law. In one of his expositions of the First Commandment, he says:

God says: I will be thy God, will make thee blessed. I will help thee, and that of pure grace; thou shalt not merit it of me, nor set up any worship in thine own self-sufficiency. Thou shalt not have that glorying before me, that thou shouldest purchase anything of me by thine own merit; I will not have regard to thy merit. I will be thy God, I will give thee everything for nothing.[92]

Or again, Luther tells us that 'the Law spiritually understood is the same as the Gospel';[93] and it is not difficult to see how this can be so. The Law spiritually understood requires us to be actuated by perfect love, a love that excludes all legalistic considerations of merit and self-interest in our dealings with others. Now since the Law is an expression of the will of God, must not this mean that God Himself is moved by nothing else but just such love? Otherwise, how should He will and command it? The Law, therefore, implies the Gospel, in which God Himself displays toward us precisely the love that He requires of us in His Law. He who commands us to love our enemies has shown us how, by loving us who were His own. He has not done it out of obedience to any commandment, but out of His eternal and spontaneous love, from which both His Law and His Gospel proceed.

It is only because men are sinners, because their wills are moved by other considerations than perfect love, that the will of God confronts them in the double form of Law and Gospel. There is no disunity in the Divine nature, although there is doubtless tension between the *opus alienum* and the *opus proprium Dei*. This tension is so great in the eyes of sinful men, that they are prone to call it contradiction; and they frequently seek to resolve it either by reducing the Gospel to terms of the Law, or by repudiating the Law entirely in favour of the Gospel. But Luther never tires of insisting that we must keep the middle way between these two extremes of legalism and antinomianism. We must preach both the Law and the Gospel as the twofold Word of the Living God, whereby He summons all men to repent and believe.

19. THE SACRAMENTAL WORD

Without the Word of God, according to Luther, man's 'general' knowledge of God leads only to false religion and idolatry. But there has never been a time, he tells us, when God has not spoken His Word in some way or other to men; and there has always been some true religion in the world, for there have always been some who have believed God's Word.[94] With the Word, moreover, God has always given some external sign, 'so that men, admonished by the external sign and work or sacrament, may the more certainly believe that God is favourable and merciful'.[95] Such signs were the rainbow after the Flood, circumcision given to

Abraham, the sacrifices of the Old Covenant. Such was, above all, 'the Son lying in the manger', the Incarnate Word; and such are, for us, Baptism, the Eucharist, and the power of the Keys or Absolution.[96] The importance of these sacramental signs is indicated when Luther says:

God has from the beginning of the world dealt with all saints through His Word, and has given along with the same, external signs of grace, etc. This I say, that no one may undertake to deal with God without these means, or to build himself a special way to heaven; otherwise he will do despite and break his neck. So the Pope with his followers has done and still does, and today the Anabaptists and other sectaries do.[97]

The Sacraments, in other words, guard against two main errors. First, they exclude all rationalistic and legalistic attempts to 'climb up into heaven' (the error of the Papists); and secondly, they are opposed to a purely 'spiritual' interpretation of religion, which lays all stress on the individual believer's 'inward experience' (the error of the sectaries). They also prevent us, we may add, from ever regarding the revelation of God in Christ as simply the 'teaching of Jesus', or the Christian faith as merely a set of doctrines, a theoretical belief about God. A Sacrament, says Luther, is a 'sign of the Divine will'[98] which betokens His real presence among men,[99] and can be called an 'epiphany' of God.[100]

We have not space here, nor is it necessary for our purposes, to give a complete exposition of Luther's doctrine of the Sacraments. Instead, we may notice a few fundamental principles of his thought.[101] First of all, it must be emphasized that what constitutes the Sacrament is not the material sign itself, but the Word which accompanies it and gives it its significance.[102] Each Sacrament is instituted by a special pronouncement of Christ the Word—Baptism by His command to the apostles to baptize in the threefold Name, and His promise that the baptized believer shall be saved;[103] the Eucharist by His words of institution, with the promise of the forgiveness of sins and the command to 'do this' in memory of Him;[104] Absolution by His word about loosing and binding.[105] It is this simple insistence on the words of the historical Christ that most particularly gives rise to the frequent allegation of literalism in Luther. But we must remember that for him these words come by no mere hearsay or traditional report, but are 'living things', *res viventes*, which give life to those who hear and believe them here and now.[106] Similarly, the Sacraments are no mere ritual acts of memorial performed by men, but they are *opera Dei*, works of the living Christ and God.[107] Where there is Baptism in the Triune Name, there the Divine Majesty Himself is present,[108] and is in fact Himself the baptizer;[109] the officiating minister is but a *larva Dei*, the mask or veil of God, so to speak. Likewise, in the Eucharist, Christ Himself is present as the Host, who distributes His own gifts through the minister to His guests.[110] Everything, however, depends upon the Word. Where the Word is proclaimed, Christ is present; where it is not, He is not.[111]

At this point it is interesting to consider Luther's doctrine of the Real Presence in the Eucharist. It was developed in opposition, on the one hand, to the views of Zwingli and the Swiss reformers, and on the other, to the Romanists with their doctrine of the Mass. With the rights and wrongs of the controversies in which it involved him, especially with the Swiss, we are not here concerned, nor yet with the course of its development. What is important is that Luther believed himself to be defending vital interests of the Christian faith, and we shall try to see these from his point of view. That is to say, we shall not regard his doctrines of Consubstantiation and of the Ubiquity of Christ's Body as essays in metaphysics, but as assertions of religious conviction. Luther does not attempt to give a theoretical, rational explanation how Christ is present in the Sacrament,[112] but he is determined to maintain the full reality and significance of the Presence against views that seem to him inadequate.

The ubiquity of Christ's body is asserted by Luther against the Zwinglian view that, since the body of the risen and glorified Christ is in heaven, seated at the right hand of God, it cannot possibly be localized in the Sacrament on earth. Luther replies that Christ's body cannot be localized even in heaven, for as God is omnipresent and His right hand is everywhere,[113] so also Christ's body is ubiquitous. God, says Luther, is 'unrestingly active in all His creatures'.[114] But this omnipresent God, as we have already seen, is for Luther no other than the God revealed in Jesus Christ, the incarnate God, who just by His incarnation reveals Himself as 'uncreated love'. Luther's assertion of the ubiquity of Christ's body at the omnipresent right hand of God, is fundamentally a defence of his conviction that wheresoever God is at work, He is at work in love. It is exactly similar to his idea that the creatures as the *larvae Dei* may be said to contain Christ. Now we recall that through the creatures, according to Luther, God is manifested so that all men have at least some awareness of Him, though they do not rightly understand Him. They do not know Him as He is in His inmost nature, except as He condescends to them, draws near to them, and above all *speaks* to them.[115] This He has done decisively in the historical Incarnation of the Word; but He had not omitted to do it, in a variety of ways, before that point in time and space, nor has He ceased to do it since. Otherwise, He would not be true to His own revealed nature of love. He does it now by means of the Word and Sacraments, in which we see His glory and hear Him speak to us;[116] but the glory we see and the words we hear are those of the incarnate,[117] not of the discarnate God, whom no man hath seen nor can see. That is why Luther insists that the true and complete body of Christ is present in the Eucharist. If it were not, then Christ Himself, with the fullness of His grace, would not be there.

It should by now be clear why Luther so obstinately refused to accept the Zwinglian rendering of Christ's words, 'This is my body', as 'this represents my body'. If the bread and wine of the Eucharist only *represent* the body of Christ, which is thought of as seated up in heaven, then the Sacrament is no longer a manifest sign of the presence of the true, gracious God, the incarnate God, among men. We must take the words as they stand, Luther insists, emphasizing 'this *is* my body'. He then goes on to express his view of the relation between the body and blood of Christ and the bread and wine in terms of consubstantiation. This is exactly parallel to his conception of the Person of Christ,[118] which we have already compared to his thought of the relationship between Christ and the believing soul.[119] That is to say, it expresses the same fundamental conviction about the nature of the religious relationship and God's dealings with men. Luther rejects the Roman doctrine of transubstantiation; there can be no confusion of the creature with the Creator; neither can be turned into the other. But Luther is no Deist, and for him it is characteristic of God to descend into the midst of the created world and meet men there, using the creatures as instruments or channels of His activity.[120]

He can therefore conceive of the incarnate God as presenting Himself to us in and with the bread and wine, which we may thus regard as *larvae* or *involucra Dei*, 'masks' of God. Luther's terminology may not appeal to us, but if we will refrain from reading into it metaphysical intentions quite foreign to him, we can at least see that the underlying convictions it is meant to safeguard are both important and consistent with his theology as a whole.

The Sacraments, we have said, are in Luther's view *opera Dei*, works of God. In connexion with this, the following points should be noticed, which again are one and all the logical outcome of his fundamental religious position. In the first place, he rejects the idea that the Sacrament is effective *ex opere operato*. The mere performance of the rite does not of itself effect the religious relationship; it does not secure for us a 'gracious God', as Luther would say; it is in no sense an instrument placed in man's hands by which he can influence God. For the same reason, Luther rejects the doctrine of the Mass as a sacrifice that men can offer to God so as to secure His love and favour.[121] God's love and favour are free and universal; but in the Mass He has given us a manifest sign and token of them, which may be described, not as a sacrifice, but as a 'testament', because in and through it He has willed to impart to us a share in the divine, victorious life of the Redeemer. We receive the promised benefits, however, only if we believe the Word of promise that is spoken to us in the Sacraments, and without which they are not sacraments at all. Indeed, it is possible to receive the benefits of the Sacrament even apart from the external, sacramental 'sign'.

Although Luther holds that the Sacraments are generally necessary, and can say to those who ignore or reject them that they can have no dealings with God apart from them, yet he maintains that the benefits of the Sacraments may be received in the absence of the signs, provided that we do not despise these latter but have the sacramental faith.[122] At the same time, he guards against any possibility of thinking that our faith is constitutive of the Sacrament, by teaching the *manducatio indignorum*. He maintains that even to the unworthy, that is, the impenitent and unbelieving, the true body and blood of Christ are given in the Eucharist, although such persons receive them to their own condemnation, since they do not receive them in faith. Similarly, he holds with regard to Baptism, that it is not of the utmost importance whether the baptized person has faith or not. It is not the faith that constitutes the Baptism, although without faith its benefits are lost. The Sacraments are constituted, not by any willing or doing of men, nor yet by their receiving faith, but by the Word spoken by the Incarnate God, present among men in the fullness of His redeeming grace.[123]

20. THE WORD AND THE SPIRIT

Christ's revelation of God is not, for Luther, something given merely once long ago, but something He continually gives. Moreover, just as the decisive revelation in the past was identical with the redemptive activity of the Incarnate, so is that given in the present. This is illustrated by the significance Luther ascribes to the Sacraments, a significance determined, of course, by their constitutive Word.

When God, who is the real agent in Baptism, baptizes us, the purpose of this is to 'confer salvation'. Now 'to be saved', Luther explains, 'is to be released from sin, death, and the devil, and to be brought into Christ's kingdom and to live with Him there for ever'.[124] Of the Eucharist he says:

here in the sacrament thou wilt receive from Christ's mouth forgiveness of sins, which includes and brings along with it God's grace, His Spirit, and all His gifts, protection, refuge, and strength against death, the devil, and all misfortunes.[125]

The Gospel sacraments, in other words, offer to us precisely what is offered in the preaching of the Word: participation in Christ's victorious strife against the 'Tyrants'. The symbolism of the Baptismal rite, which sets its seal on the whole life of the Christian, indicates the practical implications of this participation. It means

nothing else than the killing of the old Adam in us and the resurrection of the new man, both of which will continue in us all our life long; hence a Christian life is nothing else but a daily baptism, once begun and daily continued.[126]

Baptism thus 'signifies two things—death and resurrection; that is, full and complete justification', says Luther, referring us to

M

Romans 64, and then explaining that this 'justification', though it begins here on earth, is finally completed only when we literally and physically die.[127] Unlike Baptism, the Eucharist is a rite to be repeatedly observed, and 'it is well-named food for the soul, which nourishes and strengthens the new man in us'.[128] Here Christ imparts to us a share in His own victorious life, pledging Himself to fight with us and for us and in us against sin and death and all evil.[129] All this, moreover, is the work of 'the overflowing goodness of the incomprehensible God, lavished upon us through Christ', which moves us to love Him in return so that the Sacrament can be well styled 'a fount of love'.[130] By this Divine love, here given to us, 'all self-seeking love is uprooted and gives place to love which seeks the common good of all';[131] and the 'fruit' of this Sacrament is 'that we should treat our neighbour even as God has treated us'.[132] That is what it means, then, to share in Christ's victory; that is the essential 'benefit' of the Sacraments.

What is offered to man in the Sacraments, of course, can only be received by faith, and that for two main reasons. In the first place, it is neither evident to the senses, nor capable of rational proof, that it is the living God who here speaks His gracious Word to men; and in the second place, it is not by any willing or doing of men, however well-meant and well-executed, that God is moved to speak his Word of grace.[133] Here again we have strong evidence of the intensely personal nature of Luther's conception of the religious relationship. Man is in no sense in control of God, nor, it can be added, does God force Himself upon man. Neither the Word nor the signs furnish a coercive demonstration of the Divine presence and will. Yet in and through them God quite really confronts men with the inescapable alternative of faith or unbelief. By faith here Luther obviously does not mean merely the holding of orthodox opinions, for even the devil himself holds those; but he means the application quite personally to oneself of the salvation promised by the Word.[134] This, he knows, is no easy thing.

The slender capacity of man's heart [he says] cannot comprehend, and much less utter that unsearchable depth and burning zeal of God's love toward us—and verily the inestimable greatness of God's mercy not only engendereth in us an hardness to believe, but incredulity itself.[135]

Hence in the *Short Catechism* he declares:

I believe that I cannot of my own understanding and strength believe in or come to Jesus Christ my Lord, but that the Holy Ghost has called me by the Gospel and illuminated me with His gifts, and sanctified me in the true faith.[136]

Again and again Luther asserts that we can have no assurance that the promise of the Gospel is the Word of the living God to us, unless the Holy Spirit says in our heart, 'that is God's Word'.[137] Faith itself, therefore, is the gift and work of God; and if we find that we do not and cannot believe, there is nothing we can do except confess this to God and pray for faith, crying, 'Help thou my unbelief'.[138]

When through the outward preaching of the Word and the inward witness of the Holy Spirit, faith is created, that which is promised in the Gospel becomes effective for the believer. Christ, says Luther, enters by the Gospel through a man's ears into his heart and dwells there; nor does He come empty-handed, but brings with Him His life, Spirit, and all that He has and can.[139] It is a fundamental principle for Luther that in faith itself Christ is present (*in ipsa fide Christus adest*), so that 'when we believe that Christ came *for us*, He dwells in our hearts by such faith and purifies us daily by His own proper work'.[140] This means that the believer, who is united with Christ 'even more closely than the husband is coupled with his wife', must naturally share in Christ's conflict and victory.[141] For the marriage of the believing soul to Him is a matter 'not only of communion, but of a blessed strife and victory and salvation and redemption'.[142] The indwelling of Christ 'redeems us from the bondage of Egypt, makes us free, gives power to do good'.[143] Risen and ascended though Christ is, 'He sitteth not idly in heaven: but is present with us, working and living in us';[144] and His life and work are no theoretical or abstract notions, but a matter of His 'true and substantial presence'.[145] Hence, what was done once historically, Luther insists, 'is always done spiritually in every Christian'.[146]

For as Christ came once corporally at the time appointed, abolished the whole law, vanquished sin, destroyed death and hell; even so He cometh spiritually without ceasing, and daily quencheth and killeth those sins in us.[147]

What Luther thus says of the indwelling Christ, he can also say of the Holy Spirit. For not only has the Spirit the function of convincing us of the truth of the Gospel, but He 'makes us holy'.[148] Like Christ, He dwells in believers, 'not merely as to His gifts, but as to His substance'.[149] Nor does He dwell idly in them, for He 'is a living, not a dead thing'; and just as life is never actionless, even when a person is asleep, 'so the Holy Spirit is never actionless in the godly, but is always working something pertaining to the kingdom of God'.[150] The purpose of His working is our sanctification, which He accomplishes by applying, so to speak, the redemptive activity of Christ in our lives.[151] The immediate effect of it is a declaration of hostilities between the 'flesh' and the Spirit (Galatians 5 17); and this is nothing else but a continuation of the warfare in which Christ on the Cross won the decisive, though by no means the last, battle.[152] The conflict in the believer, moreover, is not won in a moment, and 'the more godly à man is, the more doth he feel that battle';[153] yet so long as he is united by faith with the victorious Christ, its final outcome is certain. The Christian is not one who is perfect, but one who fights; and daily the new man in Christ must arise and subdue the old Adam. Then

the sanctification, once begun, daily increases, [for] the Holy Spirit is continually at work in us, by means of the Word of God, and daily bestowing forgiveness on us, till we reach that life where there is no more forgiveness, all persons there being pure and holy.[154]

Just as Christ, who for our sake 'took upon Him our person', had literally to suffer and die in order to triumph over the 'Tyrants', so we also must pass with Him through physical death before sin is finally and utterly destroyed. Meanwhile, God pardons the sin that remains in us, 'for Christ's sake', the Christ who through the Spirit ceaselessly fights to overcome our sin, so that 'the heart daily grows in the Spirit that sanctifies us'.[155]

The work of the Word and the Spirit, it should be noticed, is not effected apart from the Church.[156] It is the 'proper work' of the Spirit 'to make the Church',[157] which Luther defines as 'the community of saints'[158] and as 'a Christian, holy people which believes in Christ'.[159] This people is the 'special community' of the Spirit in the world, and 'the mother that conceives every Christian by the Word of God, which He reveals and preaches'.[160]

Outside the Church, Luther maintains, there is no salvation—because there is no Saviour.[161] Christ is to be found only where the Word is preached, and the Word is not preached except in the Christian Church. We have heard Luther urge seekers after salvation to 'run to the manger' and there behold Christ. He turns this into an entirely practical injunction, when he asks: 'What is the manger, but the gathering of the Christian people for the preaching?' and assures us that 'he who goes to the preaching goes to this manger'—so long as it is preaching about Christ.[162] It is the preaching about Christ, the proclamation of the Word, that is constitutive of the Church; for if the Church is the mother of Christians it is not the mother, but the daughter of the Word.[163] Nothing else is absolutely essential, and where the Word is lacking, nothing else is of any avail.[164] Wherever the Word is preached, however, there is always the Holy Ghost, and there are also at least some who believe;[165] for it is impossible that the Word of God should return unto Him void.[166] The Word may not be altogether purely preached, and the faith may be very small and feeble; yet where the Word evokes faith in any degree, there is the Church. Hence Luther can say:

If I were the only one in the whole world who retained the Word, I alone should be the Church, and should rightly judge about the whole of the rest of the world, that it was not the Church.[167]

The Church, as Luther understands it, means essentially the whole company of Christian believers,[168] which as a spiritual fellowship is indivisibly one, although physically it is dispersed throughout the world and embodies itself in different congregations or churches.[169] Now this Church, says Luther, 'keeps all the words of God in her heart', and the churches 'assuredly have Christ with them'. 'Therefore, he who is to find Christ, must first find the churches'; he 'must not trust to himself, nor build a bridge of his own to heaven by his own reason, but go to the churches, attend them, and inquire'.[170] Since, however, the mere assembling of men in congregations that claim the Christian name is no sufficient guarantee that they are of the Church, Luther enumerates certain 'marks' by which we can be assured of finding the *communio sanctorum*, even though we cannot precisely determine who belong to it and who do not. Of these marks he usually names the preaching of the Word, Baptism, and the Lord's Supper, which in his view are infallible signs of the presence of Christ.[171] In his treatise *On the Councils and the Churches* (1539), however, he adds a number more, including the 'Keys', or the power of discipline in the Church; the Ministry, which is necessary for the due administration of Word, Sacraments, and the Keys; Public Worship, with prayer, praise, and thanksgiving; and the 'Holy Cross', or suffering in the form of persecution, temptation, and all kinds of evil, which Christians must expect the world, the flesh, and the devil to inflict upon them. Now just as we have already seen that the Sacraments are constituted by the Word, so it can be said that all these other marks of the Church are, in their several ways, so bound up with the Word that where it is absent they entirely lose their Christian significance. Luther is therefore able to say that 'if there were no other mark than this one [the Word] alone, it would still be enough to show that there must be a Christian church there'.[172]

The Word, according to Luther,

is the high, chief, holy possession from which the Christian people takes the name 'holy', for God's Word is holy and sanctifies everything it touches; nay, it is the very holiness of God. [Moreover] the Holy Ghost Himself administers it, and anoints and sanctifies the Church, that is, the Christian, holy people with it.[173]

For His sanctifying work the Spirit also employs, besides the Word, those other 'marks' of the Church which we have noticed, and which Luther describes, like the Word itself, as 'holy possessions'.[174] The purport of this sanctification is to enable us increasingly to fulfil the commandments of God, not merely according to the letter, but also according to the spirit, of the Divine Law. We do not fulfil them perfectly, as Christ has done, and we need forgiveness inasmuch as we fall short; but we constantly seek to do so 'until at last we become quite holy and need no more forgiveness'. 'To that end', says Luther, 'it is all directed.'[175] We must therefore examine ourselves in the light of God's commandments, to see how the Spirit's work progresses, and how much yet remains to be done, lest we grow careless and think we have already reached the goal.[176] 'We are constantly to grow in sanctification and ever to become more and more "a new creature" in Christ. The word is *Crescite* and *Abundete magis*.'[177] Our sanctification, moreover, finding expression in our outward life and our relationships with our neighbours, can be said to be an additional mark of the Church, although it is not so clear and certain as those already named.[178] The Church, therefore, can be defined as a

holy people in which Christ lives, works, and reigns *per redemptionem*, through grace and forgiveness of sins, the Holy Ghost *per vivificationem et sanctificationem*, through daily purging out of sins and renewal of life, so that we do not remain in sin, but can and should lead a new life in good works of all kinds.[179]

This is not the place for a full discussion of Luther's doctrine of sanctification, but in the light of what has been said, the unprejudiced will be able to assess the value of Wesley's judgement, which is too often quoted by Methodists as if it were the last word on the subject. 'Who has wrote more ably than Martin Luther on justification by faith alone?' Wesley asks, 'and who was more ignorant of the doctrine of sanctification, or more confused in his conception of it?' He then advises us, if we would be thoroughly convinced of Luther's 'total ignorance with regard to sanctification', to read over 'without prejudice' his *Commentary on Galatians*.[180] Those who are inclined to follow Wesley, as Wesley thought the Moravians followed Luther, 'for better, for worse', are quite naturally reluctant to believe that he could be mistaken; but it must be pointed out that part of the evidence quoted above is drawn from Luther's *Galatians* itself, and it could be multiplied many times. This is the more significant, inasmuch as the greater part of the Epistle Luther is expounding is primarily concerned with the doctrine of justification. But the fact is, that for Luther justification and sanctification, although distinguishable in theory, are quite inseparable in practice. Indeed, they might well be said to be simply different aspects of the same thing.[181] Just when his attention is most concentrated on the question of justification, therefore, Luther cannot help also speaking of sanctification, even when he does not actually use the word.[182]

Justification means, for Luther, participation in Christ's victorious strife against sin and all evil; it means that God in Christ still comes, through the Spirit, to dwell with sinners and to continue in their hearts and lives His redeeming work. It is thus that the believer comes to possess a 'righteousness not his own', a *iustitia externa et aliena*, a righteousness not of works, but of faith.[183]

Christ apprehended by faith, and *dwelling in the heart* [Luther teaches], is the true Christian righteousness, for the which God counteth us righteous and giveth us eternal life. [184]

Christ is that righteousness of God whereby He justifies sinners,[185] and inasmuch as we are still infected with sin, this Divine right- eousness is 'imputed' to us, and our sin is 'not imputed'—so long as we have faith, and Christ dwelling in our hearts by faith. Our sin, in other words, is forgiven, although it does not thereby cease to be sinful and hateful to God, who wills it to be utterly destroyed.[186]

Luther's view may be summarized, and its essential significance expressed, in the following way. The 'true and substantial' presence of Christ, or of the Spirit, in the believer's heart, means nothing else but the presence of that Divine love which is of the very 'substance' of God. That is why, as Luther never tires of asserting, faith, like its Creator and Lord, 'is not idle', but cease- lessly engaged in the labour and service of love.[187] The conflict of the 'flesh' and the Spirit, the mortification of the Old Adam and the rising of the New Man, means nothing else but the struggle between human self-love and the Divine in the believer's life. The daily growth in sanctification can only mean the increasing mastery of Divine love, of God Himself, who in His grace both forgives the selfishness that still remains to resist His good will, and increasingly purges it away. So the Christian becomes an in- creasingly effective channel and instrument of God's own goodness and love, until at length the last subtle vestiges of self-love are destroyed through death, and perfection, in the strictest and fullest sense of the word, is reached in the world to come, when God is all in all.

21. THE AUTHORITY OF THE WORD

The Word that speaks of a 'gracious God', who out of mere love 'justifies sinners', is difficult to believe. 'The matter of justifica- tion', Luther says, 'is brittle.' He assures us, however, that it is brittle, 'not of itself, for of itself it is most sure and certain, but in respect of us . . . because we are brittle'. Our human 'reason' and 'conscience' protest that the almighty and righteous God cannot come down to the level of humanity, still less have fellowship with *sinful* man, and their protests are not easily dismissed. 'Whereof', says Luther, 'I myself have good experience.'[188] He never finds it a simple and obvious thing to take the Word of Divine love and grace as addressed quite personally to himself. Nevertheless, he expounds his doctrine of justification to others as something 'most sure and certain', only urging them to strive and pray, as he himself does, for justifying faith.[189] The question therefore arises, on what grounds Luther can be so confident of the truth of his doctrine. What authority does he claim for setting it up as of the very essence of Christianity and opposing it to what he condemns as the Roman corruption of the Faith?

It has been argued[190] that Luther was one of those who require external authority in religion, so that when he rejected contemporary ecclesiastical authority, he had to find some substitute for it. This he sought in an infallible Word of God, which he identified with those parts of the Bible in which he could discover the Pauline doctrine of justification. Of the truth of this doctrine he was convinced because he thought it gave the correct interpretation of his religious experience, which had brought peace to his distressed heart and conscience. This he was sure was the authentic Christian experience, and since it had been mediated to him, or so he believed, solely through Scripture, it led him to maintain the sole authority of Scripture. Luther's convictions thus rest ultimately upon his own individual religious experience, and 'instead of an objective religion we find a blank subjectivism, heavily, but not impenetrably, disguised'.[191] Now if this interpretation of Luther were correct, it would stand in flagrant contradiction of all we have hitherto seen of his own most cherished principles. His strictly and consistently theocentric outlook would rest upon an egocentric foundation. We need only recall his description of 'two sorts of men in respect of faith, and what true faith is',[192] to see how intolerable such a situation would have been to Luther. It might, of course, be suggested that that was precisely why he felt the need of an external authority; yet even if that were so, it must be said that the authority he sets up is of a very different kind from the one alleged above.

In his thesis *That Doctrines of Men are to be Rejected*, Luther discusses the statement of Saint Augustine: 'I would not have believed the Gospel if the authority of the whole Church had not moved me.'[193] Of this he says, among other things:

we must not understand St. Augustine to say that he would not believe
the Gospel unless he were moved thereto by the authority of the whole
Church. For that were false and unchristian. Every man must
believe only because it is God's Word, and because he is convinced
in his heart that it is true, although an angel from heaven and all the
world preached the contrary. . . . In this way Augustine also had to
believe, and all the saints, and we too, every one for himself.[194]

Saint Augustine's meaning, Luther says, must be that he finds the
Gospel nowhere except in the Church, and that the unanimous
acceptance of it by the universal Church is an 'external proof of
faith, by which heretics are refuted and the weak strengthened in
faith'.[195] In this context Luther rejects the authoritarian pretensions of the Papacy on the ground that the Roman See is not the
'whole Church', not universal Christendom; but of more importance for our purposes is the view he takes of external authority as
such. Even the unanimous testimony of the whole Church could
never be for him more than confirmatory of a conviction already
in some measure reached on other grounds.

Now it would be entirely out of harmony with what Luther
has just said, if he had sought to invest the Scriptures with the
same kind of authority as he denied to the Papacy. It is true that
he more than once asserts that his doctrine is securely founded on
Holy Scripture, and that nothing must be believed or taught as
Christian, if it has not its warrant in Scripture. But he is invariably
thinking of Scripture as a witness to Christ, a vehicle of the Word.
His quarrel with Rome, as we have already had occasion to
state, was not so much about the authority, as about the interpretation, of Scripture. He is certain that his interpretation is
right, and he will not be moved, even if a thousand biblical texts
are quoted against him; for he has on his side Christ, the Lord of
the Scriptures, whom the Scriptures cannot contradict.[196] To
have Scripture without the knowledge of Christ, he declares, is to
have no Scripture, for Scripture, rightly understood, contains
nothing but Christ.[197] When Luther asserts, therefore, that 'there
is no other evidence (*gezeugnis*) of Christian truth on earth but the
Holy Scriptures',[198] he does not mean that he himself believes, or
that anyone else must believe, what the Bible says, simply and
solely because the Bible says it. He means first, that the New
Testament preaching and the Old Testament promises that
confirm it contain the sole original testimony we possess to the

Incarnate Word. The Scriptures can therefore be described as 'in truth the spiritual body of Christ'.[199] Secondly, he holds that Scripture must be interpreted by Scripture and not, for instance, by Tradition or the teaching of the Fathers, who themselves point us to Scripture as primary.[200] Hence he opposes the sole authority of Scripture to that claimed for the decrees of Popes and Councils, and still more to that accorded to Aristotle in scholastic theology. But, for Luther, all authority belongs ultimately to Christ, the Word of God, alone, and even the authority of the Scriptures is secondary and derivative, pertaining to them only inasmuch as they bear witness to Christ and are the vehicle of the Word.

If Luther, then, does not hold his doctrine true because Scripture contains it, but rather says that, because it is true, Scripture cannot contradict it, on what grounds is he convinced of its truth? To maintain that it is on the ground of his own 'religious experience' of inward peace, is to override his own testimony. When he says: 'I speak from experience', he is generally describing the difficulty he never ceased to feel in applying the message of Divine grace to himself; and although he doubtless speaks from experience when he describes the peace and joy that faith can bring, or urges us to examine ourselves and see whether we feel the Spirit in our hearts crying 'Abba, Father',[201] yet in no case does he argue from such experience for the truth of his teaching.[202] Furthermore, although he well knows how to fulfil the pastoral duty of comforting troubled hearts and consciences, he lays far less stress upon the peace and joy they may experience, than upon the fact that the Holy Spirit, received by faith, 'makes a quite different, new man', who thinks, judges, wills, desires, loves, behaves, in another way than before.[203] If this 'new man' feels peace in his heart, it is because he is at peace with God; but that means he is committed to a daily conflict with the world, the devil, and his own 'flesh', in which his feelings may be anything but constant.[204] If in this conflict he has joy, it is chiefly the joy of knowing that 'for us fights the proper Man', who undoubtedly 'shall conquer in the battle'.[205] For Luther, it is of secondary importance that the Gospel gives believers a sense of peace and joy. What chiefly matters is that it 'makes us new sons and such as thereafter think the things that are of God',[206] and that the 'new man' created by the Spirit loves God and keeps His commandments.[207] But the

Spirit's work in us is not completed in a moment, and our faith must not be governed by our own perception of its effectiveness, for unless we have faith, it cannot proceed at all.

Luther never tires of telling us that we must not rely upon what we feel and perceive and experience. To do so is to follow the bent of the natural man, who walks by sight and not by faith at all,[208] for 'faith rests in those things which cannot be beheld nor laid hold of by any sense of the body or soul, stands in that persuasion which it has conceived concerning God, and commits itself wholly unto it'.[209] Luther's own 'persuasion concerning God', therefore, which is summarily expressed in his doctrine of justification, can hardly have been based upon his 'religious experience', especially when we remember that he taught it with conviction to others, even at times when he personally found it very difficult to commit himself 'wholly unto it'. How he could do so, he himself explains.

This is the reason [he says] that our doctrine is most sure and certain, because it carrieth us out of ourselves, that we should not lean to our own strength, our own conscience, our own feeling, our own person and our own works: but to that which is without us, that is to say, to the promise and truth of God, which cannot deceive us.[210]

If these words reflect, as they may, Luther's own 'experience' at times of unclouded faith, it is more important that they represent the essential purport of his doctrine, which is quite independent of his or any man's experience. This, moreover, is entirely in harmony with his consistently theocentric point of view and his tireless campaign against human self-centredness.

Luther's doctrine of a gracious God who justifies sinners, as we have tried to show, is essentially a challenge to men to acknowledge God as God, to recognize His true nature and let Him be God for them. Luther is certain this doctrine is solidly supported by all Scripture—and if Scripture texts are quoted against it, he will reject the construction put upon them. He is sure it is the doctrine of universal Christendom—and if the Pope and his followers, or any other men, deny it, they are self-excluded from the one, holy, catholic, and apostolic Church. It is attested, he maintains, by the witness of the Spirit in every believer's heart—yet it does not depend upon any man's experience of this. If the preaching of it provokes hostility, Luther reminds us that the true

Church has always suffered persecution, and the Christian, like his Lord, must bear the cross. 'Reason' and 'conscience', including Luther's own, may protest against it, but their protests only reveal the corruption of the human heart, that will not let God be God.

No mere man, Luther is convinced, could speak the Word of love and grace that is addressed to us in Christ. Such love is 'not of works nor human, yea not of angels nor heavenly, but God Himself'. It is the very essence of divinity, the decisive demonstration of the sovereignty and righteousness of God. If 'reason' asserts that the God of almighty majesty could not come down from heaven and be made man, it presumes to limit Him and denies His omnipotence. If 'conscience' insists that He is too pure and holy to have dealings with sinners, it likewise limits Him and makes Him no better than a self-righteous man. The natural man dreams God to be such a one as himself, preoccupied with His own beatitude, pharisaic in His own righteousness, representing Him in effect as one who must say to sinners: 'Come not near to me, until thou art worthy of me, for I am holier than thou.' But the Word that is spoken to us in Scripture, Sermon, and Sacrament, saying: 'I am come not to call the righteous, but sinners', and: 'Be of good cheer, thy sins are forgiven thee', is no such figment of human imagination, for it surpasses man's highest thought. It is a Word that 'resounds down from above', proclaiming the glory of God, condemning all our human pride, and summoning us to repent and believe—to let God be God even for us. This Word, which is the inspiration and guide of Luther's entire reforming work, needs no external authority to attest it; for it is self-authenticated as the Word of the one, true, living God, who, as He created us out of nothing, has redeemed us for nothing, and will also save for nothing as many as ever are saved.

NOTES

1. *Gal.* E.T. 269(iv.6): 'No man can understand what God's will is, and what pleaseth Him, but in His good Word.' ibid. 157(iii.6) 'when he will measure God without the Word, and believe Him according to the wisdom of reason, he hath no right opinion of God in his heart, and therefore he cannot think or judge of Him as he should do.'

2. *Gal.* E.T. 278(iv.8f.): 'Therefore whosoever will worship God *without His Word*, serveth not the true God, but that which by nature is no God. . . . For *without Christ* there is nothing else but mere idolatry' (*italics* mine). *W.A.* X.1; 158.16: '. . . that Christ is Himself the Word.' ibid. XLII.8.24f.: 'The Father through the Son, whom Moses calls the Word, creates heaven and earth out of nothing.' cf. Prenter, *Spiritus Creator*, 120–5.

3. *W.A.* XI.223.1f. *B.o.W.* 26: 'Take Christ out of the Scriptures, and what will you find remaining in them?' cf. *Römerbr.* 240.10ff.: 'The whole Scripture is about Christ alone everywhere, if we look to its inner meaning, though superficially it may sound different.'

4. *B.o.W.* 24ff.

5. *W.A.* X.1; 81.20f. cf. ibid. XLII.166.40f.: 'Wherefore, we must look to the light of the Gospel, as I have said above, for this illumines the darkness of the Old Testament.'

6. ibid. 8f. cf. *W.M.L.* VI.379: 'He is the man to whom it all applies.'

7. *W.A.* X.1; 576.12ff.

8. op. cit. 626.2ff.

9. op. cit. 15.1ff.

10. op. cit. 625.19ff.: 'For in the New Testament the preaching must be done orally with the living voice publicly, and must bring forth into speech and hearing what before was hidden in the letters. . . . Christ Himself did not write His doctrine, as Moses did his, but gave it orally, also orally commanded to do it and gave no command to write it.'

11. op. cit. 626f.

12. op. cit. 625.13f.

13. *W.M.L.* VI.367-82 (Old Testament); 439-44 (New Testament).

14. ibid. 439f.

15. ibid. 442.

16. ibid. 368.

17. ibid. 378.

18. ibid. 440f.

19. ibid. 379f. Luther allows a limited use of the allegorical method of interpretation (which he otherwise rejects), provided it is employed in the same way as the New Testament writers use it—i.e. to 'find Christ' in the Old Testament.

20. ibid. 373ff.

21. ibid. 439.

22. *W.A.* XI.30.17f.: 'Thus evangelical preaching is nothing else but the knowledge of Christ.'

23. op. cit. 48.27ff.: 'For the Gospel teaches nothing else but Jesus Christ, who is the Son of God and a man, who assumed His whole life, passion, etc., for my sake, and obtained my reconciliation to the Father.'

24. op. cit. 98.5ff.; 131.17ff.

25. *B.o.W.* 125: 'I call both the Law and the Gospel the words of God.'

26. *E.A.* xx.1.114; I.241—quoted from Herrmann, *Communion*, 186. The Gospel story of the words and deeds of Christ is never for Luther simply a tale of long ago; it is 'things that are alive to make us alive' (*res viventes ut vivificent nos*)—*W.A.* XL.2; 259.

27. Luther naturally connects John 1 with Genesis 1, and Christ the Word is the agent of creation. We recall also that the creatures as the *larvae Dei* 'as it were contain Christ'.

28. *W.A.* XLII.110.16ff.: 'This Word was for Adam Gospel and Law.' But Satan, Luther explains, incited Adam to doubt, and so to disbelieve, that God really meant it; then disobedience followed automatically. It was thus that Adam lost the true knowledge of God and fell into idolatry.

29. Christian preaching is always for Luther the proclamation of the 'benefits' of Christ—what He has done and suffered, and how He has triumphed, on our behalf, not His own. The merely historical presentation of Christ, as we have seen, Luther does not admit to be Christian preaching.

30. R. E. Davies, *The Problem of Authority*, 36f., argues that Luther identifies the Word of God with the entire Old Testament, as containing both Law and Gospel, and with those parts of the New Testament which contain the Gospel, rejecting those which do not, as not part of the Word. He suggests that it is surprising that Luther does not show similar discrimination in the case of the Old Testament. To this it may be said: (1) This view ignores Luther's distinction between Old Testament as Scripture and New Testament as preaching. Since the Apostles were sent to preach the Gospel, Luther can easily distinguish them from preachers, like Saint James, who do not preach it, and who therefore, in Luther's view, lack apostolic authority. But that is not necessarily to say that Saint James and his kind preach no part of the Word. Although the Epistle of James was rejected by the ancients, Luther says, 'I praise it and hold it a good book, because it sets up no doctrine of men and lays great stress upon God's law'—and this despite the fact that it wrongly teaches justification by works (*W.M.L.* VI.477). Now God's law, wherever it is found, is surely part of His Word, even though it is only preparatory in relation to the Gospel, as the Old Testament is preparatory to the New Testament. Mr. Davies's identification of 'not apostolic' and 'not part of the Word' (p.33) seems therefore unjustified. (2) For Luther, the Old Testament is Scripture in the strict sense of the term, both because it is essentially something written and because it is referred to as authoritative by Christ and His apostles. But Scripture is not the Word, nor is its authority that of the Word Himself; it is essentially a witness to Christ and it derives its authority from Him, for He is Lord of the Scripture as of all else. If Luther had identified the Word with the written documents, he could not have ventured to find historical mistakes in them, nor yet to give parts of them only modified praise, as Mr. Davies admits he does—especially when he calls even Saint James's 'strawy epistle' a 'good book'! Nor, again, would he have ventured to distinguish, as he does, between much that he regards as having been of only local and temporary significance in the Old Testament, and what he considers to be still relevant for Christians (*W.M.L.* VI.376). Loofs, *D.G.* 744ff., gives evidence enough to refute the idea that Luther was undiscriminating in his use of the Old Testament. The literalism with which Mr. Davies charges him, therefore, seems unsubstantiated.

31. There is no stronger evidence of the intensely personal nature of God's dealing with men, as Luther conceives it, than the large place occupied in his thought by the conception of the Word. Speech is characteristic of persons, as opposed to animals or things, and it is superior to all other forms of communication as a medium of personal relationship. (cf. H. H. Farmer, *The Servant of the Word* 44-55). This conception is reflected even in Luther's thought of the creative activity of God; for 'to create', he says, 'means to command' (*schaffen heisst gebieten*) *W.A.* XII.328.16.

32. *Gal.* E.T. 60f.(ii.6). Notice also that Luther speaks of Christ as 'enwrapped' in the 'swaddling-clothes' of Scripture—an idea exactly similar to that of the *larva* or *involucrum*.

33. *Sermons*, 71.

34. *W.A.* XXXVII.136.

35. *Works*, I.315 (*Journal* for 15th June 1741). Wesley, however, has not only failed to grasp Luther's meaning, but he has not even given him credit for what he actually says. In view of its length, he can hardly have reached the end of Luther's *Galatians* on a journey from Nottingham to London, unless he read it very cursorily indeed.

36. *Gal.* E.T. 251(iv.3).

37. ibid. 218(iii.19).

38. ibid. 121(ii.21).

39. ibid. 167(iii.10).

40. ibid. 279(iv.9).

41. ibid. 252(iv.3).

42. ibid. 58(ii.4f); 88(ii.16); 98(ii.21); 223(iii.20); 332(v.4); etc.

43. ibid. 252.

44. loc. cit.

45. ibid. 326(v.1).

46. ibid. 78(ii.16): 'Wherefore if thou couldest do the works of the Law according to this commandment: "Thou shalt love the Lord thy God with all thy heart," etc. (which no man ever yet did or could do), yet thou shouldest not be justified before God: for a man is not justified by the works of the Law.'

47. ibid. 207(iii.19): 'For, like as this consequence is nothing worth : Money doth not justify, or make a man righteous, therefore it is unprofitable; The eyes do not justify, therefore they must be plucked out; the hands make not a man righteous, therefore they must be cut off. So this is naught also: The Law doth not justify, therefore it is unprofitable. For we must attribute unto every thing his proper effect and use. We do not therefore destroy or condemn the Law, because we say that it doth not justify; but we answer otherwise to this question, To what end then serveth the Law? than our adversaries do . . .'

48. ibid. 326(v.1).

49. ibid. 353(v.12).

50. ibid. 236(iii.23).

51. ibid. 279(iv.9).

52. ibid. 208ff(iii.19); 184(iii.12); 230ff.(iii.23).

53. See pp. 112–15 *supra*.

54. cf. Wingren, *Kallelsen*, 153: 'For Luther, the Law is not something capable of definitive statement; it is not codified anywhere, whether in the Bible or in any other book. When a person in authority exercises his office as a co-operator with God, then *demands* are made through him upon those under him. Every *larva* of God is such an embodied Law—parents, neighbours, etc. The Law is a sum of living points. The Law therefore continually requires something new and unexpected: we can never have done with it. . . .'

55. *W.A.* VI.24.11: 'Human law, when it does not agree with the Divine, is unjust.' cf. *Tischr.* 178f.nr.286.

56. ibid. XXXIX.1; 226.20f.

57. *Gal.* E.T. 209(iii.19).

58. See pp. 108ff. *supra*.

59. *B.o.W.* 146, 150, 154, 178, 345ff.

60. *Gal.* E.T. 213.

61. ibid. cf. 209: 'For if any be not a murderer, an adulterer, a thief, and outwardly refrain from sin, as the Pharisee did . . . he would swear . . . that he is righteous, and therefore he conceiveth an opinion of righteousness, and presumeth of his good works and merits. Such a one God cannot otherwise mollify and humble . . . but by the Law. For that is the hammer of death, the thundering of hell, and the lightning of God's wrath, that beateth to powder the obstinate and senseless hypocrites.' cf. ibid. 210, etc.

62. ibid. 209, etc.

63. ibid. 213.

64. ibid. 237(iii.24).

65. ibid. 213.

66. *W.A.* I.114.38.

67. ibid. V.525: 'The Law is not against the Promise, for it is given that it may slay, and increase sin; that is, that man may recognize by the Law, how exceedingly he is in need of the grace of the Promise . . . so that he does not grow complacent (*securus*) by trust in the works of the Law, but should seek something far other and better than the Law, that is, the Promise. For if the Law could have given life, we should be righteous; but now it rather slays and makes us the more sinful; and just thereby it serves the promises, inasmuch as it makes them to be the more strongly desired, and destroys root and branch all righteousness of works.'

68. ibid. I. 105. 6ff.: 'The Gospel has a twofold office. The first is to interpret the old Law, as the Lord in Matthew 5 interprets that commandment, "Thou shalt not swear falsely, thou shalt do no murder, thou shalt not commit adultery", and so to lead us from the literal to the spiritual understanding of it. . . . But this understanding of the Law spiritually is far more deadly, because it makes the Law impossible to fulfil, for no one is without anger, no one without *concupiscentia*. . . .'

69. op. cit. 113.4ff.: 'For just as the work of God is twofold, namely, proper and strange, so also the office of the Gospel is twofold. The proper office of the Gospel is to proclaim the proper work of God, i.e. grace. . . . But the strange work of the Gospel is to prepare a people perfect for the Lord, that is, to reveal sins and to pronounce guilty those that were righteous in their own eyes. . . .'

70. op. cit. 112.84ff.: 'But He cannot come to this His proper work, unless He undertakes a work that is strange and contrary to Himself, as Isaiah 28 says: A strange work is His that He may work His own work. His strange work is to make men sinners, unrighteous, miserable, foolish, lost. Not that He actually makes them such Himself, but that the pride of men, although they are such, will not let them become or be such, so much so that God . . . uses this work to show them that they are such, in order that they may become in their own eyes, what they are in God's eyes.' cf. op. cit. 540.8ff.: 'When God begins to justify a man, first He condemns him, and him whom He wills to build up, He destroys, whom He wills to heal, He smites, whom to make alive, He kills . . . in a word, God works His strange work, in order that He may work His own work.' cf. *W.A.* V.63.5ff.

71. op. cit. 113.23ff.: 'So the Gospel sounds most harsh in its strange tones, and yet this must be done, that it may be able to sound with its own proper tones. . . . Behold, the Law says: "Thou shalt do no murder, thou shalt not steal, thou shalt not commit adultery." Here the proud, who are righteous with the righteousness of works, and have not done these works, already live at ease (*securi*) as though the Law were fulfilled, nor are they conscious of any sin in themselves, but of much righteousness. To those who thus presume, there comes the interpreter of the Law, namely, the Gospel, and says: "Repent ye, for the kingdom of heaven is at hand." In saying to all men, "Repent!" it undoubtedly declares all to be sinners, and so it brings sad and unwelcome tidings, which is *Cacangelium*, i.e. bad news and a strange office. When, however, it says, "The kingdom of heaven is at hand", this is good news and a pleasant and joyous preaching; it is the proper office, namely, of the Gospel.'

72. *Tischr.* 173.nr.274; 175.nr.277; *B.o.W.* 169; *Sermons*, 69.

N

73. *W.A.* I.105.19ff.

74. op. cit. 616.20ff.; *Gal. E.T. passim.*

75. *S.W.* I.88f.: 'The Christian, therefore, is not righteous *formally*, not righteous according to *substance* or *quality* . . . but righteous according to a relation to something; that is, with reference to the Divine grace and free remission of sins, which belong to them who acknowledge their sin, and believe that God favours and pardons them for Christ's sake. After we have attained unto this righteousness by faith, then we have still need of . . . the Holy Spirit . . . that gift and power which might dwell inwardly in the heart and purge away the remainder of sin, which began to be buried in baptism but was not yet fully buried.' (It should be remarked here that Luther does not conceive of pardon and the gift of the Spirit as two separate things. They are rather two aspects of the same thing—justification.)

76. *W.A.* XXXIX.1; 83.39f.

77. op. cit. 14: *iustificatio est revera regeneratio quaedam in novitatem.*

78. op. cit. 83.16f.

79. ibid. 39f.

80. That the Gospel gives what the Law demands, can be said to be a fixed principle of Luther's thought. But the Gospel does not give in response to the demands of the Law and in order that man may be justified by the fulfilment of the Law. On the contrary, the fulfilment of the Law is made possible only by the justification of man and his deliverance from the Law by the Gospel. In other words, it is most important to observe that the Gospel is not to be understood as the answer to a legal question.

81. *Gal.* E.T. 312(iv.27); *W.A.* XXXIX.1; 219f.

82. ibid., 240(iii.25).

83. *W.A.* I.113.3.

84. op. cit. 112.37ff.

85. ibid. XXIII.517.2ff.: '. . . wrathful love. For when love is angry, it does no injury; but when hatred and envy is angry, it corrupts and destroys as far as it can. For love's anger seeks and wills to sunder the evil that it hates from the good that it loves, in order that the good and its love may be preserved.' cf. ibid. X.1; 266.6ff.: 'So we see how true love is at once both a great foe and friend, how severely it punishes and how sweetly it helps; it has a hard shell, but a sweet kernel; it is bitter to the old man, but very sweet to the new man.'

86. cf. *Gal.* E.T. 369(v.17): 'Sin is truly sin, whether a man commit it before he hath received the knowledge of Christ or after. And God always hateth sin: yea all sin is damnable as touching the fact itself. But in that it is not damnable to him that believeth, it cometh of Christ, who by His death hath taken away sin.'

87. *S.W.* I.68: 'But if God be *thus* just, that he punishes justly, or according to desert, who can stand in the sight of a God just in this sense? For we are all sinners. . . . Be such justice, therefore, and such a just God, far removed from us. . . . Because, since God has sent Christ as a Saviour, His will is, most truly, not to be just *in punishing according to desert*, but He wills to be, and to be called, just, as *justifying those who acknowledge their sins*, and to have mercy upon them.'

88. *W.A.* X.1; 106.3: 'Divine righteousness, that is, the Divine grace, which justifies us through faith.' *S.W.* I.173: '. . . thy righteousness, that is, thy grace, whereby thou pardonest sins, and hast mercy.' cf. p. 148 *supra*, n. 199.

89. See n. 85 *supra*. Luther distinguishes between *ira severitatis*, and *ira misericordiae* (*W.A.* III.69.24), i.e. the 'wrath of severity' and the 'wrath of mercy'. The former may be said to be that which is directed quite simply to the destruction of the 'old Adam', whilst the latter ministers to the creation and perfecting of the 'new man in Christ'.

90. op. cit. 322.2: '. . . that only *grace (that is, Christ)* and nothing but grace avails' (*italics* mine).

91. cf. ibid. V.82.14ff.: 'The words of this verse are words . . . of most robust faith, which, looking through the darkness of tempest, death and hell, recognizes even the God who abandons as Protector, recognizes the God who persecutes as Helper, and recognizes the God who damns as Saviour.'

92. Quoted from Nygren, *Urkristendom*, 126f. cf. *W.A.* V.171.11ff.; 346.7ff.; XIV.640.30ff. In times of spiritual distress, Luther returns again and again to the First Commandment, with its assurance: 'I am *thy* God', which he understands in the sense given above—and which he says he finds by no means easy to believe (*W.A. Tischr.* II.303.24). Holl, *Ges. Aufs. I.* 73, suggests that here Luther felt himself immediately confronted by God without the mediation of Christ. But this ignores the fact that he could not have interpreted the First Commandment as he does, apart from his understanding of Christ. The Commandment has become for him one of the *larvae Dei* which 'as it were contain Christ'.

93. *W.A.* III.96.26.

94. Luther's *Commentary on Genesis* is from one point of view largely an account of the conflict between true and false religion, the true and the false Church. He finds the true Church already in Paradise, where God's Word of both Gospel and Law was spoken to Adam.

95. *W.A.* XLII.184. cf. 624.6ff.: 'For from the beginning of the world, divine wisdom has thus ordained and disposed, that there should always exist some public sign, to which all peoples might look, and even the Gentiles might find, worship and adore the true God, although not all who had that sign believed and had fruit of it unto righteousness.'

96. ibid. 184ff.; 294ff.; 624ff. Luther gives various lists of these 'signs', but those named above are most typical and constant.

97. ibid. LI.287f.

98. ibid. XLII.626.39f.

99. ibid. 625.15f.: 'For when God reveals Himself in some sign, of whatsoever kind it may be, He is to be apprehended in it.'

100. ibid. 626.32ff.

101. For Luther's view of the Sacraments, see *W.M.L.* I.49-72 (*Treatise on Baptism*); 287-326 (*Treatise on the New Testament*); II.7-34 (*A Treatise concerning the Blessed Sacrament and concerning the Brotherhoods*); 167-296 (*The Babylonian Captivity of the Church*); 387-425 (*The Eight Wittenberg Sermons*); VI (the relevant sections from *Luther's Liturgical Writings*); and his explanation of Baptism and the Sacrament of the Altar in the two *Catechisms*. For an interpretation of his doctrine of the Eucharist, cf. Y. Brilioth, *Eucharistic Faith and Practice*. The development of Luther's thought is clearly traceable in the sources named, and the account of it given above represents his mature position.

102. *W.A.* XI.432.19; 433.18f.

103. Matthew 28:18ff., Mark 16:15f.

104. Matthew 26:26ff.; Mark 14:22ff.; Luke 22:19ff.; 1 Corinthians 11:23ff.

105. Matthew 18:18. Luther rejected the sacrament of Penance, but retained the 'Power of the Keys', the authority of the Pastoral office to declare and pronounce unto all men being penitent the absolution and remission of their sins. It is for him an essential part of the Ministry of the Word. cf. *W.A.* XLII.636.32ff.: 'We have several visible tokens: first, Baptism itself, adorned with a most sweet and solemn promise, that if we believe, we shall be saved. But since in this weakness of ours we easily slip, there are added to Baptism the Keys, or the Ministry of the Word (for these are not to be separated), which itself also is a visible token of grace, bound up with the voice of the Gospel according to Christ's institution: "What things soever ye shall loose on earth shall be loosed in heaven." When thou apprehendest this word by faith, thou art restored again to grace. . . .'

106. See the first section of this Chapter, n. 26. cf. *W.M.L.* VI.443: 'If I had to do without one or the other—either the works or the words of Christ—I would rather do without His works than His preaching; for the works do not help me, but His words give life, as He Himself says.' By 'works' here Luther means Christ's historical acts, His miracles, and so forth.

107. *W.A.* XI.33.8f.: 'the Sacrament, Baptism, which are works of God.'

108. ibid. 453.1.

109. *W.M.L.* II.224.

110. *W.A.* XI.447.9f. cf. *W.A.* XLII.667.18ff.: 'Thou hearest indeed a man when thou art baptized, when thou usest the holy Supper; but the Word which thou hearest is not man's, but it is the Word of the living God. He baptizes thee, He absolves thee from thy sins, He commands that thou shouldest hope in His mercy.'

111. ibid. X.1; 711.14f.: 'Where, however, the Gospel is preached . . . there is certainly Christ . . . whether it be in Turkey, Russia, Bohemia, or anywhere else. It is not possible that God's Word should be proclaimed, and God, Christ, and the Holy Spirit not be there. On the other hand, it is not possible that God, Christ, Church, or anything blessed should be there, where God's Word is not proclaimed, even if they performed all miracles.'

112. *W.M.L.* II.20: 'What does it matter? It is enough to know that it is a divine sign, in which Christ's flesh and blood are truly present—how and where, we leave to Him.' ibid. 193: 'What matters it if philosophy cannot fathom this?' ibid. 192: 'Why do we not put by such curiosity, and cling simply to the word of Christ, willing to remain in ignorance of what here takes place, and content with this, that the real body of Christ is present by virtue of the words [i.e. the words of institution]? Or is it necessary to comprehend the manner of the divine working in every detail?'

113. *W.A.* XXIII.132.

114. ibid. XVIII.710.38f.: *inquietus actor in omnibus creaturis suis.* cf. *W.A.* XXIII.134.

115. cf. *W.A.* XIX.492: 'For although He is everywhere in all the creatures and I might find Him in the stone, in the fire, in the water, or even in the rope . . . yet He willeth not that I should seek Him there without the Word and cast myself into the fire or water, or hang myself on a rope. He is everywhere, but He will not that thou shouldest feel after Him everywhere, but where the Word is; there do thou feel after Him, then thou wilt rightly lay hold of Him. Otherwise thou temptest God and settest up idolatry. Therefore hath He appointed for us a certain way, how and where He is to be sought and found, namely the Word.'

116. *W.A.* XLII.514.31ff.: 'We, however, see this glory face to face, we hear God speak to us and promise remission of sins in Baptism, in the Supper of His Son, in the true use of the Keys.' cf. 658.39f.

117. cf. op. cit. 659.1ff.: 'But what is it that He speaks with us? Does He terrify? Does He threaten? Does He accuse? By no means; but there perpetually sounds that voice in the Church: "Son, be of good cheer, thy sins are forgiven thee; I am favourable to thee through my Son; thou shalt be heir of eternal life", etc.'

118. *W.M.L.* II.193: 'Therefore it is with the sacrament even as it is with Christ . . . both natures are there in their entirety, and it is truly said, "This man is God", and "This God is man". . . . Even so, in order that the real body and the real blood of Christ may be present in the sacrament, it is not necessary that the bread and wine be transubstantiated and Christ be contained under their accidents; but both remain there together, and it is truly said, "This bread is my body, this wine is my blood", and vice versa. . . . At the same time, I permit other men to follow the other opinion . . . only let them not press us to accept their opinions as articles of faith.' Both in his Christology and in his Eucharistic doctrine, Luther observes the Chalcedonian adverbs.

119. See p. 127 *supra.*

120. See pp. 78ff. *supra* and n.123 *infra.*

121. cf. Nygren, *Agape and Eros*, II.ii.477-81.

122. The ubiquity of Christ's body is relevant here.

123. *W.A.* XLII.170.20ff.: 'We must therefore everywhere regard and honour the Word, by which God lays hold of and as it were puts on (*induit*) the creatures; and we must make a difference between the creature and the Word. In the sacrament of the Supper are bread and wine, in Baptism is water. These are creatures, but laid hold of through the Word. But as long as the creature is laid hold of by the Word, so long it is and does what the Word promises. . . . Baptism has the promise, that with the Holy Spirit it regenerates; in the Lord's Supper, besides the promise of the remission of sins, there is also this, that with the bread and wine there is truly exhibited the body and blood of Christ. As Christ says: This is my body, which is given for you; this cup is the New Testament in my blood, etc. In this way also it can be said that the human nature in Christ does not redeem us, but because the human nature is bodily laid hold of by the divinity, and Christ, God and man, is one person, therefore the redemption holds good.'

124. *W.B.* 133.

125. ibid. 153.

126. ibid. 140. Note also that 'Baptism includes the third sacrament, which has been called repentance . . . for what does repentance mean but earnestly attacking the old Adam in us and beginning a new life? . . . Therefore Baptism will always hold good; and though some fall away and sin, they can always return to it in order to subdue again the old Adam. . . . So that repentance is nothing but a return and re-entry into Baptism.'

127. *W.M.L.* II.230; cf. I.58ff.; cf. *Sermons*, 23f.

128. *W.B.* 146.

129. *W.M.L.* II.17: 'Christ . . . by His love, takes upon Himself our form, fights with us against sin, death, and all evil; this enkindles in us such love that we take His form, and through the interchange of His blessings and our misfortunes are one loaf, one bread, one body, one drink, and have all things in common.' ibid. 417: 'God is with you and stakes all His treasures and His blood for you, as if He said: "Fall in behind me without fear or delay, and then let come what may to attempt thy harm, let devil, death, sin, and hell and all creation try it, I shall go before thee, for I will be thy captain and thy shield." '

130. *W.M.L.* II.206.

131. ibid. 26.

132. ibid. 420.

133. *Gal.* E.T. 46(i.16): '[The Gospel] is a kind of doctrine that is not learned or gotten by any study, diligence, or wisdom of man, nor yet by the law of God, but is revealed by God Himself . . . first by the external Word: then by the working of God's Spirit inwardly.'

134. *W.A.* X.1; 331.11ff., 15ff. *W.A.* XI.109.6ff.: '. . . so that I do not only say, "Christ is God and man", but I glory that Christ is mine and all that is His is mine.'

135. *Gal.* E.T. 196f.(iii.14).

136. cf. the *Greater Catechism*, where Luther says that, just as 'we could never recognize the Father's grace and mercy except for our Lord Jesus Christ, who is a mirror of His Father's heart', so 'of Christ we should know nothing were He not revealed to us through the Holy Spirit'. cf. *W.A.* XI. 52f.; cf. 48.27ff.: 'What He did for our sake, He has given to us, but it does not become ours (*non obvenit nobis*) unless the Spirit comes into the heart. The Holy Spirit brings Christ, who reconciles us with the Father.'

137. *E.A.*[2] 13.320—see Loofs, *D.G.* 743.

138. *W.M.L.* II.21: 'If you cannot believe, pray for faith, as was said above in the other treatise.' cf. ibid. I.228; *Letters*, 177f.

139. *W.A.* X.1; 48.16ff., 49.1ff., cf. 619.17ff.

140. op. cit. 160.22ff.

141. *Gal.* E.T. 110(ii.20).

142. *W.M.L.* II.321. It is important to notice how readily Luther links the thought of faith-union with Christ with that of conflict and victory.

143. *W.A.* X.1; 52.9ff.; cf. XI.98.17ff.; cf. *Sermons*, 70.

144. *Gal.* E.T. 245(iii.28). cf. *W.A.* XL.1; 546.5ff.; XXVIII.142.9f.; XI.98.17ff.

145. ibid. 246.

146. ibid. 233(iii.23).

147. ibid. 241(iii.25).

148. *W.B.* 101.

149. *S.W.* I.153.

150. ibid. 154.

151. *W.B.* 101: 'But how is this hallowing accomplished? Answer: In the same way as the Son acquired His title of Lord, by redeeming us, through His birth, death, resurrection, etc., so the Holy Spirit accomplishes our sanctification by the following means: through the community (*Gemeine*) of saints or Christian Church, through the forgiveness of sins, the resurrection of the body, and the life everlasting; that is, by leading us into His holy community, into the bosom of the Church, through which He teaches us and brings us to Christ.'

152. cf. *Gal.* E.T. 248(iv.3): 'Indeed once with His own blood He redeemed and sanctified all; but because we are not yet perfectly pure (for the remnants of sin do yet cleave in our flesh, which striveth against the Spirit—Hebrews 1014; Galatians 517), therefore daily He cometh unto us spiritually, and continually more and more accomplisheth the appointed time of His Father.'

153. ibid. 368(v.17).

154. *W.B.* 104.

155. *S.W.* I.158.

156. *W.B.* 101-6 (Exposition of the Third Article of the Creed in the *Greater Catechism*); *W.M.L.* V.264-97 (Discussion of the Church and its marks in the treatise *On the Councils and the Churches*, 1539).

157. *W.A.* XI.53.32f. The other two works of the Spirit are to forgive sins and to raise the dead.

158. *W.B.* 103. Luther thinks that *communio sanctorum* would be better translated *Gemeine* (community, or congregation) of Saints, rather than *Gemeinschaft* (communion) of Saints.

159. *W.M.L.* V.265.

160. *W.B.* 102. For the Church as 'our Mother' cf. *W.M.L.* I.257; II.52.

161. *W.A.* X.1; 140.16f.; *W.M.L.* II.373.

162. op. cit. 82.9ff.

163. ibid. XLII.334.12f.

164. op. cit. 424.5ff.: 'Therefore the Church, not fixed in place and persons, is only there where the Word is; where the Word is not, although there are titles and offices, yet there is not the Church, since God is not there.' cf. *W.B.* 102: '. . . where Christ is not preached, there is no Holy Spirit to form the Christian Church, to call and to gather it together, without which none can come to the Lord Christ.'

165. *S.W.* I.451: '. . . where the Word of God is preached, there its fruits must of necessity follow. Since, therefore, we have the Word of God, it of necessity follows that the Spirit of God is with us. And where the Spirit is, there, of necessity, faith must exist, how weak soever it may be and imperceptible. And therefore, it cannot be denied, that there are Christians among us.'

166. *W.M.L.* V.271.

167. *W.A.* XLII.334.30ff. cf. 333.41: 'For numbers do not constitute the Church.'

168. ibid. X.1; 140.14: 'The Church is not wood and stone, but the company (*Hauf*) of Christ-believing people.' op. cit. 378.11ff.: '. . . the Christian Church, that is, all believing men.' cf. *W.A.* XI.53.20ff.

169. It should be observed that it is not our intention here to give an account of Luther's doctrine of the Church, which would require more space than can be allowed, even if this were the place for it.

170. *W.A.* X.1; 140.7ff.

171. ibid. XLII.625.22ff.: 'Christ is to be sought there, where He has manifested Himself and willed to be known, as in the Word, in Baptism, in the Supper: there He is certainly found. For the Word cannot deceive us.'

172. *W.M.L.* V.271. Luther continues: 'For God's Word cannot be present without God's people, and God's people cannot be without God's Word. Who would preach or listen to preaching, if no people of God were there? And what could or would God's people believe, if God's Word were not there?'

173. ibid. 270. cf. *W.A.* XI.53.26f.: 'It is called "communion of saints" because it is sanctified by God, because the holiness which God has, He gives to them.'

174. *Heiligthum* or *Heilthum* is Luther's word. It was also the word for 'relics', the wonder-working objects of reverence that were so eagerly collected and preserved in the medieval churches—sacred objects such as alleged portions of the Cross, or the bones of some saint. Luther has this idea in mind, when he enumerates the true 'holy possessions' of the Church.

175. *W.M.L.* V.287.

176. ibid. 288.

177. loc. cit. *Crescite* = 'grow' (2 Pet. 318); *Abundete magis* = 'Abound more and more' (1 Thess. 41).

178. loc cit. The reason is 'because the heathen have practised these works and sometimes appear holier than Christians. Nevertheless their actions do not come so purely and simply from the heart for God's sake, but they seek some other end thereby, since they have no real faith and no true knowledge of God. But the Holy Ghost is here [i.e. in the Church] and He sanctifies men's hearts, and brings these fruits out of good, fine, hearts, as Christ says in the parable, in Matthew 13(23).' In other words, even the heathen can 'do the works' of the Law, but only those who have received the Holy Spirit can even begin to 'fulfil' the Law.

179. ibid. 266. cf. 265: 'Therefore it is called a Christian people and has the Holy Ghost, who sanctifies it daily, not only through the forgiveness of sins, as the Antinomians foolishly believe, but by the abolition, purging out, and slaying of sins, and because of this they are called a holy people.'

180. *Works*, VII.204 (Sermon CVII.5). Dr. W. E. Sangster, in *The Path to Perfection*, 98ff., quotes Wesley's criticisms of Luther on this subject at some length, and claims that A. Harnack, *H.D.* VII.267 (E.T.), 'has substantially admitted this defect' in Luther. Those who refer to the passage in Harnack, (contrasting it perhaps with p. 209), may judge whether it yields very 'substantial' support. For evidence on the other side, Dr. Sangster refers us to Th. Harnack, *Luthers Theologie*, II.460ff., but he appears to regard this as of no 'substantial' importance. Luther himself does not seem to have been consulted. Wesley, of course, had looked at the *Galatians*, but it is difficult to believe that he ever read as far as Chapter 5; and his own doctrine of perfection on the one hand, and the erroneous views of professed Lutherans, to which he rightly objected, on the other, must have made it difficult for him to read Luther quite 'without prejudice'. He was, however, far too great and humble a man to wish to perpetuate a false judgement, and he would forgive the present writer for pointing it out.

181. cf. Köberle, *Rechtf. u. Heilig.* 123: 'Along with the imputative conception of divine righteousness, there is always found in Luther, from the first, the renewal of life that begins and increases in faith, although the righteousness of faith always has priority over the newness of life. Luther understood in a unique way how to keep distinct in thought what was for him a real unity—an indication that even from a systematic standpoint he was not so careless as he is often represented to be. . . . Luther at all times firmly maintained, even if with varying emphasis, the intimate union of justification and sanctification, while at the same time making a clear theological distinction between the ideas.' Köberle goes on to say that it was Melanchthon who put asunder what Luther thus joined together, and he makes the following interesting comparison: 'Melanchthon says for grace "forgiveness". Luther says for grace "forgiveness and sanctification"; Osiander, "sanctification and forgiveness"! Catholicism says for grace only "sanctification".'

182. It is after all quite possible to speak of a thing without naming it, and when Luther says, for instance, that believers have a *good will* (*Gal.* E.T. 369(v.17)), and that faith must issue in love, or it is not true faith (ibid. 340 (v.6)), what is he doing if not speaking of sanctification?

183. cf. pp. 38f. *supra.* cf. *W.A.* X.1; 84.1ff.: '. . . not our works, but Christ's, make us blessed. Now these are of two kinds. . . . The first are those which Christ has done personally without us, which are the chief works, in which we believe; the second are those He works in us toward our neighbour in love.'

184. *Gal.* E.T. 83(ii.16). cf. 108 (ii.20): '. . . [Paul] teacheth what true Christian righteousness is, namely, that righteousness whereby Christ liveth in us, and not that which is in our person.' This righteousness, Luther says, is the whole theme of the Epistle to the Galatians—op. cit. lxxiii; cf. 6(i.1).

185. *Römerbr.* 83.33: '*Christ alone is* both *His righteousness* and His truth. . . . But to God be praise and glory for ever, who has given all these things in Him and with Him, so that we through Him might be righteous and true. . . .' Note also the following: *W.A.* X.1; 106.3: '*Divine righteousness, that is divine grace*, which justifies us through faith. . . . God's grace is our righteousness, which is called God's righteousness, because He gives it to us out of grace . . .'; ibid. 322.2f.: '. . . that *grace alone* (*that is, Christ*), and nothing but grace, avails.' (*italics* mine).

186. On 'imputation' see *Gal.* E.T. 84f.(ii.16); 150ff.(iii.6); 173(iii.10); 369(v.17); etc.

187. *Gal.* E.T. 340(v.6): '[Paul] speaketh here of faith . . . that after it hath justified, it is not idle, but occupied and exercised in working through love. Paul therefore in this place setteth forth the whole life of a Christian man, namely, that inwardly it consisteth in faith toward God, and outwardly in charity and good works toward our neighbour.' cf. 100(ii.18): 'Now after that a man is once justified, and possesseth Christ by faith, and knoweth that He is his righteousness and life, doubtless he will not be idle, but as a good tree he will bring forth good fruits. For the believing man hath the Holy Ghost, and where the Holy Ghost dwelleth, He will not suffer a man to be idle, but stirreth him up to all exercises of piety and godliness, and of true religion, to the love of God, to the patient suffering of afflictions, to prayer, to thanksgiving, to the exercise of charity toward all men.'

188. cf. *Gal.* E.T. 25(i.6): 'We also do daily prove by experience, how hardly the mind conceiveth and retaineth a sound and steadfast faith.'

189. ibid. 39(i.11f.).

190. R. E. Davies, *The Problem of Authority*, 1-61.

191. ibid. 57.

192. See p. 42 *supra.*

193. *W.M.L.* II.427-55; cf. 273f.

194. ibid. 452f. cf. 274: 'But, as Augustine elsewhere says, the truth itself lays hold on the soul and thus renders it able to judge most certainly of all things; but the truth it cannot judge, but is forced to say with unerring certainty that it is the truth. For example, our reason declares with unerring certainty that three and seven are ten, and yet it cannot give a reason why this is true, although it cannot deny that it is true; it is taken captive by the truth and does not so much judge the truth as it is judged by the truth. Thus it is also with the mind of the Church, when under the enlightenment of the Spirit she judges and approves doctrines.'

195. ibid. 453. Luther's interpretation of Augustine's words may not be quite correct, but it is nearer the truth than that which has been commonly read into them. In their original context in the *Contra Epistolam Manichaei* (v.6), they are not intended to represent Augustine's own position, but are put into the mouth of a simple Christian who is engaged in a dispute with a Manichaean. Augustine himself did not in any case come to believe the Gospel in the way the quotation suggests, as anyone who knows a little of his spiritual pilgrimage is aware.

196. *Gal.* E.T. 179(iii.10). cf. *W.A.* XXXIX.1; 47.3ff.: 'And Scripture is to be understood, not against, but for Christ. Hence it must either be referred to Him, or it must not be held to be true Scripture.'

197. *W.A.* X.1; 628.6f.

198. op. cit. 80.16f.

199. *W.M.L.* III.16. There is here, no doubt, a hint of Scripture as a *larva Dei*.

200. ibid. 332-42.

201. *W.A.* X.1; 370.18ff.

202. As R. E. Davies, op. cit. 39, admits.

203. *W.A.* X.1; 233.19ff.; 328.11ff.

204. A man's psychological condition, that is to say, is no certain proof of his theological situation, his relationship to God.

205. *M.H.B.* 494.

206. *W.A.* XI.15.3f.

207. op. cit. 111.17ff.

208. cf. *W.A.* X.1; 611ff.

209. *S.W.* I.464. cf. *Gal.* E.T. 265(iv.6): 'We must not judge therefore according to the feeling of our own heart, but according to the Word of God . . .'; ibid. 271(iv.7): 'We must not measure this thing by our own reason or by our own feeling, but by the promise of God.'

210. *Gal.* E.T. 268(iv.6) *W.A.* XL.589.

O

LITERATURE CITED

(Abridgements of titles used in the footnotes are indicated where necessary in square brackets)

Aulén, G., *Christus Victor* (London, 1937).
Den kristna gudsbilden (*The Christian Picture of God*). (Stockholm, 1927.) [*Gudsbilden.*]

Baillie, J., *Our Knowledge of God.* (Oxford, 1939.)

Billing, E., *Vår kallelse* (*Our Vocation*). 4th edn. (Stockholm, 1920.)

Boehmer, J., *Luther and the Reformation in the Light of Modern Research.* (London, 1930.) [*Luther.*]

Brilioth, Y., *Eucharistic Faith and Practice, Evangelical and Catholic.* (London, 1930.)

Bring, R., *Dualismen hos Luther* (*Dualism in Luther*). (Stockholm, 1929.)
Förhållandet mellan tro och gärningar inom luthersk teologi (*The Relation between Faith and Works in Lutheran Theology*). (Lund, 1933.) [*Tro och g.*]

Brunner, E., *Das Gebot und die Ordnungen.* (Tübingen, 1933).

Burnaby, J., *Amor Dei, A Study of the Religion of St. Augustine.* (London, 1938.)

Calvin, J., *Institutes of the Christian Religion.* 2 vols. 6th American edn. (London, 1935.)

Cave, S., *The Doctrine of the Person of Christ.* (London, 1925.)
The Doctrine of the Work of Christ. (London, 1937.)

Davies, R. E., *The Problem of Authority in the Continental Reformers.* (London, 1946.)

Farmer, H. H., *The Servant of the Word.* (London, 1941.)

Franks, R. S., *A History of the Doctrine of the Work of Christ.* 2 vols. (London, 1919.) [*Work of Christ.*]

Froude, J. A., *Life and Letters of Erasmus.* (London, 1900.)

Hare, J. C., *Vindication of Luther against his recent English assailants.* 2nd edn. (Cambridge, 1855.) [*Vindication.*]

Harnack, A., *History of Dogma.* 7 vols. (London, 1894-9.) [*H.D.*]

Harnack, Th., *Luthers Theologie*. 2 vols. (Erlangen, 1862.) (New edn., Munich, 1926-7.)

Hazlitt, W., *The Table Talk of Martin Luther*. (London, 1902). [*Table Talk*.]

Herrmann, W., *The Communion of the Christian with God*. 2nd English edn. (London, 1906.) [*Communion*.]

Hildebrandt, F., *Melanchthon, Alien or Ally?* (Cambridge, 1946.)

Hirsch, E., *Luthers Gottesanschauung*. (Göttingen, 1918.)

Holl, K., *Gesammelte Aufsätze zur Kirchengeschichte, I, Luther*. 6th edn. (Tübingen, 1932.) [*Ges. Aufs. I.*]

Holmquist, Hj., *Kirkehistorie (Church History)*. 2 vols. 2nd, revised edn., by Jens Nörregaard. (Copenhagen, 1931, 1935.) *Luther, Loyola, Calvin*. 3rd, revised edn. (Lund, 1926.) [*Luther*.]

Köberle, A., *Rechtfertigung und Heiligung*. 3rd, revised edn., (Leipzig, 1930.) [*Rechtf. u. Heilig.*]

Köstlin, J., *The Life of Luther*. (London, 1898.)

L'Estrange, R., *Twenty Select Colloquies out of Erasmus*. (London, 1680.) [*Colloquies*.]

Lindsay, T. M., *A History of the Reformation*. 2 vols. (Edinburgh, 1906.) [*Hist. Ref.*] *Luther and the German Reformation*. (Edinburgh, 1925.) [*Luther*.]

Loofs, F., *Leitfaden zum Studium der Dogmengeschichte*. 4th, revised edn. (Halle, 1906.) [*D.G.*]

Mackinnon, J., *Luther and the Reformation*. 4 vols. (London, 1925ff.)

Niebuhr, R., *The Nature and Destiny of Man*. 2 vols. (London, 1941, 1943.)

Nygren, A., *Agape and Eros, a Study of the Christian Idea of Love*. 3 vols. (London, 1932, 1938-9.) *Etiska grundfrågor (Fundamental Problems in Ethics)*. (Stockholm, 1926.) *Urkristendom och Reformation (Primitive Christianity and Reformation)*. (Lund, 1932.)

Obendiek, H., *Der Teufel bei Martin Luther, eine theologische Untersuchung*. (Berlin, 1931.) [*Der Teufel*.]

Patterson, R. L., *The Conception of God in the Philosophy of Aquinas.* (London, 1933.)

Prenter, R., *Spiritus Creator, Studier i Luthers Theologi (Creator Spirit, Studies in Luther's Theology).* 2nd edn. (Copenhagen, 1946.)

Sangster, W. E., *The Path to Perfection.* (London, 1943.)

Temple, W., *Nature, Man, and God.* (London, 1934.) *Malvern 1941.* (London, 1941.)

Troeltsch, E., *The Social Teaching of the Christian Churches.* 2 vols. (London, 1931.)

Törnwall, G., *Andligt och världsligt regemente hos Luther (The Spiritual and Temporal Regimes in Luther).* (Stockholm, 1940.) [*Andl. o. världsl.*]

Watson, P. S., *The State as a Servant of God.* (London, 1946.)

Wesley, J., *Works.* 3rd edn. with the last corrections of the author. 14 vols. (London, 1829.)

Wingren, G., *Luthers lära om kallelsen (Luther's Doctrine of Vocation).* (Lund, 1942.) [*Kallelsen.*]

INDEX OF SCRIPTURE REFERENCES

INDEX OF FOREIGN WORDS AND PHRASES

INDEX OF PROPER NAMES

INDEX OF SUBJECTS

MAGNIFICAT, 42
Majesty of God, 6, 19, 61, 78, 85, 94f.,
  102f., 129, 132, 135, 137, 162, 177
Manger, 149, 161, 169
Marks of the Church, 169ff.
Marriage, 30 (n. 42), 127, 167
Masks of God, 78, 80, 162ff. (v. Crea-
  tures, Veils)
Mass, 120ff., 162, 164
"Mediated immediacy," 80, 104, 113
Mediation, 78ff., 112ff.
Mediator, 94f., 123 (v. Christ)
Mental images, 85
Mercy, 61f., 120ff., 123
Mercy-seat, 135
Merit, 35, 44, 46ff., 54, 61, 94, 117, 120,
  159f.
  of Christ, 118, 120ff., 125
  of Christians, 121, 123
  of congruence, 16, 52
  of worthiness, 16, 52
Metaphysics, 24, 59, 126, 162, 164 (v.
  Speculation)
Methodism, Methodist, 3, 171
Middle way, 135, 160
Ministry, 170
Miracles, 104
Mirror, 103, 136, 138 (n. 16), 185
  (n. 136) (v. Creatures, Glass)
Monophysitism, 126
Moralism, 35ff., 62, 96
Moravians, 3, 171
Mystery, 138 (n. 14)
Mysticism, 6, 19, 94ff., 101 (n. 107)

NAKED GOD, 78, 94f.
Natural God, 75, 105, 112
  Law, 83, 111-16, 155
  light, 86f.
  man, 80, 84f., 91f., 103, 130, 176
  religion, 91
  theology, 24, 76, 80, 83f.
  work of God, 156
Nature, 111, 116, 139 (n. 31)
  of God, 156, 159 (v. Essence, Substance)
New Man, 53, 158, 165f., 168, 172, 175
  Creature, 48, 157, 170
  Testament, 149-52
Nominalism, 13, 15, 17f., 25, 52, 77,
  97 (n. 12)

OCCAMISM, 18
Offices, 112-16, 155
Official morality, 111, 115
Old Adam, 158, 165, 168, 172
  Testament, 93, 149-52
Omnipotence, 6, 82, 134, 136, 177
Omnipresence, 162f. (v. Ubiquity)

On the Councils and Churches, 170
Ordinance of God, 51, 84, 112f., 114f.
Original sin, 16, 49, 157
'Ornament of grace', 15, 20
'Our theology', 22, 136

PAPACY, PAPISTS, 4, 6, 10f., 14, 91f., 99
  (n.57), 113, 117, 120, 161, 174
Paradise, 22, 142 (n. 88), 151, 183 (n. 94)
Passion of Christ, 19, 133
Patristic theory, 6, 118
Pelagianism, 49, 53
Penal theory, 118f., 129
Penance, 17, 183 (n. 105) (v. Repent-
  ance)
Penitence, 17ff.
Perfection, 108, 140 (n. 54) (v. Love)
Person of Christ, 96, 163
Petition, 36, 40f.
Philosophy, 5, 55f., 63, 82, 184 (n. 112)
Pilgrimages, 113
Point of contact, 85
Pope, Popery, 4, 96, 120, 161, 175f.
Power of Keys (s.v. Keys).
Prayer, 36, 39ff., 167, 173
Preaching, 149-52, 169
Predestination, 7, 18f., 52, 82, 135
Prescience, 82
Presumption, 135
Pride, 16, 31 (n. 48), 87, 109, 130, 157f.,
  177
Private judgement, 13f., 31 (n. 48)
Promises of God, 21, 150ff.
Proper office of Christ, 104f., 127, 157
  office of Gospel, 157
  use of Law, 156
  work of God, 124, 156-60
  work of Holy Spirit, 168
  work of Christ, 91, 116-32, 167
Propitiation, 121, 144 (n. 130)
Protestantism, 10, 13, 76, 110
Providence, 36
Psalms, 20, 28 (n. 19), 31 (n. 57)
Punishment, 45f., 136, 159

RATIONALISM, 95f., 161
Real Presence, 162ff.
Reason, 76ff., 86ff., 95, 103, 111, 135,
  138 (n. 13), 153, 169, 172, 177
Redemption, 118, 132, 168, 171
Reformation, 10-15, 63f.
Regeneration, 64, 157
Relics, 187 (n. 174)
Religion, 4ff., 34-8, 60, 62, 115
  and ethics, 46ff., 115f., 154
  of the Papacy, 6, 15, 22, 33
Repentance, 19, 160, 177, 185 (n. 126)
Resurrection, 117, 121, 131f., 158, 165
Revelation, 24, 56f., 76ff., 79, 92f., 97
  (n. 15), 102ff., 112, 132, 138 (n. 15)